Decide to be
Awesome !

E
" Mr Awesome "

THE
13 STEPS TO
RICHES

Featuring Erik Swanson & Michael E. Gerber

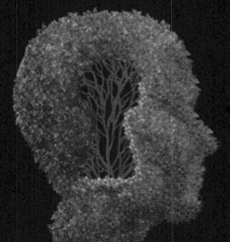
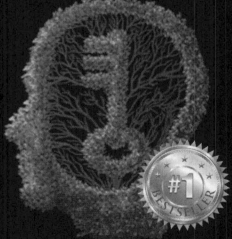

SPECIALIZED KNOWLEDGE
VOLUME 4

HABITUDE
WARRIOR

#1 BESTSELLER

BEYOND

Library of Congress Control Number: 2022900067

Paperback ISBN: 978-1-637922-48-4

Hardcover ISBN: 978-1-637922-49-1

TESTIMONIALS
THE 13 STEPS TO RICHES

"What an honor to collaborate with so many personal development leaders from around the world as we Co-Author together honoring the amazing principles by Napoleon Hill in this new book series, *The 13 Steps to Riches*, by Habitude Warrior and Erik "Mr. Awesome" Swanson. Well done "Mr. Awesome" for putting together such an amazing series. If you want to up-level your life, read every book in this series and learn to apply each of these time tested steps and principles."

Denis Waitley ~ Author of *Psychology of Winning & The NEW Psychology of Winning - Top Qualities of a 21st Century Winner*

"Just as *Think and Grow Rich* reveals the 13 steps to success discovered by Napoleon Hill after interviewing the richest people around the world (and many who considered themselves failures) in the early 1900's, *The 13 Steps to Riches*, produced by Habitude Warrior and Erik Swanson takes a modern look at those same 13 steps. It brings together many of today's personal development leaders to share their stories of how *the 13 Steps to Riches* have created and propelled their own successes. I am honored to participate and share the power of Faith in my life. If you truly want to accelerate reaching the success you deserve, read every volume of *The 13 Steps to Riches*."

Sharon Lechter ~ 5 Time N.Y. Times Best-Selling Author. Author of *Think and Grow Rich for Women*, Co-Author of *Exit Rich, Rich Dad Poor Dad, Three Feet from Gold, Outwitting the Devil* and *Success and Something Greater* ~ **SharonLechter.com**

"The most successful book on personal achievement ever written is now being elaborated upon by many of the world's top thought leaders. I'm honored to Co-Author this series on the amazing principles from Napoleon Hill, in *The 13 Steps to Riches*, by Habitude Warrior, Erik "Mr. Awesome" Swanson."

> *Jim Cathcart* ~ Best-Selling Author of *Relationship Selling* and *The Acorn Principle,* among many others. Certified Speaking Professional (CSP) and Former President of the National Speakers Association (NSA)

"Some books are written to be read and placed on the shelf. Others are written to transform the reader, as they travel down a path of true transcendence and enlightenment. "*The 13 steps to Riches*" by Habitude Warrior and Erik Swanson is the latter. Profoundly insightful, it revitalizes the techniques and strategies written by Napoleon Hill by applying a modern perspective, and a fearsome collaboration of some of the greatest minds and thought leaders from around the globe. A must read for all of those who seek to break free of their current levels of success, and truly extract the greatness that lies within. It is an honor and a privilege to have been selected to participate, in what is destined to be the next historic chapter in the meteoric rise of many men and women around the world."

> *Glenn Lundy* ~ Husband to one, Father to 8, Automotive Industry Expert, Author of "The Morning 5", Creator of the popular morning show "#riseandgrind", and the Founder of "Breakfast With Champions"

"How exciting to team up with the amazing Habitude Warrior community of leaders such as Erik Swanson, Sharon Lechter, John Assaraf, Denis Waitley and so many more transformational and self-help icons to bring you these timeless and proven concepts in the fields of success and wealth. *The 13 Steps to Riches* book series will help you reach your dreams and accomplish your goals faster than you have ever experienced before!"

> *Marie Diamond* ~ Featured in *The Secret*, Modern Day Spiritual Teacher, Inspirational Speaker, Feng Shui Master

"If you are looking to crystalize your mightiest dream, rekindle your passion, breakthrough limiting beliefs and learn from those who have done exactly what you want to do - read this book! In this transformational masterpiece, *The 13 Steps to Riches*, self-development guru Erik Swanson has collected the sage wisdom and time tested truths from subject matter experts and amalgamated it into a one-stop-shop resource library that will change your life forever!"

Dan Clark ~ Speaker Hall of Fame & N.Y. Times Best-Selling Author of *The Art of Significance*

"Life has always been about who you surround yourself with. I am in excellent company with this collaboration from my fellow authors and friends, paying tribute to the life changing principles by Napoleon Hill in this amazing new book series, *The 13 Steps to Riches*, organized by Habitude Warrior's founder and my dear friend, Erik Swanson. Hill said, 'Your big opportunity may be right where you are now.' This book series is a must-read for anyone who wants to change their life and prosper, starting now."

Alec Stern ~ America's Startup Success Expert, Co-Founder of Constant Contact

"Finally a book series that encompasses the lessons the world needs to learn and apply, but in our modern day era. As I always teach my students to "Say *YES*, and then figure out how", I strongly urge you to do the same. Say YES to adding all of these 13 books in *The 13 Steps to Riches* book series into your success library and watch both your business as well as your personal life grow as a result."

Loral Langemeier ~ 5 Time N.Y. Times Best-Selling Author, Featured in *The Secret*, Author of *The Millionaire Maker* and *YES! Energy - The Equation to Do Less, Make More*

"Napoleon Hill had a tremendous impact on my consciousness when I was very young – there were very few books nor the type of trainings that we see today to lead us to success. Whenever you have the opportunity to read and harness *The 13 Steps to Riches* as they are presented in this series, be happy (and thankful) that there were many of us out there applying the principles, testing the teachings, making the mistakes, and now being offered to you in a way that they are clear, simple and concise – with samples and distinctions that will make it easier for you to design a successful life which includes adding value to others, solving world problems, and making the world work for 100% of humanity... Read on... those dreams are about to come true!"

Doria Cordova ~ CEO of Money & You, Excellerated Business School, Global Business Developer, Ambassador of New Education

"Success leaves clues and the Co-Authors in this awesome book series, *The 13 Steps to Riches*, will continue the Napoleon Hill legacy with tools, tips and modern-day principals that greatly expand on the original masterpiece... *Think and Grow Rich*. If you are serious about living your life to the max, get this book series now!"

John Assaraf ~ Chairman & CEO NeuroGym, MrNeuroGym.com, New York Times best-selling author of *Having It All, Innercise,* and *The Answer*. Also featured in *The Secret*

"Over the years, I have been blessed with many rare and amazing opportunities to invest my time and energy. These opportunities require a keen eye and immediate action. This is one of those amazing opportunities for you as a reader! I highly recommend you pick up every book in this series of **The 13 Steps to Riches** by Habitude Warrior and Erik Swanson! Learn from modern day leaders who have embraced the lessons from the great Napoleon Hill in his classic book from 1937, *Think and Grow Rich*."

Kevin Harrington ~ Original "Shark" on *Shark Tank*, Creator of the Infomercial, Pioneer of the *As Seen on TV* brand, Co-Author of *Mentor to Millions*

"When you begin your journey, you will quickly learn of the importance of the first step of *The 13 Steps To Riches*. A burning desire is the start of all worthwhile achievements. Erik 'Mr. Awesome' Swanson's newest book series contains a wealth of assistance to make your journey both successful and enjoyable. Start today... because tomorrow is not guaranteed on your calendar."

Don Green ~ 45 Years of Banking, Finance & Entrepreneurship, Best-Selling Author of *Everything I know About Success I Learned From Napoleon Hill* & *Napoleon Hill My Mentor: Timeless Principles to Take Your Success to the Next Level* & *Your Millionaire Mindset*

Our minds become magnetized with the dominating thoughts we hold in our minds and these magnets attract to us the forces, the people, the circumstances of life which harmonize with the nature of our dominating thoughts.

(Napoleon Hill)

NAPOLEON HILL

I would like to personally acknowledge and thank the one and only Napoleon Hill for his work, dedication, and most importantly believing in himself. His unwavering belief in himself, whether he realized this or not, had been passed down from generation to generation to millions and millions of individuals across this planet including me!

I'm sure, at first, as many of us experience throughout our lives as well, he most likely had his doubts. Think about it. Being offered to work for Andrew Carnegie for a full 20 years with zero pay and no guarantee of success had to be a daunting decision. But, I thank you for making that decision years and years ago. It paved the path for countless many who have trusted in themselves and found success in their own rights. You gave us all hope and desire to bank on the most important entity in our world today - ourselves!

For this, I thank you Sir, from the bottom of my heart and the top of all of our bank accounts. Let us all follow the 13 Steps to Riches and prosper in so many areas of our lives.

~ Erik "Mr Awesome" Swanson
13 Time #1 Best-Selling Author & Student of Napoleon Hill Philosophies

CPL. HUNTER LOPEZ, 22

It is our distinct honor to dedicate each one of our *13 **Steps** to **Riches*** book volumes to each of the 13 United States Service Members who courageously lost their lives in Kabul in August, 2021. Your honor, dignity, and strength will always be cherished and remembered. ~ Habitude Warrior Team

Cpl. Hunter Lopez, 22, of Indio, California, a rifleman.

His awards and decorations include a Certificate of Appreciation, Marine Corps Good Conduct Medal, Letter of Appreciation, Meritorious Mast, National Defense Service Medal, Sea Service Deployment Ribbon, Global War on Terrorism Expeditionary Medal and Global War on Terrorism Service Medal. Additional awards pending approval may include Purple Heart, Combat Action Ribbon and Sea Service Deployment Ribbon.

THE 13 STEPS TO RICHES
FEATURING:

DENIS WAITLEY ~ Author of *Psychology of Winning & The NEW Psychology of Winning - Top Qualities of a 21st Century Winner,* NASA's Performance Coach, Featured in *The Secret* ~ www.DenisWaitley.com

SHARON LECHTER ~ 5 Time N.Y. Times Best-Selling Author. Author of *Think and Grow Rich for Women,* Co-Author of *Exit Rich, Rich Dad Poor Dad, Three Feet from Gold, Outwitting the Devil* and *Success and Something Greater* ~ www.SharonLechter.com

JIM CATHCART~ Best-Selling Author of *Relationship Selling* and *The Acorn Principle,* among many others. Certified Speaking Professional (CSP) and Former President of the National Speakers Association (NSA) ~ www.Cathcart.com

MICHAEL E. GERBER ~ New York Times Bestseller of the mega best selling theory for over two consecutive decades… E-Myth books. ~ www.MichaelEGerber.com

GLENN LUNDY ~ Husband to one, Father to 8, Automotive Industry Expert, Author of "The Morning 5", Creator of the popular morning show "#riseandgrind", and the Founder of "Breakfast With Champions" ~ www.GlennLundy.com

MARIE DIAMOND ~ Featured in *The Secret*, Modern Day Spiritual Teacher, Inspirational Speaker, Feng Shui Master ~ www.MarieDiamond.com

DAN CLARK ~ Award Winning Speaker, Speaker Hall of Fame, N.Y. Times Best-Selling Author of *The Art of Significance* ~ www.DanClark.com

ALEC STERN ~ America's Startup Success Expert, Co-Founder of Constant Contact, Speaker, Mentor, Investor ~ www.AlecSpeaks.com

ERIK SWANSON ~ 13 Time #1 International Best-Selling Author, Award Winning Speaker, Featured on Tedx Talks and Amazon Prime TV. Founder & CEO of the Habitude Warrior Brand ~ www.SpeakerErikSwanson.com

LORAL LANGEMEIER ~ 5 Time N.Y. Times Best-Selling Author, Featured in *The Secret*, Author of *The Millionaire Maker* and *YES! Energy - The Equation to Do Less, Make More* ~ www.LoralLangemeier.com

DORIA CORDOVA ~ CEO of Money & You, Excellerated Business School, Global Business Developer, Ambassador of New Education ~ www.FridaysWithDoria.com

JOHN ASSARAF ~ Chairman & CEO NeuroGym, MrNeuroGym.com, N. Y. Times best-selling author of *Having It All, Innercise,* and *The Answer.* Also featured in *The Secret* ~ www.JohnAssaraf.com

KEVIN HARRINGTON ~ Original "Shark" on the hit TV show *Shark Tank,* Creator of the Infomercial, Pioneer of the *As Seen on TV* brand, Co-Author of *Mentor to Millions* ~ www.KevinHarrington.TV

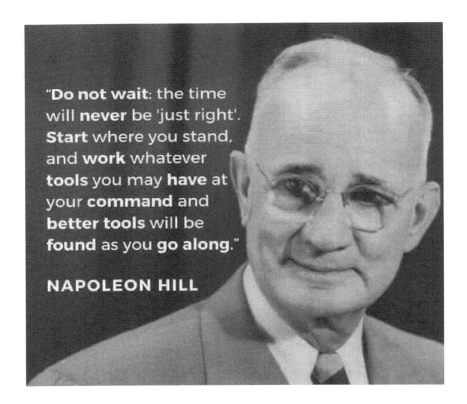

"Do not wait: the time will never be 'just right'. Start where you stand, and work whatever tools you may have at your command and better tools will be found as you go along."

NAPOLEON HILL

CONTENTS

INTRODUCTION

by Don Green

ERIK SWANSON & DON GREEN

Once you give yourself the gift of reading Erik Swanson's newest book series, *The 13 Steps to Riches*, you are sure to realize why he has earned his nickname, *"Mr. Awesome."* Readers usually read books for two reasons – they want to be entertained or they want to improve their knowledge in a certain subject. Mr. Awesome's new book series will help you do both.

I urge you to not only read this great book series in it's entirety, but also apply the principles held within into your our life. Use the experience Erik Swanson has gained to reach your own level of success. I highly encourage you to invest in yourself by reading self-help materials, such as *The 13 Steps to Riches*, and I truly know you will discover that it will be one of the best investments you could ever make.

Don Green
Executive Director and CEO
The Napoleon Hill Foundation

Michael E. Gerber

WELCOME TO A
SPECIAL NEW WORLD

It has been thought by those at the heart of our business universe that general knowledge is essential for a business' success. Meaning, knowing how to do all of the essential things a company is both created to do and, in the course of growing in its market, forced to do, whether to compete successfully with all the others attempting to secure a foothold in that world each has designs to successfully inhabit, or whether, even more hopefully, to wrest a leadership role in that marketplace by overcoming all other competitors' efforts at same.

It's the general knowledge that begs this conversation, the belief that knowing how to do everything "generally" will forge a truly competitive enterprise into a market leader. Or, if not that, at least make one out to be competitive.

So it is that a summary review of all companies within any market, no matter what the product or service, no matter what its intention is, no matter how much experience may be put into play, that summary will reveal a surprising to most of us, realization that in the main, each and every one of those companies, look, act and feel very much the same.

Oh, yes, their name is different. Ford is Ford. Chevrolet is Chevrolet. And so forth and so on.

But despite the apparent differences between a Ford Mustang and a Chevrolet Corvette, when you walk into their dealerships, or watch their advertising, or talk to one of their salespeople, or go into their service centers, what you'll find will be, without question, very much the same.

Indeed, it's the un-bewildering sameness of the world of companies on our planet which is an almost eerie repository of the un-bewildering sameness of all our people, no matter their race, no matter their sex, no matter their politics, no matter their insistence that they're indelibly unique, one and all, as original as the day they were born. Uniquely, Sam, Uniquely Alex, Uniquely Jezebel, uniquely their own.

Oh, if that were only true! What we find, unfortunately, is exactly the opposite. Glaringly opposite.

The extreme ordinariness of our paths, of our choices, of our employment, of our work, of our creativity, of our discipline, of our hopes and intentions, flails out at even the most casual observer, especially when we're engaged in the pursuit of the special in the world of our so-called entrepreneurs.

I say so-called entrepreneurs, because that resides at the heart of the matter, the heart of the absence of Specialized Knowledge.

The heart of the dissolute fact that the reality of Specialized Knowledge is that in the broad universe of commercial activity here in America and, even more distastefully, throughout the rest of the world, Specialized Knowledge is looked upon, if it's looked upon at all, as a foreign, unnecessary, foolish idea wresting for too much time, too much capital, and far too much insistence upon creativity than is necessary to do business at all.

In this book, *The 13 Steps To Riches - Volume 4 Specialized Knowledge*, we deal with that subject in a most specialized manner. We look upon Specialized Knowledge through the lens of a universal creator.

A universally inspired mindset that looks upon all things from the perspective of What, Why, Who and How? What are you there to do? Why are you there to do it? Who is responsible, and who is accountable for doing it? And How, pray tell, do you get it done?

In each and every case above, there is a special answer to those four questions, and a general answer to those four questions.

Answer them generally, and I will show you a company struggling to get by, if even that. Answer them specially, and I will show you a company in the process of transforming their marketplace and the people who live and work in it.

Allow me to demonstrate the difference:

In the general case, the What do you do might be said, to sell and distribute light fixtures to the residential marketplace in Detroit. In the special case, the What do you do might be said, in the very same industry, to transform the state of light fixture distribution worldwide.

In the first case, we have an ordinary business doing ordinary work in an ordinary way. In the second case, we have an extraordinary business doing extraordinary work in an extraordinary way.

The first company has a strategic objective, exactly the same objective that every one of its competitors have within that very same marketplace.

The second company has a dream, an outsized objective through which to literally transform how light fixtures are designed, built, marketed and supported, worldwide. The first company is driven by a general description. The second company is driven by a special description.

To fulfill the first company's strategic objective, general knowledge implemented efficiently and effectively will earn it a competitively secure space in its local market.

To fulfill the second company's dream, Specialized Knowledge –

Marketing Knowledge, Financial Knowledge, Enterprise Development Knowledge, Engineering Knowledge, Digital Knowledge, etc., etc., will earn it a leadership role in the worldwide community of the light fixture industry.

The difference between the two, is extreme!

The first calls for transactional skills. The second calls for transformational skills. The first is led by a transactional leader. The second is led by a transformational leader.

The way in which the people in each of those entities is inspired, led, taught, trained, managed, and developed are completely foreign to each other. Very much like a McDonald's store is remarkably different than a Starbucks store. Very much like the founder of McDonald's set out in his uniquely differentiated manner through which to design, build, launch and grow the only company of its kind in the world.

Just as did, however differently, the founder of Starbucks set out in his uniquely differentiated manner through which to design, build, launch and grow the only company of ITS kind in the world.

Astonishing, yes?

This is how we do it here, yes?

And in each of the above cases, it comes down to the very words a young women uses at the counter, to greet a new customer, to greet a returning customer, to respond to a concern any one customer might have about any one problem every single one of their customers has had, and might have, from the very first day in service, to the very day they're experiencing it, the minute by minute Special Operation of their Very Special company, doing their Very Special things they do, in their almost infinitely Special way of doing them, every single one of them, every single day, by every single employee, for one solitary, exclusively original purpose, to reinstate the McDonald's Brand, the Starbucks Brand, in the hearts and minds of those they were created to serve.

Which is after all what a Brand is, once said and done, isn't it? It's a Special Way of being in the world. And if it isn't, then what? Then failure, of course. Because that's why the vast majority of new businesses fail, 70% of all those started up in their very first year! 95% of which fail before they reach their 10th anniversary. Which then explains why Specialized Knowledge is not only important, but essential.

Because it is only Specialized Knowledge which distinguishes special companies and special people from everyone else. Welcome to the conversation. Welcome to a special new world. Welcome to a special new you!

Wishing you the most special of experiences as you visit the most special authors in this book series who follow in my footsteps in this journey.

Michael E. Gerber ~ Creator of The E-Myth.

MICHAEL E. GERBER

Michael E. Gerber is the author of the N.Y. Times mega-bestseller, for two consecutive decades, "The E-Myth Revisited" and nine other worldwide best-selling E-Myth books concerning small business entrepreneurship, leadership, and management.

Additionally, Michael E. Gerber has written 19 industry-specific E-Myth Vertical books co-authored by industry experts, for Attorneys; Accountants; Optometrists; Chiropractors; Landscape Contractors; Financial Advisers; Architects; Real Estate Brokers; Insurance Agents; Dentists; Nutritionists; Bookkeepers; Veterinarians; Real Estate Investors; Real Estate Agents; Chief Financial Officers; and soon to be, HVAC Contractors and Plumbers.

His mission is "to transform the state of small business worldwide™."

Erik "Mr. Awesome" Swanson

YOU ARE SPECIAL!

You may be asking yourself why I would say that, especially if I don't even know you. How could I possibly know that YOU are special when there are close to 8 billion people in the world? How could I say that you are special when I don't know if you have been struggling through the past few years, or have encountered huge setbacks recently? How could I say that if I didn't know that your successes have been really tough to accomplish and had taken much longer than you expected? You may be thinking that if I only 'knew you' that I would never in my wildest dreams come up with a saying such as: "You are special!"

Yet, I am here to tell you that indeed…YOU ARE SPECIAL!

This is such a vital concept to accept. It's vital to all of your successes in every area of your life. If you truly look at the possibilities that sit in front of you each and every day, you will be astonished.

Think about it. Just the mere fact of your existence is astonishing. I mean, it literally takes on average over 100 million little guys to swim upstream, if you know what I mean. Over 100 million of them and yet just one is needed to create your existence. That is special!

Now, why would I mention all of that when we are discussing the concept of 'Specialized Knowledge?' Well, you see, the way I figure is that we need to come to the realization that we truly are a gift to the world. The more you believe this, the easier it is to realize we must focus our energy and efforts into a special and certain field of knowledge to excel in such a magical way.

Too many people in the world simply go about their lives without harnessing their true magic or gift. They tend to stay in the general knowledge pool.

There are two types of knowledge, as Napoleon Hill describes. One is general knowledge, and the other is Specialized Knowledge. Hill mentions that people tend to believe the statement that 'knowledge is power,' yet it's not true. Knowledge is only 'potential power.'

It's time for you to vow to be an expert in your field. The beautiful part of this is that you can do this in a couple different ways. The first way is to dive deep into absorbing as much knowledge in a specific subject as to be more advanced in that field than others around you. This will make you more desirable in business, for example, and organizations will seek you out as the expert in that field. The other way is to create what I call my 'Ambassador Team' or 'Dream Team.'

Your Ambassador Team or Dream Team is a group of individuals who are your 'Go To' team to educate you in those specific areas in which they are experts in. You draw from their expertise and apply their knowledge to the specific answer you are seeking. This requires that you are able to organize it and also possess the knowledge in how to put this it all into action.

Your Dream Team is also referred to as a Master Mind Group. This is a group of individuals who all possess their own Specialized Knowledge in certain fields. It is very important to organize this group in such a way that all of the actual Specialized Knowledge in the group points to a specific definite purpose.

I have a friend who is a very famous real estate investing coach who often tells me that he has over 7 or 8 Masters from highly sought-after universities. When people ask him how he accomplished that at such a young age, he replies that he personally doesn't hold any of those degrees. He hires his team under him in his company and has them on his payroll. So, it's as if he has 7 or 8 Masters underneath him.

There's a saying that explains you should never strive to be the smartest man in the room. It's smarter to surround yourself with others who are smarter than you so that you can draw from their Specialized Knowledge.

Once I realized the value of leveraging this strategy, I started to seek out how to create, develop, harvest, and sustain a successful Master Mind Group.

It took some time and trial and error. But, now I run a very successful Master Mind Group called the Habitude Warrior Mastermind (www. HabitudeWarriorMastermind.com), in which we have over 100 members, all focusing on the growth of great habits and attitudes. We draw off of each other's expertise or Specialized Knowledge to reach a common goal or definite purpose. Each of us contribute counsel from our own real-life experiences and expertise. Feel free to join us for a session and see if it resonates with you. Make sure you mention this particular book and chapter for you to receive one free session with us: www.RideAlongGuestPass.com

It's truly amazing to see the growth of each member. Wow, what a blessing to create these masterminds and attract such beautiful human beings who all have one major goal in mind—to assist and cheer on the growth of their fellow members!

Once I saw the true success of our Habitude Warrior Mastermind, I decided to create another group that focuses on the growth of professional speakers and authors. It's called the Global Speakers Mastermind. We bring in top Speakers and Mentors from around the world to share, teach, and inspire each of us in our growth as a Speaker, Mentor, and Author. If you are an aspiring speaker who knows the true value of consistently learning and sharpening the saw in your field, feel free to check it out. (www.DecideTobeAwesome.com)

Another great friend of mine who is a highly paid and sought-after Professional Speaker colleague of mine has a fantastic strategy. He vowed to himself to read 3 books per month. The first book is on his specific field in order for him to consistently sharpen his saw in his own Specialized Knowledge. The second book that he reads each month is a book teaching him to become a better parent to his children on a consistent basis. And the third book he reads each month is on a subject that he doesn't have any prior knowledge. This is so cool. He is constantly enhancing his Specialized Knowledge each month and at the same time he is learning new, general knowledge in which he can apply as well. Brilliant!

Mastering the strategy of Specialized Knowledge will forever change your life! It will truly bring up your worth and value in the world. You will soon realize that YOU are now the 'GO TO' person everyone else seeks out.

ERIK SWANSON

About Erik "Mr. Awesome" Swanson: As an Award-Winning International Keynote Speaker and 13 Time #1 Best-Selling Author, Erik "Mr. Awesome" Swanson is in great demand around the world! He speaks to an average of more than one million people per year. He can be seen on Amazon Prime TV in the very popular show SpeakUP TV. Mr. Swanson has the honor to have been invited to speak to many universities such as University of California (UCSD), Cal State University, University of Southern California (USC), Grand Canyon University (GCU), and the Business and Entrepreneurial School of Harvard University. He is also a Faculty Member of CEO Space International and is a recurring keynoter at Vistage Executive Coaching. Erik also joins the Ted Talk Family with his latest TEDx speech called "A Dose of Awesome."

Erik got his start in the self-development world by mentoring directly under the infamous Brian Tracy. Quickly climbing to become the top trainer around the world from a group of over 250 handpicked trainers, Erik started to surround himself with the best of the best and soon started to be inviting to speak on stages alongside such greats as Jim Rohn, Bob Proctor, Les Brown, Sharon Lechter, Jack Canfield, and Joe Dispenza... just to name a few. Erik has created and developed the super-popular Habitude Warrior Conference, which has a two-year waiting list and includes 33 top-named speakers from around the world. It is a 'Ted Talk 'style event which has quickly climbed to one of the top 10 events not to miss in the United States! He is the creator, founder, and CEO of the Habitude Warrior Mastermind and Global Speakers Mastermind. His motto is clear... "NDSO!": No Drama – Serve Others!

Author's Website: *www.SpeakerErikSwanson.com*
Book Series Website & Author's Bio: *www.The13StepstoRiches.com*

Jon Kovach Jr.

WORLD'S GREATEST ATHLETE

"A jack of all trades is a master of none but oftentimes better than a master of one."

In the track and field sport of Decathlon, one athlete must master the elements of 10 track and field events. Those events include: 100m, long jump, shot put, high jump, and 400m on the first day and 110m hurdles, discus, pole vault, javelin, and 1500m on the second day, traditionally in that order. "World's Greatest Athlete" is awarded to whoever wins the Decathlon.

In high school, I openly competed in the 100m, 200m, 400m, 800m, 1500m, long jump, high jump, triple jump, and some shot put and discus throw. Although my mom was a hurdle champion in her youth, I had little to no experience competing in hurdles, and I had no training in the javelin. But the one event that intimidated me the most was pole vault—running full speed while bending a carbon fiber pole and flinging your body over a small resting bar elevated by some medal stands high up in the air. And once you've cleared the bar at the apex, you then free fall to a soft mat and somehow land on your back. It's one of the most technical sports I've ever witnessed. Despite my intimidations, I had one goal, "World's Greatest Athlete."

I had recently returned home from the Philippines, where I felt called to serve a two-year mission trip for The Church of Jesus Christ of Latter-day Saints. My scholarship options I once had in 2008 dissolved as I was now 21 years old and two years behind on my technical training. The mission trip was a sacrifice I was willing to make at the time, but it ultimately made my journey to becoming "World's Greatest Athlete" a lot harder.

I contacted my old high school, remembered as a celebrity alumnus. Having been voted homecoming king and prom king multiple times, elected as the senior class president, and also nominated as a captain of the football team and track team, I was easily welcomed back to the track squad as an assistant coach where I could condition with the athletes and train for the decathlon while in this transitional period of life.

I hadn't been accepted into a college at this point, given my ecclesiastic sacrifice. However, I was aware that if you didn't train for a school, you could still compete at open national track meets for adults through the United States of America Track & Field Association (USATF). In May of 2011, Colorado State University announced its hosting of an open track meet where I could compete in the decathlon and qualify for the USA Olympic Trials. I believed that this was my ticket back into the track and field world. I could compete and show multiple coaching squads my skillsets and strengths, get accepted on to a university track squad, obtain specialized training, and work my way to the Olympics. That was my plan.

Like hopping on a bicycle, I quickly got back into great physical shape to compete with the Division I athletes. My sprint speed was back up to max velocity. I put muscle back on where I previously had fat from eating rice for every meal in the Philippines. I worked on my flexibility and form for the hurdles and javelin (my weak spots). I practiced my shot put and discus techniques. I was feeling great with my leg strength for the jumping events. But still in my mind was that intimidating and technical event of pole vault.

I consulted with the high school pole-vault coach and worked on my form. I collected tips from my friends who had competed in this event before. I even studied hours of the event on YouTube.

The drills and training were unlike any other I had experienced. It required precision, grace, timing, and finesse. Each day that I practiced, I got better, but faced one inevitable fact: that I was going up against Division I athletes who have been training and competing in the pole vault for years. I hadn't even cleared an open height in competition before.

April 22, 2011, came. Competition day. I competed as best I could have in each event and even better than I imagined. I broke a personal record in the long jump and high jump competition. I was top 3 ranked in the shot put and the 1500m. Then, it was time for the pole vault. After a few stiff run-throughs, I stepped away from the competition for a quick minute to say a prayer. In my prayer, I released my fears by giving gratitude for all my training up until this point.

At this Pac 12 and Mountain West Division I Conference track meet, I was up against the toughest decathletes in the Intermountain West; Colorado State University, Colorado University, and Air Force Academy athletes. Then I heard my name, "Kovach on deck!" I grabbed my pole vault and positioned myself on the platform, ready to take on my biggest physical challenge ever. "Kovach is up!" I lifted the pole, sprinted down the platform with 100m speed, planted the pole in the hole, leaped upward, bent the flexible bar, and flew vertically into the sky upside down. I was 10 feet off the ground, floating high above the mat and platform and then flopping over the high bar, free-falling to the mat. Ten feet and one inch; a new personal record and the first time I had ever placed in the top 5 for an event I only started to learn two months prior.

After landing on the mat, I said out loud, "that was so much fun!" A roar from the crowd burst into applause after I rolled off the mat to retrieve my pole. The coaches and athletes were all standing to applaud as well. I hadn't realized until then, but while warming up I told another competitor that I had never pole vaulted before in my life, and this was my first time competing in it. I guess word got around because people lined up to see me try—I guess new pole vaulters are entertaining and comical to watch. Boy, were they surprised, as was I.

I was proud of my accomplishment. I placed 7th overall in the decathlon competition without a coach or specialized training. Pole Vault taught me one of the biggest life lessons that day—anyone can learn and become good at anything with enough knowledge, preparation, experience, and a passionate attitude to achieve it. At the risk of becoming a one-dimensional type of person rather than a dynamic person, people too often focus on one thing they are good at but lack the dynamics of curiosity and inquisitiveness. Don't get me wrong, they become masters of those one or two things over time, but still limit their abilities by creating a proverbial glass ceiling above their potential and success.

Throughout my continued collegiate journey, I discovered the power of a mastermind, a group of people who gather in the spirit of harmony to help each other solve unanswered challenges in their lives and businesses. I became obsessed with the mastermind methodologies. I studied them. I practiced facilitating them. I started writing about them. Seven years later, I've contributed over 7,000 hours to mastering the mastermind process, make it my own, and now teaching people the outstanding results and benefits of its implementation and effects. In Malcolm Gladwell's book Outliers, he talks about the all-time greatest humans in their specific trades, services, and expertise and how they all became the greatest as a result of acquiring Specialized Knowledge and experience while dedicating 10,000+ hours in pursuit of mastering that one thing. In my professional pursuit to master the mastermind methods, I've transmuted my power and energy as an Olympic hopeful and competitive Division I athlete into my absolute passion.

In the pursuit of my new passion, this ultimately brought an end to my track career. Although I still haven't hung up the track spikes just yet, I've still competed in 200-mile Ragnar races, played recreational sports, and have coached several state champions in an effort to pass on my Specialized Knowledge to others as they've chased their various dreams. My hope has been to help average athletes become elite, top-performing athletes through their mindset and belief systems, then a specialized training system.

People lack the skill of organizing and using their knowledge after they acquire it. I learned that day at my decathlon trial that I (like everyone else in the world) have the ability to pick up a pole vault, compete, and place in the top ranks amongst other top athletes just by studying it and acquiring an inkling of experience. I asked myself, "imagine what I could do with that same power as I harness it for good and educate people on things that will also change their lives."

Although my professional passions transitioned me away from becoming "World's Greatest Athlete," I have found limitless fulfillment in serving others through the mastermind methodologies. However, I still get the urge to train again and fulfill that unfinished dream... To be continued.

"An educated man is not necessarily one who has an abundance of general or Specialized Knowledge. An educated man is one who has developed the faculties of his mind that he may acquire anything he wants or its equivalent without violating the rights of others." —Napoleon Hill

As you read through the various chapters in this book, you will be amazed at all the expert contributions on the subject of Specialized Knowledge from the founding principles that Napoleon Hill wished to bestow us on the road to thinking and growing rich. No other book in this world will have as many examples, stories, teachings, and diverse perspectives on this topic of acquiring knowledge in pursuit of riches. I invite you to study this volume intently.

JON KOVACH JR.

About Jon Kovach Jr.: Jon is an award-winning and international motivational speaker and global mastermind leader. Jon has helped multi-billion-dollar corporations, including Coldwell Banker Commercial, Outdoor Retailer Cotopaxi, and the Public Relations Student Society of America, exceed their annual sales goals. In his work as an accountability coach and mastermind facilitator, Jon has helped thousands of professionals overcome their challenges and achieve their goals.

Jon is Founder and Chairman of Champion Circle, a networking association that combines high-performance-based networking activities and recreational fun to create connection capital and increases prosperity for professionals.

Jon is the Mastermind Facilitator and Team Lead of the Habitude Warrior Mastermind and the Global Speakers Mastermind & Masterclass founded by Speaker Erik "Mr. Awesome" Swanson.

Jon speaks on a number of topics including accountability, The 4 Irrefutable Laws of High Performance, and The Power of Mastermind Methodologies. He is a #1 Best-Selling Author and was recently featured on SpeakUp TV, an Amazon Prime TV series. He stars in over 100 speaking stages, podcasts, and live international summits on an annual basis.

Author's website: *www.JonKovachJr.com*
Book Series Website & Author's Bio: *www.The13StepsToRiches.com*

Amado Hernandez

SPECIALIZED KNOWLEDGE IS A GAME OF POKER

"If you're playing a poker game and look around the table and can't tell who the sucker is, it's you." That statement has been attributed to actor and film director, Paul Newman, but the concept has been expressed by many people through the years, including Warren Buffett. Buffett said similarly, "If you've been in the game for 30 minutes and you don't know who the patsy is, you're the patsy."

What's more valuable in a poker game and in stock market investing? Is it general knowledge about poker or stocks? Or is it Specialized Knowledge about poker or stocks? Or is it possible that it's something entirely different?

Knowledge, general and specialized, has become a commodity that to most is synonymous with the word "Google." In fact, a Google search of "Specialized Knowledge" returns 400,000,000 results (0.94 seconds) and, finally, doesn't really tell you much. So, let's forget about Google and get back to the poker game and the stock market.

Self-awareness is the most valuable knowledge that a poker player, stock market investor, or almost everybody can acquire, which is Specialized Knowledge about themselves. And the second most valuable Specialized

Knowledge is awareness about the other people in the game, in the market, or in our lives.

Optimal self-awareness encompasses a complete understanding of ourselves; ultimate Specialized Knowledge about our own traits, behaviors, and especially, feelings. It's a psychological state where we are in touch with, and in control of, everything we think and everything we do.

I have repeatedly failed, often miserably, over the past five decades. But it is my failures as well as my successes that have provided the knowledge I have about myself. This self-awareness has empowered me to develop specialized skills that enable me to make a positive impact on the lives of others. And, just as valuable, inspire me to help others realize their own dreams.

We all have a moral obligation to continually pursue self-awareness because self-awareness is not a destination; it is an ongoing journey. What's the alternative to self-awareness? Is it self-ignorance? Who wants to be the sucker in the poker game?

There are countless areas of Specialized Knowledge, but there are only three types: (1) Personal, (2) Professional, and (3) Cultural. The value of Specialized Knowledge ranges from worthless to priceless. And the value can go from one extreme to another virtually overnight, especially Specialized Knowledge in the professional category.

Personal Specialized Knowledge includes everything we have learned about ourselves. It's unique in that we are the only ones in the universe who know, and will ever know, everything about ourselves. It starts with our memory, but memories without understanding and action (like history) are entirely worthless.

My ongoing quest for greater and more valuable self-awareness is like Don Quixote's idealistic quest in his life. Don Quixote believed only what he chose to believe and saw the world much differently than most other people. Don Quixote was proud and idealistic and, ultimately, wanted to save the world.

Saving the world may be well beyond my realm of desire, expectation, and capabilities. Yet, positively impacting the world is what I do best, and I am as passionate about it as Don Quixote was about tilting at windmills. So, my pursuit of Specialized Knowledge of myself (aka self-awareness) is like Lexus' "Relentless Pursuit of Perfection."

How do you validate "self-awareness"? Self-awareness opens with self-love and closes with self-honesty, and embraces everything in between. Self-honesty may be the most difficult part of the equation. Self-honesty is all about living in the present, recognizing our own weaknesses and forgiving ourselves and others for having flaws. It's about accessing the elements of our lives that give us strength and thanking God for them. Kind of like Frank Sinatra's "ac-cen-tu-ate the positive, eli-mi-nate the negative."

Professional Specialized Knowledge is what we need to have for our "day job." It can come from formal education (high school, college, trade school or professional training, real estate school), corporate training, and professional coaches and mentors. This type of Specialized Knowledge is highly fluid. Think about the jobs that have disappeared or are rapidly disappearing. They include, but are in no way limited to taxi drivers, librarians, cashiers, rapidly disappearing stockbrokers, real estate agents, and mortgage loan officers. That's why most people realize that "A-B-C" also means "always be changing" (careers). While you may not always be changing your career, you need to always be modifying and growing it.

The third type of Specialized Knowledge is cultural awareness. It is the easiest and most fun of all three. My cultural awareness begins with a thorough understanding of my Latino Community and Southern California, and extends around the world. As a Latino, I understand the not-so-subtle differences between tortillas and arepas, tacos and pupusas, blanco, reposado, and anejo. It's usually not as simple as the difference between chile verde (green) and chili rojo (red), or the difference between tortillas de maize (corn) and tortillas de harina (flour).

Understanding, REALLY understanding, the Specialized Knowledge of my Latino culture means understanding that there is Salsa, Pasodoble, Bachata, Tango, Merengue, Cumbia, ChaCha, Mambo, Reggaeton, Bossa Nova, Rumba, Son Cubano, Vallenato, Banda, Norteiio, Quebradita, Mariachi, and even more. There are songs and dances and countless variations of all of them. Those are just a few examples of my Specialized Knowledge about mi Cultura Latina (Latin Culture).

So what's the bottom line? The bottom line is "Specialized Knowledge" can mean whatever you want it to mean. And its value can be whatever you want it to be. For me, Specialized Knowledge is not an end, it is a means. Specialized Knowledge empowers me to continually develop the personal and professional skills that I need to succeed as an entrepreneur and dealmaker.

What is the most valuable Specialized Knowledge that I have? Remember the reference to the poker table? Have you ever played poker (or watched a poker tournament)? If your answer is "yes" then you probably know what a "tell" is. A "tell" in a poker game is a player's behavior, demeanor, body language, or often facial expressions (micro-expressions) that give away their poker hand or what their next move might be. You know what Kenny Rogers sang in *The Gambler*, "Son I've made a life out of readin' people's faces. Knowin' what the cards were by the way they held their eyes."

Specialized Knowledge, in its purest form, is a treasure. It's a treasure if, and only if, we effectively use it. The true value of Specialized Knowledge is when you can contribute to society and the market rewards you. With Specialized Knowledge, you can greatly leverage the law of reciprocity because you have something proprietary that others may not have.

One practical example of Specialized Knowledge that many people take for granted (maybe because it was easily given to them) is speaking a second language. My professional career has been greatly boosted by my fluency (writing and speaking) in both English and Spanish.

Mastering Specialized Knowledge is impossible without having a solid understanding of general knowledge. But what is the "X-factor" that acts as a catalyst to bring people together? The "X-factor" is charisma. Along with passion, charisma is what monetizes Specialized Knowledge.

Like me, by now you have probably been saturated with thinking about "Specialized Knowledge" in all its various forms. So let's get physical about Specialized Knowledge and take immediate action.

Grab a piece of paper. It doesn't matter what, type, color, or size. Either lined or unlined. It is okay if it's blank. Fold the piece of paper into 3 sections approximately the same size (either vertical or horizontal is okay). On the first side, write "NOW" at the top of the page. Label the three sections: "PERSONAL" - "PROFESSIONAL" - "CULTURAL". Do the same thing on the other side and write "THEN" at the top of that page.

Keeping it as simple as possible, complete each section on the "NOW" side with a brief description of the Specialized Knowledge that you have, how you acquired it, and how valuable it is to you (rate from 1 to 10 with 10 being the highest).

On the reverse side (the side labeled "THEN"), complete all three sections with a brief description of the Specialized Knowledge you plan on acquiring, when and how you plan on acquiring it, and rank it (1 to 10) on how valuable you believe it will prove to be.

I hope that my few words about Specialized Knowledge, if nothing else, will inspire you to dig deep into your heart, mind, and soul and begin (or intensify) your quest for personal growth and self-discovery. Reach for the stars. Dance on the edge. And hold on tight to your dreams. Remember what Paul Coelho said in The Alchemist, "Dreams are the language of God."

AMADO HERNANDEZ

About Amado Hernandez: Amado was born in Mexico of humble beginnings and raised in Los Angeles, California. As an avid reader, Amado always focused on self-development. He coaches sales professionals to make six and seven figures in real estate.

Amado believes in a progressive culture, one people-centric where clients' dreams come true and salespeople thrive; at the end of the day, we all want to be respected and pursue our happiness. My goal is to leave a legacy-making a difference in people's lives.

With 33 years of Real Estate experience, Mr. ABC Amado Hernandez successfully operates and grows his Excellence Empire Real Estate Moreno Valley office. Broker/Owner Amado first opened his doors in 1995, and Excellence currently has over 60 offices in Southern California, Las Vegas, Merida Yucatan, Mexico, and over 900 Agents. He is also part owner of a highly successful Mortgage company Excellence Mortgage and owner of Empire Escrow Services. Mr. Amado is also involved with his community and currently serves as Director at Inland Valley Association of Realtors and will be the President-Elect for IVAR in 2022.

Author's Website: *www.ExcellenceEmpireRE.com*
Book Series Website & Author's Bio: *www.The13StepstoRiches.com*

Angelika Ullsperger

TURNING KNOWLEDGE TO POWER

Imagine you're in an empty room and your mind, a blank slate. You're handed a dictionary and must memorize the entirety of it before you can leave. The book in front of you exudes knowledge, some of which dates back to before the common era. Over 230,000 entries fill the pages to the brim, a pure wealth of knowledge you have been gifted with. Upon leaving, you are placed as the head of an immensely successful business and it's up to you to run it. Would you have any idea what to do?

"Knowledge is only potential power. It becomes power only when, and if, it is organized into definite plans of action, and directed to a definite end." Knowledge is only as useful as the action you take. What do you need to take action? The knowledge of the process, steps, and skills that are necessary to turn knowledge into power. Knowledge provides strength to navigate through the world. Any problem you have can be aided with knowledge, but it is specific knowledge that will do so.

For a while, I gathered knowledge but made it nowhere. As fun as it is to learn, I was not aware that I needed knowledge that allowed me to take action. Until learning this, I was unable to move forward. To help you get past an obstacle that I and many others have run into, my goal is to provide you with some knowledge that helps you to progress forward.

By the end of this chapter, aim to have a plan in mind to acquire the Specialized Knowledge that you need to take action and move forward.

You could have access to every ingredient known to man, but without the knowledge to cook recipes, you won't be able to make a 5-course meal. So, where and how will you learn?

Today, the acquisition of knowledge has changed immensely from when *Think and Grow Rich* was written in 1937. The most important means of receiving dependable knowledge according to Hill was:

One's own experience and education…

Experience and education available through cooperation of others (Master Mind Alliance) Colleges and Universities...

Public Libraries (books and periodicals in which may be found all the knowledge organized by civilization) Special Training Courses (night schools and home study schools).

Every means listed is still monumentally beneficial but now, with the creation of the internet, you have access to all of these options and more for receiving knowledge. There are learning materials across all media, and they are available on the internet. Documentaries, podcasts, masterclasses, textbooks, instructional videos; the list goes on. There is a place to learn anything. Every manner Hill listed as an important source for knowledge can be accessible online, in many instances for free. It could be faster to hire a coach or pay for a class, but for those who are not yet in the position to do so, and even for those who are, you still have many options and cost-effective sources to benefit from. Numerous places such as banks, stock brokerages, social media websites, your local library, or your local government business page all provide learning resources you can benefit from at no cost.

You may not have the funds to invest in yourself significantly (yet!) but chances are you have a tablet or smartphone. One free vein of knowledge is in applications. Applications such as TED, Khan academy, Sololearn, and Coursera provide free reputable knowledge. The library is reputable for the wide access it provides to sources of information. There is an app for that, too.

The information you need is out there, but first, you must decide what information you need.

In 1993, 56 years after the publication of *Think and Grow Rich*, the world wide web (www.) made the internet available to the public. Since then, the internet has exploded with data.

The internet has exposed the world to an almost infinite amount of knowledge. For comparison, the average phone in 2021 has anywhere from 32 gb to 128 gb of memory. The IDC (The International Data Corpration) states that all the data across the world totaled 33 zettabytes (zb) in 2018 and by 2025 will total up to 175 zb.

Just 1 zettabyte is equal to one trillion gigabytes.

IF you tried to download zettabytes, it would take you 1.8 billion years. With such an incomprehensible amount of data, there is bound to be false information readily accessible. With such an influx of new information, now, more than ever, it is absolutely paramount to consider and analyze the source of the information you are getting. It is important you keep an open mind, but look with a critical eye.

Be aware of biases.

When searching for information, you must keep in mind the biases that exist. For one, there is confirmation bias. Confirmation bias causes us to look for and interpret information that supports our beliefs or causes us to reject information that objects to our beliefs. If we aren't careful, we can unintentionally filter out valid information. We all are guilty of having bias from time to time, and the best we can do is work to acknowledge and avoid falling victim to our biases again. Whether its realized or not, many news sources have biases as well and in turn provide incorrect or misleading information. Always be sure to view a variety of news sources so you can verify the information. Even better, chances are you can find the source. If there is no link to a source, you can always rely on Google to search for the original source.

A great way to avoid biases and cover blind spots can be through accountability and masterminds, which are even more accessible now, thanks to the internet. No matter how smart you are or how much time you have, you can only acquire thorough knowledge on so many topics. No matter what you experience, you can only encounter so much. No matter how much Specialized Knowledge you collect, you will need the Specialized Knowledge of others. This is one way mastermind members create an abundance of value. When the group works together to combine their knowledge, skills, and power, everyone wins. Not only is there shared benefit for the group, but the entirety of the world benefits, for you have strengthened your power to think, create, and accomplish that which would be otherwise impossible.

The best teams are embodied with individuals who each specialize in a different field. Even world leaders have a variety of advisors who are masters in their respective fields. The phrase "knowledge is power" never specified whose knowledge you may draw from. This is good for you because you don't have to settle. Find what you truly enjoy, something that sparks joy, something that you want to explore every inch of, and master it. When you specialize in a subject, you stand out. At the end of the day, you can specialize in more than one thing, but you will find it works best to focus on mastering subjects one at a time. For those who have trouble focusing on a single aspect for long periods, pick no more than three subjects to explore and master. It may be tempting to do more, but it can create disorganization and/or burnout.

Think and Grow Rich provided specific knowledge of ideas—ideas that helped every author in this series grow into the successful person they are today. These ideas open your mind to what types of knowledge you will need to progress. Without the knowledge they were provided and the time they took to comprehend and apply it, you would not be reading this book. Every book in this series contains Specialized Knowledge; knowledge that will help you progress in the direction of your desires.

You could spend all of your free time using various media to gather knowledge, but most importantly, you need to make sure you're getting the specific knowledge you need to take actionable steps. Anyone can provide you with information, but it is up to you to take action. Or as Greg Reid would say, "You can lead a person to knowledge, but you can't make them think."

You must take the time to sit with yourself to process, ponder, and plan. You may not figure it all out at once, and that is okay. Figure out what knowledge you need to make a plan with actionable steps you can start immediately. Please get out either a pen and paper or open your notes app on your phone and answer the following:

What are your end goals?

What do you know?

What do you need to know to take action? Why?

From whom or where can you obtain this knowledge?

Is this a trustworthy source?

What action steps can you take when you put this book down?

For further guidance, the Specialized Knowledge in an upcoming book in this series, Organized Planning, will help you create a more clear, organized path for you to take action along.

So far, with the knowledge and guidance from this book, a mastermind or accountability partner, and the burning desire you have forged, you have both the knowledge and the power to decide your next step and take it!

ANGELIKA ULLSPERGER

About Angelika Ullsperger: Angelika is a serial entrepreneur from Baltimore, Maryland. She is a fashion designer, model, artist, photographer, and musician. Angelika has extensive and well-rounded professional experience having worked as a business owner, carpenter, chef, graphic designer, manager, event planner, sales and product specialist, marketer, and coach. Angelika is now a #1 Best-Selling Author in the historic book series, The 13 Steps To Riches. She is a life-long learner with a sincere and genuine interest in all things of the world with a major interest in the formal subject of abnormal psychology, neuroscience, and quantum physics.

Angelika prides herself as someone who has saved lives as a friend, first responder, EMT, and knowledgeable suicide prevention advocate. With a vast knowledge and experience in multiple professions, Angelika is also a proud honorable member of Phi Theta Kappa, The APA, the AAAS, and an FBLA (Future Business Leaders Association) Business Competition Finalist. She is Certified in basic coding and blockchain technology. Amongst the careers and vast experience, Angelika is an adventurer and avid dog lover.

Her ultimate goals and dreams are to make a lasting positive impact in people's lives through her wealth of knowledge and skillsets.

Author's Website: *www.Angelika.world*
Book Series Website & Author's Bio: *www.The13StepstoRiches.com*

Dr. Anthony M. Criniti IV

KNOWLEDGE IS NOT POWER

Think and Grow Rich by Napoleon Hill is one of the best classic books to teach someone about how to become a financial success (as well as a success in other areas of life). In there, you will find his thirteen steps to riches and each one has its own separate chapter and analysis. The subject of our book is to interpret his fourth step to riches: Specialized Knowledge. Let's review some of his major conclusions.

First, Hill distinguishes the difference between creating wealth with general knowledge and Specialized Knowledge. "General knowledge, no matter how great in quantity or variety it may be, is of but little use in the accumulation of money." (Hill, 2011, p. 116). He cites examples of the professors in universities who teach general knowledge of every subject possible, yet have very little money. As a former professor, I know the harsh realities of this subject very well. Despite the impact that they have on so many students and their intense effort to reach the highest levels of academia, the pay for untenured professors can be hard to feed a family with.

Instead of general knowledge, Hill advocates for Specialized Knowledge as the path to riches. "Knowledge will not attract money, unless it is organized, and intelligently directed, through practical plans of action, to the definite end of accumulation of money. Lack of understanding of this fact has been the source of confusion to millions of people who falsely believe that "knowledge is power." It is nothing of the sort! Knowledge is only potential power." (Hill, 2011, p. 116). Yes, indeed—knowledge is not power. Millions of people hold cell phones in their hands armed with the accumulation of the knowledge of humanity. This does not make them any smarter. Instead, what matters is their understanding of that knowledge and how to apply it.

Let's take a look at another example. According to *The Necessity of Finance,* "The major goal of finance is to continuously maximize wealth for an individual, a group, or an organization." (Criniti, 2013, p. 18). If I gave someone all of my finance books to read and a million dollars to invest in her business, this does not mean that in a year from now she will still have this exact amount (or any money at all). I have handed her knowledge and she might have memorized it line for line. Nevertheless, without the ability to understand the information presented in it and without proper implementation, it will be of little use in meeting her financial goals.

The specialist who has Specialized Knowledge should know how to put it to use. However, this does not mean that he knows how to make money with his specialty; only that he is capable of performing tasks that he was trained to do. Too many specialists fail as entrepreneurs because they confuse knowing how to apply a specialized skill with knowing how to apply the skill of making money from a business. In many cases, an individual whose only specialty might be assembly becomes the one who actually makes an idea profitable. As Hill puts it, "The accumulation of great fortunes calls for power, and power is acquired through highly organized and intelligently directed Specialized Knowledge, but that knowledge does not, necessarily, have to be in the possession of the man who accumulates the fortune." (Hill, 2011, p. 119).

Further, the unspecialized individual who knows how to make an idea profitable does not even have to have a formalized education. Hill highlights the true academic credibility of these talented moneymakers. "The man who can organize and direct a "Master Mind" group of men who possess knowledge useful in the accumulation of money, is just as much a man of education as any man in the group." (Hill, 2011, p. 119). This statement is very consistent with my conclusion in Principle 148 of *The Most Important Lessons in Economics and Finance:* "You don't need to become academically intelligent to become wealthy." (Criniti, 2014, p. 181).

There are a few other important points to discuss from Chapter 5. Next, at your first glance of this chapter, you might have been confused to think that Hill has rated general knowledge as worthless, and Specialized Knowledge as just a little more valuable. After all, he admits that you don't even need to have Specialized Knowledge to make money. With these statements, you might be tempted to wonder why you even need to go to school. However, as you read on, there is one statement that sums up his true feelings on the importance of education. Hill says, "The person who stops studying merely because he has finished school is forever hopelessly doomed to mediocrity, no matter what may be his calling. The way of success is the way of continuous pursuit of knowledge." (Hill, 2011, p. 126).

Hill's many messages on the subject can now be simplified as follows: Having knowledge is important, but understanding it is better. General knowledge is good, but Specialized Knowledge can make you more money. However, if you know how to manage people with Specialized Knowledge, then you can also make money with very little knowledge of that specialty.

Let's now reflect on the concept of purpose found in this chapter. One of the major conclusions in my last book was the deep necessity of having a purpose for both survival and prosperity reasons. From *The Survival of the Richest,* "These reasons are held deep within us, even deeper than the desires for great amounts of money, pleasure, and power. If we don't know our purpose yet, then we must search for it in order to avoid the potential fate of existential frustration." (Criniti, 2016, p. 59). Napoleon Hill has a similar conclusion as it applies specifically to education. "To a large extent, your major purpose in life, the goal toward which you are working, will help determine what knowledge you need." (Hill, 2011, p. 120). If you combine both of our conclusions, a purpose becomes the bedrock to gather the correct knowledge to learn how to survive and prosper.

An interesting observation that I found in this chapter was a glimpse of Napoleon Hill's background with marketing (which includes advertising). Hill stated that he enrolled in a home study course on advertisement (Hill, 2011, p. 124). I thought this was interesting because it helps to explain how he acquired his skillset that helped him later to market the number one best-selling book on self-development in history. It may be possible that without that course, you might not be reading this book right now. I, too, have learned that without marketing knowledge, a written book will probably live forever in obscurity.

Finally, Hill concludes the chapter preparing us for the fifth step to riches by discussing the importance of ideas. "There is no fixed price for sound ideas!" (Hill, 2011, p. 135). He makes the connection between Specialized Knowledge and imagination, paving the way for the next chapter's analysis. He says, "Capability means imagination, the one quality needed to combine Specialized Knowledge with ideas, in the form of organized plans designed to yield riches." (Hill, 2011, p. 135).

To conclude, knowledge alone is not power. True power comes when you have knowledge, understand how to use it, and actually implement it properly. Money generally follows naturally when you have obtained and applied Specialized Knowledge. However, the key lesson to this chapter is that being a specialist alone is not enough to become very wealthy. You must also learn how to run a business. This requires mastering the lessons learned from finance.

You might be the best at what you can do, but if you don't know how to allocate responsibilities to your employees, count your money, invest in your business, market your products or services, and do everything else under the sun necessary to manage your business's wealth, then your business will never reach its fullest potential (or survive long, for that matter). Ultimately, true power is derived from studying and implementing the many lessons of the very special, specialized science of finance.

Bibliography

Criniti, Anthony M., IV. 2013. *The Necessity of Finance: An Overview of the Science of Management of Wealth for an Individual,* a Group, or an Organization. Philadelphia: Criniti Publishing.

Criniti, Anthony M., IV. 2014. *The Most Important Lessons in Economics and Finance: A Comprehensive Collection of Time-Tested Principles of Wealth Management.* Philadelphia: Criniti Publishing.

Criniti, Anthony M., IV. 2016. *The Survival of the Richest: An Analysis of the Relationship between the Sciences of Biology, Economics, Finance, and Survivalism.* Philadelphia: Criniti Publishing.

Hill, Napoleon. 2011. *Think and Grow Rich.* United Kingdom: Capstone Publishing Ltd.

DR. ANTHONY M. CRINITI

About Dr. Anthony M. Criniti IV: Dr. Anthony (aka "Dr. Finance®") is the world's leading financial scientist and survivalist. A fifth generation native of Philadelphia, Dr. Criniti is a former finance professor at several universities, a former financial planner, an active investor in diverse marketplaces, an explorer, an international keynote speaker, and has traveled around the world studying various aspects of finance. He is an award winning author of three #1 international best-selling finance books: *The Necessity of Finance* (2013), *The Most Important Lessons in Economics and Finance* (2014), and *The Survival of the Richest* (2016). As a prolific writer, he also frequently contributes articles to *Entrepreneur, Medium,* and *Thrive Global*. Dr. Criniti's work has started a grassroots movement that is changing the way that we think about economics and finance.

Author's website: *www.DrFinance.info*
Book Series Website & Author's Bio: *www.The13StepsToRiches.com*

Barry Bevier

SPECIALIZED KNOWLEDGE WILL SET YOU APART

I have always loved learning, especially math and science. In high school, I generally challenged myself with the harder classes. For the most part, high school came easy for me. I loved to read and study and would spend hours doing more than was required for my classes.

I was raised in a home where getting an education was valued. Both of my parents were raised on humble family farms, where sometimes meeting basic needs was a challenge for their parents. I don't know if any of my grandparents had a high school education; I doubt it. In spite of growing up during the Great Depression, my parents completed high school and went on to further their education as much as they could. Mom attended a local business college and studied bookkeeping. Dad kept working on the farm and went to a night school to learn the refrigeration trade until WWII interrupted their lives for a few years. After the war, dad continued to farm, yet I remember him taking agricultural courses at Michigan State University to improve his knowledge and expand his business. Mom did the bookkeeping. Their additional knowledge and hard work resulted in them earning several Farm Management Excellence awards.

Even though they were not able to pursue a college degree, they saw the value of education as a means of getting ahead in life. They recognized that the extra Specialized Knowledge they had gained helped to set them apart. They encouraged my sister and I to do well in school so we would be able to get into a good college. I was blessed to have parents who had the desire for their children excel in life.

My parents put a high value on education and expected that my sister and I would attend college to get the additional education that would allow us to make a higher income and secure a better lifestyle than they felt they had. My parents took their courses with a definite plan of action in place as to how they would use it in their business.

After high school, I went on to study Civil Engineering at the University of Michigan. Even during my undergraduate work, I started to specialize in the area of geotechnical engineering, which deals with land development, structure foundations, earthquakes, landslides, and ground water resources. I then specialized even more in the study of foundations for vibrating machinery. I took the course work and developed the knowledge because it was of interest to me and challenged me. I realized how that Specialized Knowledge in the science of machine foundation vibrations would set me apart. At the time, there were very few engineers with this specialty and people with that knowledge were frequently sought after.

Having that Specialized Knowledge allowed me to travel the world, working on projects that I would not otherwise have been able to be involved with, and being in countries I likely would never have been able to experience. Like working on a hydroelectric project in Pakistan for two years that now provides essential power and irrigation water to most of the country. Like working on a landslide repair project in Peru for over a year that ultimately rescued a power plant that provides much of Peru's electricity. Not only did the Specialized Knowledge provide experiences for me, it allowed me to be of greater benefit to others. While some opportunities and events happened that I hadn't anticipated, I took the classes and developed the knowledge with a definite plan of action to get a position in an international engineering firm and eventually own my own company.

At a point in time, I had the opportunity to start my own company with a couple of partners. We were all well-versed in the technical aspects of the business, and our Specialized Knowledge in engineering was only a small part of what was required to build a successful business. We needed additional technical staff with experience. We needed people knowledgeable in bookkeeping, accounting, and tax preparation. We needed people experienced in sales and marketing. We needed people experienced in HR. We grew our company by hiring people with the skills that were required.

Living within an hour's drive of Detroit, the Motor City Capital of the World, I developed an early attraction to cars. Many family members were associated with Ford Motor Company, and Henry Ford's story fascinated me. As a youth, I questioned how a man with very little formal schooling could be so brilliant and become one of the wealthiest men of his time.

As I read and understand the principles of *Think and Grow Rich*, I've taken the time to learn a little more about Henry Ford and some of the other successful and wealthy industrialists of the 19th and 20th century that Napoleon Hill interviewed for *Think and Grow Rich*. Henry Ford had little formal education and quit school at age 15 after having gone through the eighth grade.

Many of the successful people that Napoleon Hill interviewed for *Think and Grow Rich* either didn't have much formal education or had little knowledge in the area in which they became extremely successful. Even (or perhaps especially) Andrew Carnegie, who commissioned Napoleon Hill to do the research and write *Think and Grow Rich*, knew very little about the steel manufacturing business, yet in the early 20th century, amassed a fortune equivalent to over $300 billion in today's dollars.

John D. Rockefeller, who founded Standard Oil Company when he was in his early thirties and is considered one of the wealthiest Americans of all time, only had a high school education. Cornelius Vanderbilt, who became one of the most prolific railroad barons of the 19th century, quit school at age 11 to work on his father's ferry boat in New York City. At age 16, he started his own ferry boat company and later shifted his focus to railroads, were his ruthless acumen and shrewd business practices helped him amass a fortune.

Although coming from a family of entrepreneurs in manufacturing, William Wrigley Jr. had a difficult time in school and was expelled frequently. At age 13, he convinced his father to allow him to be a traveling salesman for his father's soap company, where he developed Specialized Knowledge in sales.

From what I've learned about these few men, while they didn't have much formal schooling, they all had been given or developed special talents that set them apart. In place of schooling, they used their experience and the experience and Specialized Knowledge of others to become successful. They had a strong desire to succeed, were persistent, innovative, and surrounded themselves with others that had the knowledge required for their businesses to be successful. They had the aid of a mastermind, a group of people they surrounded themselves with, who provided the Specialized Knowledge required to achieve success.

I was introduced to Paul Martinelli through the brain health program I have recently completed. He tells his story about Specialized Knowledge that allowed him to transition from a struggling janitor making $20,000 a year to owning a successful business in a very short time. He did this by having a burning desire to accomplish more, and the assistance and power of a mastermind. At the time, he was struggling to get more business and price was an issue with getting more customers. His mastermind suggested that he needed to find something that set him apart from the competition. A way to provide more value.

This challenge occurred at the same time of the HIV epidemic in the 1980s. To set himself apart from his competition, he recognized, through suggestions from his mastermind, that with little investment, he could provide more value that would set him apart and get more customers. He could use vacuums with HEPA filters, which no one else was using at the time. He could use microfiber cleaning cloths, which do a better job of cleaning and not spreading germs, which his competition were not using. With little investment, he could use better quality disinfecting and cleaning materials that his competition were not using. These changes provided more value and were more than enough to set him apart, to allow him to get more business and raises prices.

As his business expanded, he saw the need to take care of stone floors and expanded his capabilities to polishing marble and granite floors. He gained the knowledge to provide this service. This edition to his company's services also set him apart from the competition and allowed him to get more business and increase income. The Specialized Knowledge that he gained and used to improve his janitorial services did not come from him. It came from his mastermind.

Although in my past career in engineering I gained much of my Specialized Knowledge through formal education, Specialized Knowledge does not need to be our own. It can come from others, especially masterminds. You can seek out people to associate with who can provide you with the needed knowledge or experience. And most importantly, Specialized Knowledge has little value if it is not applied through an organized plan of action.

BARRY BEVIER

About Barry Bevier: Barry Bevier is a proud father of two amazing daughters in their mid-twenties, who are pursuing their passions in psychology and architecture in Southern California. He was raised on a family farm near Ann Arbor, Michigan. Growing up, he developed his faith in God, a strong work ethic, a love for nature, and a passion to help others. After completing his master's degree in Civil Engineering at the University of Michigan, he pursued a career in engineering, which eventually brought him to Southern California.

In 2000, he married the love of his life, Linda. They shared a beautiful life for ten years, until she succumbed to the effects of lupus and 20 years of treatment with prescription medications. Since then, Barry pivoted his career path into educating and helping others. Barry has educated himself in alternative, natural modalities in wellness and became a Licensed Brain Health Trainer through Amen Clinics. He also works with a new technology in stem cell supplementation that releases your own stem cells.

Author's Website: *www.BRBevier.Stemtech.com*
Book Series Website & Author's Bio: *www.The13StepstoRiches.com*

Bonnie Lierse

DELEGATION

Did you know potential knowledge isn't power, but the USE of knowledge is the REAL power? That is said in many ways, even by Napoleon Hill. Knowledge comes in many forms. You never know how it will hit you!

I had a wonderful, loving, middle-class family growing up, including a wonderful sister and brother. We were all very close, with definitely different thought processes and personalities. I was the free spirit.

Growing up in Brooklyn, New York, my parents taught us to be loving, giving, and to serve others. They taught us what love and caring meant. They didn't have a lot, but gave everything to their family.

Knowledge is everywhere and shows up every day, in everything we do, and from others around us, as well. However, it's vital to know the difference between general knowledge and Specialized Knowledge. I had to understand both.

My mom sold the World Book encyclopedia most of her life and was very successful. She learned Specialized Knowledge in her career as an entrepreneur and manager. Talk about Specialized Knowledge! She was always reading great books with World Book. She taught me about ambition and to be a true entrepreneur. She always wanted me to focus on my passion and supported me to become highly skilled at what I did. That's where Specialized Knowledge comes into play.

When I was going through primary school, I recall that my teachers were always saying to my parents, "You are such a daydreamer!" School didn't come easily to me.

The great news is that this had nothing to do with my mastering a field I was passionate about. My schooling had nothing to do with being successful and specializing in something. I certainly did not understand or see that at that time.

The other great news was that it didn't matter that I was a daydreamer, as long as I was willing to take those dreams and put them to good use through the Specialized Knowledge I attained over the years in certain areas. We can have many strengths gained over a lifetime. Looking back, I know I did. This has nothing to do with wealth, but doing what you love.

School allows us to study and work on specific subjects, find what we connect with, and grow from there.

I was always artistic and creative. I was able to use a different type of Specialized Knowledge to see my vision. I skimmed by school with challenges, graduated high school with maybe a B average, then went to Brooklyn College for a short time, studying early childhood education, and then eventually transferred universities.

My new journey was to earn access into Pratt Institute in New York City, and it was considered a great privilege to get in. It was one of the largest Art Institutes and most prestigious schools of which I knew. A dream come true!

Soon, I graduated with a BFA degree, specializing in Graphic Design and Illustration. The new journey and career had begun.

After graduating from Pratt Institute, I went through a variety of graphic art careers. My favorite was being mentored as part of the

Screen Cartoonist Guild of Motion Pictures. I went through a wonderful specialized journeyman program.

Knowledge comes to us in so many unexpected ways. It's exciting!

As life moved on, I eventually got married to an encouraging man with whom I went to college, moved from New York to Connecticut, and had two beautiful children. To be an exceptional wife and mother requires instinct and particular knowledge. There is something new, every day. We constantly stretch with every new venture.

Life is a stepping stone of using Specialized Knowledge. It is how we grow into the person we are meant to be. I am still growing to this day, at sixty-six years young! I have chosen many forks in the road, exploring what my most Specialized Knowledge should be.

When you stop growing and stretching, you might possibly end up lifeless and dormant in many ways you don't even realize. Many individuals possess only general knowledge because they don't have or desire a particular mastery. Many people have personalities that don't like change. I THRIVE ON IT!

I personally believe with failures, come true success.

My first marriage was very challenging, so my children had to be my utmost priority. If we don't have life lessons and difficult experiences, we won't grow into our best selves. I always learned from them.

I'm grateful to my former husband, because he made me stronger, through extraordinary adversity. The negative experiences I endured with him made me seek out knowledge in order to bring out the best in me. I am blessed because my former husband and I are close today.

Even through all that, I'm blessed with exceptional grown children and young grandchildren. They too, with me, are part of a huge business leadership and mentorship team. We stretch and grow daily.

There's a saying I used to hear, "Five heads are better than one, ten are better than five" and so on. More minds equals more knowledge. Napoleon Hill always believed that. If he didn't know something, he would delegate to someone on his team who knew more.

Sometimes we use our common sense and street smarts, but many times we need to use our Specialized Knowledge.

Just before my first child was born, I decided to build an interior accessory design business. I had the encouragement of a successful and great man and friend. He said, "If you feel the passion, go for it!" I did, and it became my specialty. I thought to grow leaders.

My personal goal was to become a director by the time my son was born. The month I gave birth, I became a director. While in the hospital, I focused entirely on my gifts and knowledge of leadership and creativeness.

Yes, it took relearning a business and great knowledge of art, decorating, and business leadership to get to that point. The other proficiency I began to develop was people skills. I have been part of a multi-level marketing (MLM) company since my son was born. It's so important and vital to constantly challenge and develop yourself through Specialized Knowledge, but you must USE it, as well. I believe the right MLM can bring out your strengths, if you have access to the specialized leadership and mentorship. Otherwise, your strengths can fade away. It took ten years of developing my business, and I eventually became a district director.

I had extreme admiration for the president of the company. Unfortunately, things went wrong within the corporation itself (out of my control and his), and I knew it was time to walk away. Eventually, it closed down. It was my knowledge and instinct that told me to walk away. I never had regrets, because I knew I had grown and stretched over the years. I still admire the president to this day. Trust those instincts, they are so crucial!

Eventually, I met my present husband and moved back to New York from Connecticut. Funny, I always said I'd never move back to New York, but I did. NEVER say NEVER!

I moved to Long Island, New York. Obviously, it was meant to be. If I hadn't, I wouldn't have met an incredible friend and coauthor, Erin Ley, who contributes in this book as well.

We continuously have to attain new Specialized Knowledge on every journey and path we take.

Once on Long Island, we bought a home through a realtor, who then eventually introduced me to real estate. This was my new adventure, and I would have never thought that! Again, Specialized Knowledge to learn a new business. You guessed it—I stretched.

Are you open to growing yourself, attaining new knowledge and becoming the best you? It's what drives me. What drives you? Every lesson and failure is knowledge because it's how we grow into our best selves.

As you will learn, I love being spontaneous. Most of the steps I took in my life were partly directed by gut-instinct, knowledge, and spontaneity. It does make life interesting!

At sixty-six years young, I'm still gaining knowledge, growing, and changing.

Wisdom, I believe, comes with time and age. Don't you agree?

By the way, I am a Virginia gal now on a newer journey. Soon, you'll learn more!

This chapter is dedicated in loving memory of my husband Thomas Lierse. My best friend, soul mate and beloved husband passed away unexpectedly, November 23, 2021. I know his wings will protect and give love to those he left behind in his life! He was a very wise gent! Among many things, Tom loved our country having served in the U.S. Navy submarine division. Tom was a great writer, trumpet player, and enthusiastically loved participating in local theater productions.

Here's a Specialized Knowledge reminder to all.... don't take TIME, MONEY, ANYONE or ANYTHING for granted! Say I love you often. Spend quality time together. Smell the roses on your way to success, and look into each other's eyes regularly. Times flies so use it well! Live life and pay it forward!

BONNIE LIERSE

About Bonnie Lierse: Bonnie Zaruches Lierse, was a member of "The Screen Cartoonist Guild of Motion pictures" for many years. Also, did freelance at Sesame Street in NY. Part of her creative journey.

As an entrepreneur, was a District Director for a Interior Accessory Design company, which was her own business.

Now on her path she is a seasoned real estate agent with a 20+ years experience in real estate in the NY / Long Island vicinity. She relocated to Northern Virginia nine years ago and continued her real estate career.

Bonnie also works in business development with (LTD) Leadership Team Development and her supplier is Amway. Part of her passions is making a difference in lives of others and discovering and creating leaders.

She is blessed with five beautiful grandchildren and very close with her children and family - some of whom, are also in Virginia. Her mission, as well as passions, are leadership, mentorship, paying it forward, and changing lives one at a time.

Author's Website: *www.amway.com/myshop/SplashFXEnterprises*
Book Series Website & Author's Bio: *www.The13StepstoRiches.com*

Brian Schulman

RICHES BEYOND A BANK ACCOUNT

People think of Specialized Knowledge as technical expertise, product knowledge, being the premiere expert in your field of study or business and they're not wrong, but they're not entirely right, either.

"Dad, I'm going to play lacrosse," my son informed me.

And that was that.

The sound of a lacrosse ball banging against the side of the house became my family's constant companion during my son's freshman year of high school.

He had never played the sport before. I'm not even sure he had watched it played, but he set his sights on making the team and became a student of the game. Completely immersed in the sport, he devoured information on rules and strategies. He committed to four years of play, with practices before and after school, while maintaining his grades, a job, being a part of the school's Jazz and Marching bands, cultivating his friendships and nurturing his social life while still finding time to sleep and do homework. He researched equipment and mastered the game so much so that he began receiving awards, and his team went on to win their division. His 'riches' were not received as a paycheck or monetary compensation, his bank account did not change, but he became wealthy. His currency—Specialized Knowledge.

He had the desire to learn, the faith in himself that he was capable, and a plan of action.

Standing at Dick's Sporting Goods, the reality that Lacrosse is an expensive sport was undeniable and the full four-year commitment would be required. My son said to me, "I want these cleats." I looked at the price, and, at the time not fully understanding the depth of his desire and faith, asked him, "How are you paying for them (priced at $120)?"

My son had already formulated a plan and had put the first steps into action. Without missing a beat, he looked me in the eye and told me that he had noticed our neighbor engaging in a number of home improvement projects and seeing that he had begun working on his fence, my son had approached him. He had talked to the neighbors about painting their fence, negotiated a price that would cover not only his cleats, but his pads as well. Nevertheless, he did not have the money, YET, and was asking me to 'front him a loan'. I would be lying if I did not say that I was incredibly impressed with the detail with which he had planned and prepared! He told me when the job would be done and how long it would be before I got my money back.

I'm sure by now you have guessed the ending to this Cinderella story. I bought him the cleats and, just as promised, I had the $120 in my hand exactly when he said I would. Not only did he have the Specialized Knowledge, he had an organized system of how he would apply it.

Have you ever watched someone, in real time, develop Specialized Knowledge and systematically put it into place? Was it you?

Around the time my son took up lacrosse, I made the decision to leave my corporate job and create my company, Voice Your Vibe. In a way, our journeys were parallel. Before founding my company, I evaluated the Specialized Knowledge I possessed that I would leverage to ensure the success of my business, and how I would organize and systematically apply that wisdom.

My goal was clear: to inspire one person every day.

Here is what I knew:

I am rich in Specialized Knowledge.

- I am exceptional at "humaning" and the art of reading people. I see people's strengths and read their doubts. I introduce them to a version of themselves never before seen.

- I know how to make people feel seen and heard when building personal relationships. At the heart of it all, we all want to matter, and I make it my business to make sure people know they matter.

- I readily and easily see things in others that they don't see in themselves. I recognize the glow, the spark, and help others to recognize it in, and for, themselves.

- I have 20+ years of experience in entrepreneurship, as well as building and growing successful startups. Seeing a person's vision is innate to me. I see their perspective, where they want to go, and possess the specialized business knowledge to get them there.

- I take a vested interest. I truly care. I'm not just trying to sell someone for a buck. You feel it. You know it to be true and trust is established.

- I am a chameleon. I adapt easily to the climate in the room and the energy of whomever I am working with, all the while remaining heart and human centered. Relatable. Genuine. Caring.

- I have skills that set me apart AND that people are willing to pay for. I have a proven track record. I am the guy Fortune 500 Executives, Founders and CEOs go to, to find their digital voice, with the goal of dominating in a digital market. I have been featured in *Forbes, Thrive Global* and *Yahoo! Finance* among others.

- I am overflowing with desire, faith and commitment!

- MOST IMPORTANTLY, I care about people as human beings.

My Specialized Knowledge is selling people on THEMSELVES.
On the benefits of themselves/investing in self
On believing in themselves
On their self as the commodity that people will clamor for
On their untapped power and Specialized Knowledge
On showing up as themselves
On the fact that they are the only one that can do what 'they do', the way 'they do it'

One of the most powerful 'teachers' on how to gain and share Specialized Knowledge are those around you who serve as models. Learning from people who have blazed paths, are considered experts in their field, and value sharing their knowledge with others. However, you must remain open to who those role models are and how they show up.

I started by telling you about how my son's grit, determination and organized planning gained him the Specialized Knowledge to excel in lacrosse. My son has served as one of my greatest teachers time and time again. Lacrosse is only one example of his acquisition of Specialized Knowledge. The lessons I learned from him are as powerful as those I learned from Chairmen, CEOs, and top executives. My point being, there is something to learn from everyone; from executives to the janitor, if you are open to seeing it. Everyone is someone. The converse is true. YOU have something to offer and teach every person you come into contact with. We build Specialized Knowledge through our experiences and some of the most powerful experiences are those shared with other people. It is the experience that garners the opportunities that generate the revenue. Through the experiences, you are gaining Specialized Knowledge which makes you valuable, and because you have had experiences that others have not gone through.

An agency CEO asked me to make her a promotional video for a high-profile speaking engagement. She was willing to pay me for the video, because she knew it would take her days, if not weeks, to come up with something that was even close to the caliber of what I created. She was paying me for the Specialized Knowledge that came from thousands and thousands of hours of experience, which allowed me to produce a superior product in a fraction of the time. I turned the video around in an hour.

The perspective, Specialized Knowledge, the experience, make you valuable and people pay for that. WHY? Because Specialized Knowledge and time are two of the most valuable commodities. If I can help you get to your goal in a fraction of the time that it would take you, because I possess the Specialized Knowledge, you will pay for that.

I'm valuable to Fortune 500 companies and they are willing to pay me because I have been through everything there is to go through in the world of start-ups. I bring my Specialized Knowledge having learned from having gone through experiences that they have not.

It is my Specialized Knowledge that has had me invited to stages around the world as an International Keynote Speaker. Specialized Knowledge has led to my being recognized as one of the premiere live-streaming and video marketing experts in the world, who's insights have been featured on NASDAQ, ROKU and a #1 Best-Selling live-streaming book. My two weekly LIVE shows have been featured in *Forbes, Thrive Global, Yahoo*

Finance, an Amazon best-selling book, syndicated on a Smart TV Network and named "2020 Best LIVE Festive Show of The Year" at the IBM TV Awards. Furthermore, I've been recognized as a 'LinkedIn Top Voice', 'LinkedIn Video Creator Of The Year', one of the 'Top 50 Most Impactful People of LinkedIn' out of 800 million people (three consecutive years) and a 'LinkedIn Global Leader of The Year' (two consecutive years).

When specialized and organized, knowledge becomes powerful.

BRIAN SCHULMAN

About Brian Schulman: A 3X #1 Best-Selling Author and internationally known Keynote Speaker, Brian Schulman is known as the Godfather, and Pioneer, of LinkedIn Video and one of the world's premiere live streaming & video marketing experts who's insights have been featured on NASDAQ, ROKU and a #1 Best-selling live-streaming book.

With 20+ years of proven Digital Marketing experience strategizing with Fortune 500 brands across the globe, Brian founded & is the CEO of Voice Your Vibe, which brings his wealth of knowledge, as an advisor and mentor to Founders & C-Suite Executives by providing workshops and 1-on-1 Mastery Coaching on how to voice their vibe, attract their tribe, and tell a story that people will fall in love with through the power and impact of live & pre-recorded video.

Named "2020 Best LIVE Festive Show of The Year" at the IBM TV Awards, his global award-winning weekly LIVE shows #ShoutOutSaturday & #WhatsGoodWednesday have been featured in Forbes, Thrive Global, Yahoo Finance, an Amazon best-selling book and syndicated on a Smart TV Network. Among his many awards and honors, Brian has been named a 'LinkedIn Top Voice', 'LinkedIn Video Creator Of The Year', one of the 'Top 50 Most Impactful People of LinkedIn' for three consecutive years and a 'LinkedIn Global Leader of The Year' for two consecutive years. Beyond all the achievements and accolades, Brian is most proud of his two children and the connections and relationships he's made along the way.

Author's Website: *www.VoiceYourVibe.com*
Book Series Website & Author's Bio: *www.The13StepstoRiches.com*

Bryce McKinley

THE ART OF PERSUASION

Like Henry Ford, I made most of my money in the automotive industry. He's always been somebody that I admired. Ford once said, "Why should I clutter up my mind with general knowledge, for the purpose of being able to answer questions, when I have men around me who can supply any knowledge I require?"

I believe that Specialized Knowledge is wisdom that you can search out from others. By leveraging the information of others, you can go further, faster. Specialized Knowledge is also a transferable skillset from industry to industry. In my case, I specialize in the art of conversation and persuasion, which helps me in sales and relationship building.

The earliest memory I can recall was a specific conversation around persuasion. I was eight years old, and I had begged my parents to have a paper route. They gave me that opportunity and signed me up in northern Illinois in the Chicago area, even though you were supposed to work the paper route at ten years old. After three weeks, the route manager, Karen, came to the house to inform my parents that they would pay me for the work that I had done, but they would have to let me go.

I was devastated. However, I realized that I could use the specialized language I learned to persuade my parents and Karen and salvage the situation. I said to them, "You know, Dad, I remember you said that I could do this paper route, and I've done a great job so far. And Karen, you know I've been doing a great job, too. I've got more accounts on this route than ever. So why don't we just put it in my dad's name, and when I turn ten years old, you can give me more responsibility. Is that fair?"

I'll never forget the look on their faces. They were shocked. Karen agreed to put the contracts in my parents' names to continue working.

By the time I turned ten years old, I had five additional routes more than the other boys running paper routes, and I was making more money than my parents were making at their jobs. I delivered the papers and collected a check every two weeks.

Master a Process

If you can find the process within the knowledge you're seeking or developing, you will form great habits. After 20 years of practicing my methods, I've created a five-step process in the Art of Persuasion that I teach when I train my teams. I'll use the example of working out at the gym to explain each step of the process.

Step 1: Warm With Form.

FORM is an acronym that stands for Family, Occupation, Recreation, and Motivation. FORM split into two parts, FOR and M.

FOR is the "why" in front of their (M) Motivations.

FOR—You'll never truly solve someone's motivation if you don't know what their motivations are for or against.

M—I believe that genuinely when you add value to someone's life, it fuels their motivation.

For example, it's typical at the gym is warm up with good form and stretch, so you don't hurt yourself or pull a muscle. It's no different in conversations. If you don't Warm With Form, it can be detrimental, even harmful to a good discussion or connection.

Step 2: Bridging The Gap

Bridging the gap is helping people feel like other successful people want the same results as them. In the gym example, you bridge the gap starting with smaller weights rather than jumping straight into lifting 500 lbs. Work your way up.

You can help most people bridge the gap by helping them feel inevitably that they're going to say "yes." You can negate any potential objection by asking the questions that lead to yes, such as, "Why do you want this house today? Why do you want this car today? Why do you want to be a part of this mastermind today?" They have already felt comfortable in doing so because you've warmed them up to the scenario of saying yes.

Step 3: Asking Defeating Questions

In Asking Defeating Question, you want to challenge the beliefs of those you are persuading. But when you're doing bench presses and pushing the weight, you start to create that chemical in your body that produces what transitions into fatigue.

Defeating questions include dropping your voice pitch while simultaneously adding an uptick tonality. You can create a small belief in the other person's mind that they can't live without your suggestion. This step builds credibility and trust in conversation.

Step 4: Close/or Set Objective

Set the objective means to solve their challenge. Just like re-racking the bar or closing out your set at the gym correctly, you can set the objectives in communication. Setting the objectives in conversation helps complete the deal and solve the problems they've been struggling with. Then, offer solutions.

Step 5: Warm Down

Like you would after a good workout at the gym, you warm down with stretching. It's no different in the art of persuasion. According to this five-step process, warming down any conversation includes taking the last step of action to set your and their expectations up for success. Book another appointment, suggest the following action steps, and close people through persuasion.

This five-step process has worked for me for over 20 years. Mastering your techniques of Specialized Knowledge will earn you better results. It would be best if you mastered them, in any case.

Specialized Knowledge in Leadership

As a child, I grew up in a cult-like religion. Although I had my dislikes in that cult culture, I was fascinated with the leadership and communication tactics that pastors used to teach their sermons.

One, in particular, called a straw-man fallacy (refuting an argument by not answering the original argument), pinned people up at fault against their obedience to commandments.

You're going to heaven, or you're going to hell. It was fascinating to see pastors manipulate people. To understand their persuasiveness, I've studied pastors. Persuading and convincing someone to alter their beliefs is one of the most challenging sales to do.

I've studied the articulation of their sermons how they frame the outline of their message and then their call to action to salvation.

I believe that there is an obligation with Specialized Knowledge to use it for good.

The second person that I genuinely look up to is John Maxwell. While speaking at the same event, Maxwell recognized me from another event, and we sat down and hung out for 30-40 minutes. Maxwell is a God-believing man like me, so we both prayed over each other and the presentations we'd both be presenting that day. John Maxwell inspired me to work on the mastery of leadership with the experience of my five-step process to persuasion and what I had learned from observing pastors.

Mastering and Articulating

Our brain works like a funnel; if you don't pour out the bottom spout into others, you run over the edge at the top if you don't make room for more knowledge. Mastering the art of communication is like a funnel. When I learn something, I find as many people to pass it along to so that I can make more room for more knowledge. I believe that that is one of the Master's keys to success.

I am surprised at the amount of Specialized Knowledge that nobody knows about in this world. I didn't realize that food scientists were behind the scenes at your local Pizza Hut, Taco Bell, or KFC restaurants, constantly and daily perfecting recipes. Now, when you go to taco bell, you get any one of their 32 sauces. My sister-in-law had a part in playing as a food scientist behind the scenes, and she created all of those recent sauces in the last five years.

People can do and become whatever they want. We can choose any form of specialty.

Find someone who has already done what you are hoping to accomplish and emulate them. Even as we progress in our human evolution and technological advances, anything is possible.

There's one significant oversight of the five-step process to mastering persuasion that holds it all together, and that is called the RAQ. The acronym of RAQ stands for Repeat, Assign, Question. When you repeat (R) something back to the other person and communicate that, you assign (A) a feeling or an emotion. Then ask (Q) a question, you can maintain and guide that conversation.

An excellent example of this is when someone says something like, "Gosh, the sky looks blue today." In response to their statement, you can use the RAQ method to reply with, "The sky does look blue today. That's exciting. Are you going to go outside and enjoy the nice weather?" Repeat (R) what they said back to them and assign (A) an emotion or feeling in the context and then ask a question (Q) to validate their comment. I call it the RAQ. (1) Repeat, (2) Assign a feeling or emotion, and then (3) Ask what is so neat about it.

Using genuine sincerity to the steps above has become my superpower and has ultimately built my life and career of masterful persuasion. I highly recommend you find your one or two greatest strengths and passions and focus solely on mastering those things. Stay in your lane. Let others do and work on everything that you are not masterful at so that you, too, can lead like Henry Ford and John D. Maxwell.

BRYCE MCKINLEY

About Bryce McKinley: Bryce is an International Best-Selling Author and one of the Top 5 Sales Trainers in The World! With over 20 years of working with various Fortune 500 companies including but not limited to the likes of Ford, Nissan, Tyco, and ADT. Helping each of them transform their sales process to focus on better conversations and building better relationships.

Over 8,000 transactions in Real Estate later, Bryce is one of the leading experts in wholesaling houses with his 5 Hour Flip method and has been able to close almost every deal over the phone, only ever walking 5 properties.

Author's Website: *www.5HourFlip.com*

Book Series Website & Author's Bio: *www.The13StepstoRiches.com*

Candace & David Rose

LEARNING IS A NEVER-ENDING QUEST

Would you take your Microsoft PC to the Apple genius bar to be repaired? Probably not. As smart as those geniuses are, and even though they possess a level of general knowledge about computer repair, they would struggle with the windows environment and lack the specific or special knowledge that windows computers require. This is a surface-level example of how Specialized Knowledge is used in our everyday lives.

How is this useful to us in our search for riches?

I used to work as a supervisor for an oil and gas service company performing a variety of services on oil wells. When I first started the job, I had just a basic knowledge of the hand tools and equipment required to perform the work. As my career went forward, I started seeking more and more information on the industry. Learning all I could to make myself a more valuable employee. As I developed, I gained the Specialized Knowledge on various tasks that allowed me to advance to the supervisor position. But how does one go about gaining this knowledge?

We live in time where information is readily accessible. Most of us carry a smartphone of some type in our pocket. And have access to anything we want, instantly. How amazing is that? But having all that access is just the beginning. Napoleon Hill stated, "Knowledge is only potential power.

It becomes power only when, and if, it is organized into definite plans of action, and directed to a definite end."

After reading that, the statement from GI Joe, "Now you know, and knowing is half the battle" has a bit more impact for me. If knowing is half the battle, what is the other half of the battle? That is where organizing and putting that knowledge to action comes to play.

Being a jack-of-all-trades is great. But to better our position, becoming a master of one needs to happen. Use the information at your fingertips, and don't ever turn away advice, as all advice has some value. Be willing to know what you know, but also know what you don't know. And ask for help. Don't clutter your mind with knowledge that someone else has. For example, if you're running a cleaning business, don't seek knowledge on web development. That information won't help you become the best cleaner there is. Leverage the Specialized Knowledge of a web developer so you can focus on your own mission.

So, how does one start to gain that Specialized Knowledge? I have two steps that I believe are important to gaining the Specialized Knowledge needed to gain riches.

Step 1: Know Who To Listen To

Seems simple right? With our instant access to information, knowing who to listen to may be a bit more difficult than it seems. It takes time and effort on your part to sort through all the different things out there. As you begin sifting through the information, listen. Ask your higher power to open you mind to the intuition needed to find the place that resonates with you. Once you've found that source. Stick with it. Learn all you can from it.

Step 2: Be Teachable Or Coachable

As you start learning from a source, make sure you are open to suggestions. Many times in my life, I have encountered people who have the attitude, "I know it all" or, "You can't teach me anything new." If you reach this mindset, then you have lost. If you ever find that you are the "smartest one in the room" then it's time to find a new room. Learning and gaining knowledge is a never-ending quest.

~ David Rose

Specialized Knowledge and imagination are the ingredients that go into a unique and successful business. And everything in life is just that—A business. I regularly invite "average" people to business conferences. Often, their most consistent excuse is, "I don't have a business." False! You have a life, therefore, you have an empire (AKA a business). I have a friend who said, "I don't want to think, nor grow rich." I call rubbish on this statement! Because to not think, nor grow rich, equals not progressing. Parables and metaphors are abundant in this and all lessons.

So, how does Specialized Knowledge help you grow your empire? Let's start with defining general knowledge versus Specialized Knowledge.

General knowledge is taught in public school and universities. Specialized Knowledge is attained through either experience or mentoring.

This is why I invite "nonbusiness" owners to business conferences for mentoring. Before I began going to business conferences, I didn't even know I needed mentoring. I signed up for specialized mentoring immediately, with the statement, "I'm just a mom" when asked what I did for a business. And that is OK. Because my Family deserves THE BEST! And the more experience and Specialized Knowledge I bring to parenting, the better experience my children get. We all know that parenting is 95%

on-the-job training. So how else do I get Specialized Knowledge while it can still benefit the ones that matter most?

Specialized Knowledge includes a range of factual, theoretical, and practical knowledge, as well as competencies and skill in a particular discipline or profession.

This is why generations pass on stories and skill. Because otherwise we would have to depend solely on our general knowledge for survival. Which is fine. I mean, how many others have? But it leaves little time for progression and relaxation, right?

The wise person gets all the mentoring they can, even if it's simply to be a better/more educated member of society.

My particular fields of Specialized Knowledge are in parenting and organizing peoples' homes. My husband is a professional driver. I have a daughter who has Specialized Knowledge in food production, and another who operates the rides at Lagoon Amusement park. I promise you, I'm incredibly grateful for each and their expertise.

The statement "I don't want to think, nor grow rich" does not build an empire. It tears one down.

Many religions and philosophies teach continued acquisition of knowledge, and my personal belief system says that our sole purpose for existence is progression.

I would encourage every single one of you to make a list of what you feel you have Specialized Knowledge in, a list of what you wish you had Specialized Knowledge in, and a list of what you would like to start acquiring Specialized Knowledge on.

They say you become like the five people you spend most of your time around. If you would like Specialized Knowledge in baking, for example, maybe having one of these five be a baker is a good choice. However, surrounding yourself with anti-bakers is self-defeating, and should be avoided.

To reiterate, everyone has a business, because everyone has some Specialized Knowledge. And it is our duty to share our Specialized Knowledge with those who could benefit from our expertise.

There once was a farmer who grew the most excellent wheat. Every season, he won the award for the best wheat in the county. A wise woman came to him to ask him about his success. He told her that the key was sharing his best seed with his neighbors so they could plant the seed as well. The wise woman asked, "How can you share your best wheat seed with your neighbors when they compete with you every year?" "That's simple," the farmer replied. "The wind spreads the pollen from everyone's wheat and carries it from field to field. If my neighbors grew inferior wheat, cross-pollination would degrade everyone's wheat, including mine. If I'm to grow the best wheat, I must help my neighbors grow the best wheat, as well."

If you want to grow rich, you must use your Specialized Knowledge to help others grow rich as well.

My favorite song that reminds us to do just that is *Humble and Kind* by Tim McGraw, "Don't take for granted the love this life gives you, when you get where you're going don't forget turn back around and help the next one in line."

~ Candace Rose

CANDACE & DAVID ROSE

About Candace and David Rose: Candace and David Rose are #1 Best-Selling Authors in the 13 volume book series *The 13 Steps to Riches*. They grew up together and currently live in South Jordan, Utah, with their 6 children, 4 chickens, 4 cats, 1 dog, and a rabbit. They are both Veterans of the U.S. Army. David served as a mechanic and Candace as a Legal NCO. David is currently a Product Release Specialist, delivering liquid oxygen and nitrogen to various manufacturing plants and hospitals throughout Utah, Colorado, Idaho and Nevada. Candace is the owner of Changing Your Box Organization, where she specializes in helping people organize their space, both physically and mentally, with the ultimate goal to help you change your box and find more joy in your life. Both Candace and David are proud members of the elite Champion Circle Networking Association in Salt Lake City, UT., founded by one of our Coauthors of *The 13 Steps to Riches* book series and the Habitude Warrior Mastermind Senior Team Leader, Jon Kovach Jr.

Author's Website: *www.ChangeYourBox.com*
Book Series Website & Author's Bio: *www.The13StepstoRiches.com*

Collier Landry

THE KNOWLEDGE DICHOTOMY

Great leaders are great learners. As an entrepreneur and creative, I've struggled immensely with this concept.

I was just into my second year at musical conservatory when I came to a stark realization: my altruistic artistic vision might not add up to dollars to pay the bills. I needed to pivot in my thinking if I would succeed as a creative entrepreneur.

Growing up in a small town, my affluent and self-made neighbor Sam V. planted the first seed of that pivot. On winter break that semester, I shared with him my predicament. He said, "Collier, you need to read the book Think and Grow Rich."

I had no idea what he was talking about, but I got myself a copy immediately. After all, Sam had been a highly successful entrepreneur who was constantly growing and learning. He was a voracious reader with an open mind, and I admired that quality.

When I landed in Hollywood years later, I found myself surrounded by know-it-alls. I found myself pontificated by those who "knew the biz" of entertainment, and I quickly became frustrated. I could glean one perspective from my new reality, much to my chagrin. These people were not malleable. Their thought process was not the innovative approach I came to identify with the entertainment industry, rather an archaic one rooted in dogma and secret handshakes.

However, in that, I recognized a real opportunity. If I could change my thinking, keep my humility, and dig in to expand my knowledge, I would find success while maintaining my all-important artistic integrity.

The traumatic life circumstances of my youth forced upon me both the skill and Specialized Knowledge of resilience. Applying that made me a malleable and creative entrepreneur.

In the late 2000s, I decided to shift my focus from music to filmmaking. At that time, I was completely green in the industry. I absorbed every opportunity to be on a film set, even when it wasn't attached to a paycheck.

If Picasso had his "blue period," this was my "growing and learning" period. Adopting this mentality went from being a choice to being a necessity.

At that time, the proverbial sands were beginning to shift rapidly. The digital revolution had made itself to the film industry, just as it had in music a few years previously. Remember your first iPod?

With the rapid advancement of technology, being an independent filmmaker was becoming more accessible than ever. What would once take an entire crew and tens of thousands of dollars could now be streamlined into the efforts of a few individuals. The one caveat? You had to be willing to grow and learn. As is often said, fortune favors the prepared mind.

Still, over a decade later, so many of us in the creative world fall into that trap daily. Whether it be new challenges imposed by ever-changing social media algorithms or the fast pace of technology in the creative space, it's a problem. Many of us often fall prey to this daily.

Having a broad knowledge and specializing in one particular subject are two contradictory positions yet seemingly intertwined. Acquiring knowledge from different topics offers people extensive choices to contribute to their future careers. Juxtapose that knowledge on various subjects to being a specialist in a particular discipline, and that will play a significant role in the future, especially nowadays. I find both of these forms of knowledge valuable in people's personal and professional development, especially when viewed as a more significant part of society as a whole. Society needs specialists to study in one field to perpetuate society's general knowledge base.

Let's take a look at filmmaking. I think that this discipline requires both an overarching worldview and a specialized set of techniques to convey the intended message. This isn't just limited to filmmaking, but to all forms of digital media. The most successful people are often ones who have curated a treasure trove of techniques while maintaining an overall perspective to the message at hand. This case is the artwork.

I realize that this chapter seems to veer into "intelligentsia" territory, but this translates into all forms of business medium these days.

First, any discipline is not isolated; different subjects are almost always associated somehow. People with broad knowledge can think thoroughly and become considerate. In this way, when people face unpredictable difficulties, they can figure out more than one solution to the problems.

A global pandemic, anyone?

Real-life leadership and knowledge can be hard to come by for those who seek to advance. I believe that anyone can succeed if they prepare themselves for the next level in their careers. To do so, you must exploit every opportunity to learn. Here are a few things that I have learned along my journey.

Hone a "Growing and Learning" Mindset: Having a positive attitude towards professional development is vital. Consistently moving toward expanding your knowledge base is almost like oxygen to an entrepreneur. Set aside time to learn regularly.

Examine Your Decisions: One difference between great leaders and mediocre ones is the willingness to examine past actions and make decisions to improve. Adopt the habit of appointing a devil's advocate for all significant decisions. This examination can help you make better decisions and prevent any decision-making biases (and also prevent you from making impulse camera equipment purchases).

Read Regularly: Read widely, not only about current events but also subjects that can broaden your horizons, such as history. I am an avid reader of business books and almost always find an idea or two that I can use in my businesses. Let Audible be your friend!

Write Regularly: Writing has multiple benefits for leaders: helping them master the content, improve critical thinking skills, and enhance communication with their audiences. The more they publish, the better their writing will become. It can also help build awareness for yourself as an expert in your field.

Teach What You Know: Teaching is one of the most underused tools in leadership development. It's giving back, and there is no better way to master something than by trying to impart your knowledge and skills to others. I cannot stress this enough. It makes you think about the material in new ways. I have learned far more by sharing my filmmaking knowledge with others who are not as experienced than by keeping my nose to the grindstone. Take advantage of opportunities to teach. You won't regret it.

Build Self-Awareness: This is so key to developing professionally and personally. While it may sound cliché, self-awareness is critical to effective leadership. The best leaders are aware leaders. Learn to observe yourself as you go about your workday while simultaneously focusing on others' reactions. Then, take in what you've observed to make improvements.

Gather Feedback: No one is an island, and great leaders ask for feedback. Actively asking for feedback from your colleagues is essential to development as a leader and developing key relationships. Engagement is key to development, whether with colleagues, employees, clients, or even, yes, your social media audience.

Find Mentors: This was essential to my success, personally and professionally. Having a father who was incarcerated the majority of my life forced me to find more positive role models to fill the void. When I came to Hollywood, I asked anyone who I looked up to to be a mentor in my professional life. Not all of them leaped at that opportunity, but enough did to make an impact on my career. Choose to cultivate relationships with people who have been in your shoes. And when it comes to feedback, mentors are often able to give you objective advice that you may not get on the job. In any industry, finding someone who will provide you with honest, unvarnished input is critical.

Cultivate Peer Relationships: The entertainment industry is like being in a family. One hugely dysfunctional family! In all seriousness, developing relationships with as many people in your industry as possible is imperative to your survival. I cannot overstate this enough— this is mission critical for keeping up with developments and gaining new perspectives and ideas. The relationships I have formed within my industry have often provided tremendous value to my career and those around me. There is always someone more intelligent than you who has done it before, so take note. Whatever industry you find yourself in, be unwilling to let the fast pace of business prevent you from developing as a leader and knowledge seeker. After all, the dynamism of today's markets is why you need to keep learning in the first place.

And never let anything interfere with creativity!

Creativity is often characterized by the ability to perceive the world in new ways, find hidden patterns, make connections between seemingly unrelated phenomena, and then generate solutions.

It is the act of turning new and imaginative ideas into reality—growing and learning, followed by action.

COLLIER LANDRY

About Collier Landry: Collier is the creator and subject of Investigation Discovery's true-crime sensation A Murder in Mansfield, a documentary from two-time Oscar-winning director Barbara Kopple.

A formally trained musician and photographer, Collier segued into filmmaking as a means to creatively express and deal with his own traumatic childhood story - the premeditated murder of his mother Noreen by his father, Dr. John F. Boyle, Jr. - and to give a narrative voice to others in similar circumstances.

The film explores not only the collateral damage of violence and its traumatic repercussions but the beauty of human strength and resilience through seemingly insurmountable odds.

Collier hosts the Moving Past Murder podcast, where he shares his passionate and robust message of human resilience, hope, and personal triumph over adversity has inspired audiences across the globe.

A multiple award-winning cinematographer and director, Collier has been featured in *Variety, The New York Times, Esquire, USA Today, The Hollywood Reporter,* is a TEDx Speaker, and guest on the Dr. Phil show.

He resides in Santa Monica, California.

Author's Website: *www.CollierLandry.com*
Book Series Website & Author's Bio: *www.The13StepstoRiches.com*

Corey Poirier

MAKING THE CASE FOR SPECIALIZED KNOWLEDGE

One of my absolute favorite stories in *Think and Grow Rich* is the one of Henry Ford, and the attorneys attempting to justify the newspaper that called him an ignorant pacifist, by questioning him ad nauseam about things he had never attempted to learn personally.

The moment in that story when he replied that he may not know the answers himself, but he knows exactly how to get those answers; that was an aha moment for me.

You see, previous to hearing that, I was the person, even from a young age, trying to fill my mind with general knowledge AND trying to learn all the Specialized Knowledge available about every single thing I sunk my teeth into.

It was both exhausting and discouraging.

For instance, when I started learning to play music, I became obsessed with learning how to read music, how to tune my guitar, etc.

I struggled to ultimately discover that not only did I not have the patience to learn how to read music and tune my guitar, I didn't have the need.

Considering I could buy a guitar tuner for less than $20 that would be more accurate at tuning than my ear, and the fact that I could play music by ear and therefore didn't need to read music to play music, I finally clued into the fact that I didn't need to acquire this Specialized Knowledge to play guitar, and write, and perform music at the highest level.

Actually, upon listening to one of Johnny Cash's live CDs, I'm convinced the man didn't know how to tune his guitar, and he fared out okay.

Oh, and the end result is that I wasted much time that I could have been dedicating to writing music, rather than trying to accumulate knowledge for the sake of accumulation.

So, when I heard the Ford story, I finally knew that I no longer needed to learn every single aspect of everything I had my hands into.

This was so liberating, while also being great for my business and personal life. I should have known so much sooner, though.

You see, my grandfather was one of the best carpenters in the entire region where I grew up.

When people wanted a home built, most who didn't have Specialized Knowledge, didn't try to build their home from scratch themselves. They hired someone like my grandfather.

When they were having a home built for them, they also didn't hire my grandfather to do the plumbing. That wasn't his specialty.

I was there on many builds with him, trying desperately to come across like a competent carpenter's helper, only to come across like what I really was: a 14-year-old kid who hadn't inherited his grandfather's natural skills, and who never would be at home, building a home.

While on those builds though, I watched as person after person with Specialized Knowledge came in to handle their part of the home build.

The electrician didn't put up the walls. The plumber didn't do the electrical. My grandfather didn't handle the plumbing or the electrical.

Yet, the home got built by the homeowners, and they simply had to know where to hire those with the Specialized Knowledge, or at least how to reach out and start the process of finding them.

They ended up with a solid home, and yet, they didn't have to have the Specialized Knowledge needed to build it themselves, just like with Ford.

The fact that it didn't sink in until I read it in *Think and Grow Rich* is just another reason I love this book that has impacted my life in so many ways.

Since the aha moment, I have applied this idea that I could hire for the Specialized Knowledge, over and over in my life and business, and it has yet to fail me.

Sure, there are times when you have to try multiple people to find the person most aligned with you, or to find the person best suited for the job, but once you find that person, things get so much easier.

On that note, let me share just one example of me using this approach in my business, so you can see it in real time.

Let's take our bLU Talks brand.

With this brand, we have a book series, a podcast, a virtual stage, and a live stage as our main platforms.

Even though I know a thing or two about the book world (including writing, launching, and marketing a book) and a thing or two about podcasting (I have 3 podcasts and my first was almost 12 years ago and is still going), me trying to manage every aspect of the bLU Talks brand myself would be not only be exhausting, but also bad for business.

Instead, when it comes to the bLU Talks Brand, we have a person with Specialized Knowledge who edits the books, a person with Specialized Knowledge who formats the books, and a person with Specialized Knowledge who launches our books.

We also have a person with Specialized Knowledge who runs the live events, we have hosts on the virtual events with Specialized Knowledge around hosting, a person with Specialized Knowledge who edits the videos, a person with Specialized Knowledge who films the talks, a person with Specialized Knowledge who runs the audio, and a person with...

Okay, so you probably get the idea.

The key thing is these are all separate people.

Now, for me to operate the bLU Talks brand, I don't know how to do all of these things. And like Ford, I don't need to. I simply need to know how to find people who can.

The end result is not only us creating work and jobs for each of the people involved, but also having the best of the best managing the aspects of the brand they most enjoy, and the areas typically closest to their genius zone.

Another end result is that I don't find myself pulling my hair out on a daily basis.

Well, actually, I don't have any hair these days, but you probably get the idea here as well.

So for my money, when the question is 'how does one do a big project with many facets without losing their mind', the answer is almost always—find people who have the Specialized Knowledge and let them work their magic.

Until then, here's to your greater success.

COREY POIRIER

About Corey Poirier: Corey is a multiple-time TEDx Speaker. He is also the host of the top-rated Let's Do Influencing radio show, founder of The Speaking Program, founder of bLU Talks, and has been featured in multiple television specials. He is also a Barnes & Noble, Amazon, Apple Books, and Kobo Bestselling Author and the co-author of the *Wall Street Journal* and *USA Today* bestseller, *Quitless*.

A columnist with *Entrepreneur* and *Forbes* magazine, he has been featured in/on various mediums and is one of the few leaders featured twice on the popular *Entrepreneur on Fire* show.

Also appearing on the popular Evan Carmichael YouTube Channel, he is a New Media Summit Icon of Influence, was recently listed as the # 5 influencer in entrepreneurship by Thinkers 360, and he is an Entrepreneur of the Year Nominee—and, to demonstrate his versatility, a Rock Recording of the Year nominee who has performed stand-up comedy more than 700 times, including an appearance at the famed Second City.

Author's Website: *www.TheInfluencerVault.com*
Book Series Website & Author's Bio: *www.The13StepstoRiches.com*

Deb Scott

SPECIALIZED KNOWLEDGE, PERSONAL EXPERIENCE OR OBSERVATIONS

Napoleon Hill states, "Knowledge will not attract money unless it is organized and intelligently directed, through practical plans of action, to the definite end of accumulation of money."

I believe this to be true for any goal: financial, mind, body or spirit.

There are a lot of high-IQ serial killers out there. Knowledge has nothing to do with having intelligence or being a good person or being a happy person. I have met many smart people who do evil things with their knowledge.

You must take the knowledge you have gathered, together with your own personal experience, and map out a plan to get where you want to go. You are in California and want to get to Boston; you have knowledge a plane or car or bus is available to get there, but until you pull a map out, plan to buy a ticket and set a date to travel, your knowledge is just an unopened gift sitting on your table doing nothing for you.

Having and knowing what knowledge you need and don't need is also part of being knowledgeable.

Napoleon Hill gives a great example of Henry Ford being thought of by many in his day as a stupid man, despite the fact by any historical record, he was a huge success. In his day, Henry Ford was not formally educated, so therefore, many elites thought him to be stupid because this was their standard for intelligence.

I love how Mr. Ford responded to this insult by turning everything around—that he had the knowledge to know he could get the knowledge he needed, when he needed it, by someone else who had it. He, himself, did not have to have all the knowledge to be successful, but his success was in the fact that he knew the people who had the knowledge he needed when he needed it, and this was a key to his success. Why waste time filling up your brain with things you don't need to know, when you know someone who already has the information?

In real estate, I don't have all the answers for an entire successful transaction from contract to close, but I try to surround myself with people I know who do, so when the time comes for action, I am ready. I can't be the expert home inspector, electrician, title company, closing attorney, house cleaner, or appraiser. I can, however, surround myself with a trusted team to do efficiently and effectively what I know will need to be done in the process to bring it to a successful outcome. That is why people hire me.

It's not about being able to do everything and know everything. It is about having the self-awareness to understand what needs to be done to get where you want to go, and then surrounding yourself with the people who can make it happen.

Thomas Edison had only three months of "schooling" during his entire life. He did not lack education, neither did he die poor.

Henry Ford had less than a sixth grade "schooling," but he managed to do pretty well by himself financially.

You reading this book is gaining knowledge just like a mastermind group. You are taking the personal experience of each author and collecting the information into your own action plan merged, with your gifts, talents, dreams, and goals. The fact that you are reading this book is the promise; you have already achieved the goal.

When I was in cardiac surgery sales, I wanted to watch as many surgeries with my customers using my competitor's device. Why? Because I needed to understand the benefits, features, and deficiencies of my competitor's product vs mine. I needed to understand the surgeons' need for their patients and how I could provide a product that would best meet those needs. It was not enough that I understood my product better than any of my colleagues to be top in sales; I had to know everything about all my competitor's products, as well as my own, to be the best in my career. I needed the knowledge to best solve the surgeons' problems.

Sometimes, I think we get caught up in looking at another person from the outside and believing we understand or are seeing the truth of their inside. Identify the issue, become knowledgeable in all aspects for or against that issue, then specialize that knowledge with an action plan to obtain your goal.

Napoleon Hill breaks this goal down into easy steps.

First: Make a list of all the specialized knowledge you already have acquired. For example, from your own education and experience, through cooperation with others (such as a mastermind), other colleges or events they conducted, books or personal study, special courses or certifications.

Second: Make a list of the acquired knowledge you want to receive. Find those people who have what you want or need, and connect with them to gain those skills.

Third: Begin an Apprenticeship. This is where you work in the area, store, or company where they have what you want combined with your personal set of skills and actually apply them. Hill states this "discipline" and "finishing what you begin" in this venue can catapult you to success more rapidly.

In my own life, when I was a biology major in college, I was considering going into medical sales instead of being a medical technologist. I had volunteered one summer in my local laboratory and found it too isolating for my natural tendency to enjoy conversation with people. My father actually suggested going into medical sales as he was in sales as president of the realtors. While I was unsure about the prospect because I really didn't like salespeople, I still moved ahead with a sales internship at Wang Laboratories in Boston. I learned that I never wanted to sell computers, but I loved meeting new people and solving problems for them. As soon as I graduated from college with my biology major, I found a job in medical sales and ended up specializing and becoming an award-winning cardiac surgery devices representative for two decades. I would never had known what I could or truly wanted without placing myself in a position to experience my unique traits, with the desire to see how they worked in real-time by investing in an internship/apprenticeship.

Napoleon Hill emphasizes that it is better to delegate and pay someone to do what you are not good at or don't enjoy. I find this to be critical. I personally hate paperwork. Why would I spend all my time and energy doing something I don't like that creates frustration and stress, when I can pay someone to do the job? In real estate, we call that "hire a transaction coordinator." I am much wiser to spend my time and energy with people, helping them buy and sell, than doing the paperwork for the transaction. However, the paperwork is a key part of the process. It must be done, and be done correctly. It's worth it for me to spend the money and find an excellent transaction coordinator who loves that work in order to get the job done right and free me of the stress and time it takes to do something which frustrates me.

Ideas are the linchpin. Ideas are free. Make a list of the most outrageous ideas you have, combined with your desire, and you will know what inspires you; then you can make it happen. You can create an organized plan to manifest your material or spiritual riches—however you define riches to be for you.

If you are having difficulty, one of the best lessons I was given was to ask ten close friends the top three character traits they admired about me. Ask ten friends what type of business they see you creating with your personality. We don't always see ourselves as we are, but others can see in us the truth of who we are, which might be the very things we take for granted in ourselves. This is the huge gift!

Do it now.

DEB SCOTT

About Deb Scott: Deb Scott, BA, CPC, and Realtor was a high honors biology major at Regis College in Weston, Massachusetts, and spent over two decades as an award-winning cardio-thoracic sales specialist in the New England area. She is a best-selling author of *The Sky is Green & The Grass is Blue: Turning Your Upside Down World Right Side Up*. She is an award-winning podcaster of The Best People We Know Show. Following in her family's footsteps, she is a third generation Realtor in Venice, Florida. As a certified life coach, Deb speaks and teaches on how to turn bad situations into positive, successful results. As a top sales specialist, she enjoys teaching people "sales without selling," believing that integrity, good communication, and respect are the winning equation to all outstanding success and happiness in life.

Author's Website: *www.DebScott.com*
Book Series Website & Author's Bio: *www.The13StepstoRiches.com*

Dori Ray

GAIN MORE BY SHARING
WHAT YOU KNOW

After three short months, I could not believe that I was back in Philadelphia. When the plane landed, I don't know who jumped off faster, me or my daughter! I silently reminded God that I understood the assignment. I promised Him that this will be my best season ever. I thanked Him for the many blessings I encountered on the West Coast, even the ones that caught me blind-sided disguised as problems. I was so excited to be back with friends and family who I knew loved me beyond measure, but I was still a HOT MESS!

The years of dealing with the depression and the aftereffects had taken their toll on me. However, the short trip to California had put things into perspective a bit. I learned, in a place that was very foreign to me, the God's purpose had no boundaries. It felt great to get another fresh slate. Although I was a Hot Mess, I was now a Hot Mess On Purpose!

After arriving back in Philadelphia, I continued to write the blog. As I began to feel better, the tone of the blog began to change. When I first started to write the *Brand New Every Morning*, I was literally crying out for help. The liquid in my pen felt more like blood, sweat and tears as opposed to ink. I literally poured my heart out. Sharing with the world that I was mentally ill was absolutely LIBERATING. But it was not easy! It not only freed me, but it positioned me to be a "gateway" to freedom for many others. People were actually starting to refer to me as an "expert" on depression. Imagine that!

My blog had become so popular that people started to reach out to me to ask my opinion on how to deal with their depression. Little did they know, I was still in the beginning stages of dealing with my own. However, because of my natural gift of leadership and servant's heart, and because I was now OFFICIALLY DORI ON PURPOSE, I felt the need to oblige.

This began my personal mission on learning as much as I could about this ugly disease and ways that me and my newfound tribe could function despite the label and ugly stigma attached to our condition. I searched for any information I could find to assist in helping people rebuild their lives.

In my quest for knowledge, here are some of the most important things that I was able to share with people who tapped into my blog. These are the things that made ME feel better and I know helped countless others. If you, or someone is dealing with depression right now, this information would help you, as well.

1. Women are more likely to be depressed than men.

2. Your genes play a role.

3. You might not respond to the first treatment.

4. Talk therapy can work as well as medication.

5. Depression doesn't just get in the way of being happy. It can also interrupt your ability to think.

6. It hampers your attention, memory, and decision-making abilities

7. Things which were once very easy become extremely difficult.

8. Proper Diet & Exercise are ESSENTIAL!

For a long time, as a person who suffered from depression, I felt like I was crazy. At times, I felt like I was losing my mind. I did not understand the disease and was too sick to do the work to try to get out from under it. Having that breather in California gave me the strength I needed to move forward.

Now, equipped with my BURNING DESIRE to be free from this disease forever, I was becoming the specialist. Every new piece of information I acquired made me feel stronger. It gave me a sense of purpose. It felt great knowing I was bringing help to my community; a community full of shame, embarrassment, and hopelessness.

Each discovery gave me a major boost in my FAITH. I began to believe for bigger again. I backed up my faith with action by continuing to speak the words that would make the things that I wanted to become a reality. I took time out every day to say my affirmations, and even continued to write the blog. It felt really good to know that I was well on my way to riches by controlling my own destiny; knowing what I wanted, believing I could have it, and envisioning it before it even happened. The principles I had read about in my business books, in particular, *Think and Grow Rich*, were finally working for me!

One of the major things that I learned in dealing with my depression is that the skills that I had acquired to get rid of that ugly disease are the same skills that I would need to do any and everything that I purposed to do in life.

I was able to use these skill sets (that is having a burning desire, exercising faith, saying affirmations, using auto suggestion, and becoming a specialist) to restart my business, get my personal life back on track, rebuild my finances, and even build my social life.

It is my opinion that if it is your desire to be your best at anything, you, too must take a look at the *13 Steps To Riches*. You must determine in your heart that you are willing to follow the course necessary to achieve your dreams. There is no getting around these principles. They have been proven. They have been tested. They have been tried. In my own life, I have testimony after testimony about how, when using these principles, things always work out. However, when I have deviated away from these principles, I quickly find myself falling back into some old habits that take me back to some old places that do not fulfill any of my dreams and goals.

DORI RAY

About Dori Ray: Dori "On Purpose" Ray is a native Philadelphian. As a businesswoman, her mission is to help people transform their minds, bodies, and bank accounts!

Dori was educated in the Philadelphia Public School System. She graduated from the Philadelphia High School for Girls in 1982 and Howard University School of Business in 1986 with a BBA in Marketing. Dori is a member of Delta Sigma Pi Business Fraternity and Delta Sigma Theta Sorority, Inc.

Dori leads teams around the world. She is a sought-after Speaker and Trainer within her industry and beyond. She is an experienced Re-Entry Coach as she has helped hundreds of Returning Citizens get back on track after incarceration.

Having suffered from depression for 20 years, she always reaches back to share her story and help break the cycle of silence. Her audience loves her authenticity!

Book Dori for speaking engagements www.linktr.ee/dorionpurpose

Author's Website: *www.linktr.ee/DoriOnPurpose*
Book Series Website & Author's Bio: *www.The13StepstoRiches.com*

Elaine Sugimura

A PASSION FOR FASHION & BEYOND

I shared in earlier chapters of *The 13 Steps to Riches* that my career involved many years within the fashion industry. It all started when I accepted an invitation to a friend's wedding. I showed up in the perfect outfit: wide-brim hat with a net hanging over the front, and high-heeled shoes. I did not know many of my girlfriend's colleagues, but one woman caught my eye. She had a powerful presence, and I knew she commanded respect among the guests there. When we arrived at the wedding reception, she came up to me, and in her rich Italian accent said, "I love your fashionable style" and "who are you?" I quickly responded and accepted her invitation to visit her office to interview for a sales position. I had zero expectations and just enough moxie to get myself together and take another step in my young career to see if this was a fashionable fit.

This was the start of my career in the fashion industry. When I speak to Specialized Knowledge, this is where it all began. It was from this foundation of learning and expertise that I was able to reach the C-Suite of many brands and businesses. What was this so-called Specialized Knowledge, you ask? Well, I found myself among a group of beautiful, intelligent, aggressive, and impressive individuals who all had the same goal, which was continued growth in an up-and-coming fashion organization. The majority of the team had fashion degrees, while I concentrated on overall business. I was an outcast, yet I knew I had what was needed to climb the corporate ladder. I chose to dig my heels in and learn—learn everything I could. It meant asking a million questions and making decisions that were based on analysis and facts. We were the sole U.S. distributors of the Gucci Accessory Collection. It was a dream job, and if I succeeded here, I knew life would be interesting along the way.

What was the Specialized Knowledge I gained from the start of my career and how I applied it along the way? Well, the story begins with what we were trained to do as sales associates for this incredible luxury brand called Gucci. We were taught a merchandising method that was known in the cosmetics industry. Each sales assistant was required to work with individual retail accounts, and you learned what was at the heart of their business. From monthly inventory counts to managing their stock levels to ensure maximum sales growth opportunity is what we were expected to review on a daily, weekly, and monthly basis. This required a high level of math and analytical skills to ensure sales goals were being met. I thrived when there were new ways to analyze data, and I sought out the top sales and merchandising leaders who would continue to challenge me to find new opportunities to increase sales. I knew I reached a level of success when I was promoted to an account executive position faster than my teammates. It required traveling to New York City and being a part of a team who began training the younger staff members. I absolutely had a burning passion to be the best on the sales team. I chose to give it my all and continued to rise within the sales organization. Not too long after, I was the first to be promoted from within into a regional sales management role.

As I continued to achieve, I sat back and assessed where I was within the organization and sought out to learn more. I had mastered the sales functions and communications needed to drive and exceed sales goals on a consistent basis for my specific retail accounts. I was asked to take on additional management tasks to support the merchandising and operations teams. This required working with executive management and creating new training methods because the organization was growing exponentially, as business was on fire. Since I was the only sales manager who had risen from the ranks and actually performed the work at the micro level, it gave me the insight needed to create and implement tools for the sales team to drive increased sales. I was tasked to work with the IT department to figure out how we could create an online sales-ordering system based on the manual work we were required to perform on a monthly basis. This was my first step into proving my expertise and Specialized Knowledge. By creating the necessary training documents and performing live demonstrations, the quality of the overall sales reporting and order processing improved not just sales, but overall team morale. This new sales training program was another anchor in the foundation I was setting for myself in managing branded businesses.

My deep passion for fashion led me down a path to learn more about what I was yet to be exposed to. After accomplishing key goals within the sales and operations areas, I chose to stretch myself into learning more about merchandising, as I was always intrigued by the woman who ran this department. She was one of the top executives in the organization. She was highly intelligent, and had both a sense of style and mystique. I was interested in learning more about her success and her vision for the department. I soon found myself in a new role as director of merchandising. It was a huge goal of mine to step into this role, as I always wanted the 360-degree view of how the business operated. I was clear on how to move our accessories from the time they reached our warehouse, but did not have a full grasp of what it meant to design and merchandise a branded accessory line from season to season. When I say accessories, I mean handbags and small leather goods. I was able to take the Specialized Knowledge I had gained thus far and continue to build that foundation and deep understanding of how a fashion brand operates. I did not realize the amount of dedication and work it required to learn this part of the business. I was given the opportunity to travel to Florence, Italy, to work with the Fendi team (at this time we had given up the distribution rights for the Gucci Accessory Collection) as we now had the sole distribution rights for this brand. I honestly did not realize how fortunate I was to have this opportunity. To learn a business from the start of the process to the finish was my next goal, and I was right in the middle of accomplishing that. My dream was starting to become a reality.

You may be asking, what was required to prepare for such a trip? Well, let me first say, back then, laptops were yet to be used as a daily work tool. We created and filled our suitcases with 75-to-100-pound bound workbooks and traveled to Rome, drove 5 hours to Florence, and stayed in the corporate villa for 3 to 4 weeks each season. Pinch me! I did not realize until years later what this opportunity really meant for my career. In preparation for these trips, the workbooks were created over a 5-week period during many late nights with the team. Burning the midnight oil was common back then, and each and every page of the over 200-page workbook was reviewed and assessed by our vice president. There never was a dull moment, and always something new to learn. I had already mastered the 6-month sales plans, gross margin, gross profit, to overall profit and loss statements for each of the retailers I managed, and now within the merchandising area, I began to master the design process, analyzing pricing from cost to retail, merchandising new product collections. It was as if I learned how to build the puzzle from start to finish. I now gained the Specialized Knowledge to build a fashion brand's presence from the foundation to the sales floor. I walked away from this experience knowing I had the tools to apply to any business that required this Specialized Knowledge to flourish from the ground up. I knew I would have ongoing challenges to these tools each and every time a new concept needed to be learned.

I was fortunate to continue my fashion career as my passion for fashion is what led me down a path that now, as I look back on this fabulous journey, allows me to take all that I learned and continue to learn and build the bridge between different categories of business. Over the past ten years, I have built my consulting firm that focuses on supporting those who have never received this Specialized Knowledge in their own businesses. Somewhere along the way, they may have missed knowing what the next step should be. I am grateful for this life of mine, and I currently support an international franchise business that is in the food and beverage sector.

Yes, you can take that Specialized Knowledge and apply it to any business as the focus is not the commodity itself, but instead it is how you take that commodity and allow it to be the star. Now, I am adding one additional career path to my journey, being a coach/mentor to those who are in need and want to be inspired by this Specialized Knowledge! Hard work pays dividends, and I am living proof of that!

ELAINE SUGIMURA

About Elaine R. Sugimura: Elaine is an accomplished fashion executive turned entrepreneur who has a passion to create leaders amongst leaders. Currently, she owns several businesses and as CEO, she runs a franchise food and beverage organization that requires both strategy and execution. Fun fact: she is an adrenaline junkie—the higher, the faster, the better. Her love for adventure has led her to travel to many parts of the world by plane and automobile. She and her husband, Hiro, share their home in Northern California. They have raised two extraordinary sons and have added two beautiful daughters-in-law to their growing family.

Author's Website: *www.ElaineRSugimura.com*
Book Series Website & Author's Bio: *www.The13StepstoRiches.com*

Elizabeth Walker

THE GIFT OF SPECIALIZED KNOWLEDGE

Specialized: to be engaged in a special study or line of business

Knowledge: acknowledgement of a superior, honor, worship

Both are definitions from the etymology dictionary. What does this mean? I have an engagement in a special study or line of business while acknowledging something or someone superior to me through honoring them or worshipping them, or honoring it and worshipping it?

When I looked at the definition of these words originally, I wondered, do I have Specialized Knowledge in anything? I then realized that in every area of life that I have ever succeeded in, there has been an element of having someone I looked up to as a superior and something or someone I honored and had a sense of worship towards.

When I left school, I engaged myself in the specialized study of nursing. I acknowledged that it was a profession in which a ranking system existed. I knew right from the start that there was an ascension model, and I knew exactly what I needed to do to climb the ranks. I was engaged in Specialized Knowledge. Being the mismatcher that I am, I believed there was a faster and better way!

I was passionate about premature babies and my goal was to become Australia's leading neonatal intensive-care nurse. I was brand new, straight out of university, and yet wanted one of the most sought-after positions in the hospital. So, I went about acquiring more Specialized Knowledge. I acknowledged who the superior was, and I started to learn all about her. Her name was Madeline Longobardi, and she was passionate about nursing, passionate about education, and passionate about tiny babies. I learned everything there was to know about her and her unit. I even called and asked her why new graduate nurses were traditionally kept out of the NICU. About a week after our meeting, she called me. She said, "I've thought about what you've said, and you're right! If I recruit new graduate nurses into NICU, they can learn great habits from the start and be dedicated to a long profession in the NICU. Would you like to come in for an interview?" Of course, I ecstatically agreed and impressed the pants off her with my knowledge of her backstory and my knowledge of all the recent journal articles on neonatal intensive care. My Specialized Knowledge got me what I wanted.

The same was true when I decided to become a flying trapeze artist. I was 36 years old and yes, I had a history in trampolining and gymnastics, however flying trapeze was a whole new sport. This was a very different kind of Specialized Knowledge. I was engaged in a special study of learning how to strengthen and manipulate my body into that of a flying trapeze artist. In terms of my knowledge, I acknowledged the incredible Miguel Vazquez, arguably the world's greatest flyer in history. I watched all the old circus shows and became obsessed with Cirque du Soleil. It was a completely different pathway than that of traditional study, and yet it was Specialized Knowledge that afforded me future relationships with some of Australia's leading circus families like the Ashtons, the Wests, and the Webers. It was specifically this knowledge that opened conversations after a show with performers, which later led to being able to fly on their rigs in their circus tents!

I created a very special relationship with Stardust Circus in Australia and particularly, Yelena West, at a time in my life when I was broken from an horrific divorce. The circus was always there as an escape for my children and for me. Stardust Circus became a place where we were always welcome. Glenn and Yelena treated my children as their own, showing them the animals, and telling them off when they mucked around. Meanwhile, I got to escape on the rig, even if just for a few moments, and live, in my head at least, my dream of being a world-famous flyer! If not for my dedication to organizing my knowledge and creating these relationships, my children and I would never have had these experiences and opportunities.

Have you noticed a theme? You see in the above two examples that it was the relationships from the Specialized Knowledge which allowed me to create. Without the Specialized Knowledge, I was just another nurse with a dream, who would have had to do post-grad study and a few years on the job before I saw the inside of a NICU. Without the dedication to learning the history of flying trapeze, I was just another circus-goer with a wild imagination, thinking I could ever fly in a tent. Instead, my Specialized Knowledge created unimaginable experiences that my children, now 18 and 21, still talk about.

So, what about traditional Specialized Knowledge? The kind you get in a university or from books or colleges. I have had phenomenal experiences with that, too! I hold degrees in nursing, midwifery, and theology. I hold diplomas in aromatherapy, remedial massage, astrology, energetic healing, counselling, linguistics, embryology, and many more. All studied at highly accredited universities and colleges. This knowledge is highly transferrable once it is categorized and organized in a way that is easy to make sense of and easy to access.

In my current field of expertise, neuro-linguistic programming, I have not only studied and acknowledged those before me, but I have also looked from the worship perspective that people take on the words that others use. So many people have allowed themselves to be hurt by words. Words that don't mean and were never intended to mean the current societal definition. I have seen words destroy people, families, and communities. I made it my mission to teach people Specialized Knowledge on how to firstly communicate with themselves, and communicate with those around them in an effective and direct way that is much less likely to be misconstrued or misunderstood.

Here's the really interesting thing about Specialized Knowledge: most people think they have none. Yet you are an incredibly unique individual whose experience and individual Specialized Knowledge is something that no one else has. Your ability to see things from your perspective, to organize knowledge according to your life experience, and use it for business, or relationships, or pleasure is completely unique to you. Imagine what would happen if you could take that knowledge that you have and translate it into something the world needs and wants.

Some people believe that they need all the Specialized Knowledge to start anything of any value. What you need is a great mastermind. A collection of people all moving towards the same goal. All with their own unique individual Specialized Knowledge. All wanting to create a better world.

In my current business, we have 10 committed team members, all who have their own Specialized Knowledge, all who also run their own businesses, and are all committed to the mission. Between us all, we have the knowledge of the world. Individually, we have Specialized Knowledge. And with that, we can create anything we choose to create.

So if you're currently sitting there saying, "I don't know enough to start my business, to speak my truth, to leave my partner, to be a parent, etc." the truth is you need to use what you have, gain the first lot of knowledge you need, connect with others who have the missing pieces, and create the world's most phenomenal, completed jigsaw puzzle you've ever seen. If you've ever done a jigsaw puzzle, you know that initially it looks like a mess, and you also know the great satisfaction that comes from putting all of the pieces together. Some of you might be feeling like a mess right now; you're just a jigsaw puzzle ready to be connected. The organization of Specialized Knowledge, and the acknowledgement that you have Specialized Knowledge, is where you get to create the big picture you've been looking for. You have a gift, and that gift is your very own version of Specialized Knowledge. Gifts are meant to be open! Go ahead and open yours!

It took me a few years to realize it was my Specialized Knowledge that was at the forefront of every imagining that came true. It was indeed a dedication and organization of everything I've ever learned and a hungry desire to always learn more that allowed me to realize my Specialized Knowledge. I have watched many a person whom I thought was more knowledgeable than me, fall in a heap due to the lack of ability to transfer Specialized Knowledge. I've seen people fail from not recognizing others' Specialized Knowledge. Saddest of all, I've seen people's life force die because they were unwilling to acknowledge their own Specialized Knowledge and connect that with others to create something world changing.

People often say I'm lucky. I would say I've dedicated my time to reading, studying, modeling, collating, organizing, and creating Specialized Knowledge in order to create the opportunities that have given me an exciting and varied life that I love living!

ELIZABETH WALKER

About Elizabeth Walker: Elizabeth is Australia's leading Female Integrated NLP Trainer, an international speaker with Real Success, and the host of Success Resources' (Australia's largest and most successful events promoter, including speakers such as Tony Robbins and Sir Richard Branson) inaugural Australian Women's Program "The Seed." Elizabeth has guided many people to achieve complete personal breakthroughs and phenomenal personal and business growth. With over 25 years of experience transforming the lives of hundreds of thousands of people, Elizabeth's goal is to assist leaders to create the reality they choose to live, impacting millions on a global scale.

A thought leader who has worked alongside people like Gary Vaynerchuck, Kerwin Rae, Jeffery Slayter, and Kate Gray, Elizabeth has an outstanding method of delivering heart with business.

As a former lecturer in medicine at the University of Sydney and lecturer in nursing at Western Sydney University, Elizabeth was instrumental in the research and development of the stillbirth and neonatal death pathways, ensuring each family in Australia went home knowing what happened to their child, and felt understood, heard, and seen.

A former Australian Champion in Trampolining and Australian Dancesport, Elizabeth has always been passionate about the mindset and skills required to create the results you are seeking.

Author's website: *www.ElizabethAnneWalker.com*
Book Series Website & Author's Bio: *www.The13StepsToRiches.com*

Erin Ley

THE KEY TO SUCCESS

In *Think and Grow Rich*, Napoleon Hill states, "Knowledge will not attract money, unless it is organized, and intelligently directed, through practical plans of action, to the definite end of accumulation of money. Lack of understanding of this fact has been the source of confusion to millions of people who falsely believe that 'knowledge is power.' It is nothing of the sort! Knowledge is only potential power. It becomes power only when, and if, it is organized into definite plans of action, and directed to a definite end."

When I was being treated for non-Hodgkins lymphoblastic lymphoma in 1991, I craved learning everything I could about the mind, body, and spirit. From the hospital bed, I read tons of books and consumed tons of cassette tapes. When I was at home, I went back to college to study physical therapy. I wanted to know as much as possible about the body and how to heal it. Two years into my classes, I changed my major and graduated from Hofstra University with a bachelor's degree specializing in speech/language pathology with a minor in psychology. I graduated from college three years after I graduated from my chemotherapy and radiation treatments.

The doctors were astonished that I was able to handle as many college classes as I did during and after the two-and-a-half-year protocol, and that I survived the grueling protocol as well. Most people did not live when diagnosed with that rare pediatric cancer. Little did the doctors know, the learning I did at that time became my Specialized Knowledge that would get me through the protocol. I put into action everything I could when applicable to my health and well-being. To this degree, with regard to Specialized Knowledge, we can substitute the word "money" for "health" here.

What are you studying? It doesn't have to be a formal education. Most of my education came from outside the classroom. What is it that you have been focused on but have not yet acted upon? The action part of this is the key to success. Knowledge is a beautiful thing, and it allows us to grow, but in a limited way. When you couple knowledge with action toward a desired goal, all the while taking those action steps in faith, then you just exploded the ceiling off all limitations that had been set there before.

In the 1990's, as I was going to school and after I graduated, the doctors at Memorial Sloan Kettering Cancer Center had their patients call me at home. They wanted me to share with their patients what I learned and what got me through the protocol as well as I did. I began to take my Specialized Knowledge and share it with many cancer patients across the country. This was the beginning of my coaching practice. I did this for years for free, to give back, and then the doctors suggested I coach people for a living. At first, I thought I couldn't because it was too easy. Prior to this, I had worked on Wall Street as an account executive for a few years, and that was not easy. For some odd reason, I thought work had to be hard. Then I learned it is supposed to be easy. If it is hard, then you are in the wrong business and off purpose.

When you decide that you can do, be, and have whatever you desire, your life begins to light up. Life becomes fun. People will not understand why you are so happy all the time. When you have Specialized Knowledge backed by action with a definite goal in mind, the miracles start to happen.

I went through a tumultuous divorce a few years ago. After I quieted all the fear, lack, and scarcity that was going on in my mind, I began to do exactly what I had done during the cancer treatments. I made a crystal-clear vision for the business I wanted to resurrect. I started off with $5 in my pocket in line at the supermarket with milk and bread in my hands, praying to God the $5 would cover it, and it did. I walked out of the supermarket with my daughter and the white-hot burning desire to never have that horrible, uncomfortable feeling again. I went home and wrote out a plan for exactly what I wanted my business to look like as an Empowerment and Success Coach. I had already written three books and knew I wanted to write more. I knew I wanted to do more inspirational speaking. And I knew I wanted to pour love into the world and receive it as well. With my focus on exactly what my Specialized Knowledge was, helping people go from feeling the overwhelm, fear, and distraction to becoming focused, fearless, and excited about life and their future, I was able to grow my business to six figures in a year and a half with the help of God, coaches, and mentors.

I joined the Habitude Warrior Mastermind and that is when growing my business became fun. Erik Swanson's Mastermind's primary focus IS Specialized Knowledge. We all show up and discuss our businesses. We help each other get clear on what it is we are doing and what we want to do next. We provide and receive counsel. We hold each other accountable for the action steps necessary to move our life and business forward, directed at the definite end goal. If you are looking to grow your life and/or your business, I highly suggest you do not do it alone. It takes longer and it is not as enjoyable. There's an old proverb that says, "If you want to go fast, go alone. If you want to go far, go with a team." From my experience, nothing can be more true.

Are you working in a job you do not like? I call that a soul-suck. In *Think and Grow Rich*, Napoleon Hill wrote, "Halpin deserves credit for refusing to compromise with life by accepting and keeping a job he did not want, and that is one of the major points I am trying to emphasize through this entire philosophy—that we rise to high positions or remain at the bottom because of conditions we can control if we desire to control them. I am also trying to emphasize another point, namely, that both success and failure are largely the results of habit."

I invite you to imagine your life exactly the way you want it, beyond your wildest dreams. Now I invite you to think about the habits and beliefs that you've acquired over your lifetime that are keeping you stuck; keeping you from living that life you imagine. Once you become aware of what those limitations are, you can begin to replace them with better habits and beliefs, ones that will serve you. Then you can get into the driver's seat of your own life and become the creator of your destiny. Life will no longer drive you. Imagine the kind of work you would love to do, what you know would light you up when getting out of bed in the morning. Then acquire the Specialized Knowledge necessary to make that go from a dream to your reality, as a result of you backing that knowledge with focused, fearless action.

Henry Ford is a prime example of Specialized Knowledge. With very little formal education, he focused on exactly what he knew best and hired out the rest. One of my favorites of Ford's quotes is, "Whether you think you can or think you can't, you're right."

Once you encounter an idea that lights you up, something you would really love to do, allow yourself to purge all negative self-talk that keeps you from bringing that idea to life. Think the thoughts of "I CAN!" Speak the words of "I CAN!" Visualize your idea coming to life. Meditate on it becoming your reality. At the same time, take the time to acquire the Specialized Knowledge necessary to bring that idea to fruition. Be intentional, in an organized fashion, regarding taking massive action. Be solution focused. Be persistent. Celebrate the wins along the way. Always remember to live onward and upward!

ERIN LEY

About Erin Ley: As Founder and CEO of Onward Productions, Inc., Erin Ley has spent the last 30 years as an Author, Professional Speaker, Personal and Professional Empowerment and Success Coach predominantly around mindset, Vision and Decision. Founder of many influential summits, including "Life On Track," Erin is also the host of the upcoming online streaming T.V. Show *"Life On Track with Erin Ley,"* which is all about helping you get into the driver's seat of your own life.

They call Erin "The Miracle Maker!" As a cancer survivor at age twenty-five, single mom of three at age forty-seven, successful Entrepreneur at age fifty, Erin has shown thousands upon thousands across the globe how to become victorious by being focused, fearless, and excited about life and your future! Erin says, "Celebrate life and you'll have a life worth celebrating!"

To see more about Erin and the release of her 4th book *"WorkLuv: A Love Story"* along with her "Life On Track" Course & Coaching Programs, please visit her website.

Author's website: *www.ErinLey.com*
Book Series Website & Author's Bio: *www.The13StepsToRiches.com*

Fatima Hurd

CAPTURED FROM THE HEART

Not having finished college weighed heavily on my shoulders for many years. I was convinced that because I did not finish my degree in visual communications, I would never be worthy of a great-paying career.

I relied for many years on working my way to the top. I had the fire in me and was ambitious with a desire to excel and climb to the top at any job I held.

I would always tell myself to keep my head up and keep moving towards the goal, and that my hard work would pay off. And eventually it would, but it was not without the sacrifice of working myself to the ground being the yes-girl to overtime and taking on multiple tasks to prove my worthiness.

However, no matter how hard I worked to know everything about all the moving parts of a company, I could never advance past a managerial position into an executive role, even though I know I could be great at it.

I always felt that I would never achieve great success because my education was limited to that of a college dropout.

Then one day, I lost my job, around the time when the 2008 recession hit. It was then that I realized that not even the best education could save those executive positions from cuts that were brought on from circumstances such as a recession. If anything, executive positions were never permanent roles and were positions that were more prone to a higher turnover in the corporate world.

As I was laid off from my job at the start of the recession, little did I know what a world of opportunities it would open up for me!

The vision was not yet evident at the time, but these circumstances pivoted my life into a whole new direction that woke up the entrepreneurial spirit that was dormant inside of me.

First, it began as I turned to some amazing books for self-development. Such as *Think & Grow Rich* by Napoleon Hill, and *The Success Principles* by Jack Canfield.

As I read these books from cover to cover, I was inspired to break away from the 9-5 and focus on how I could be of service to others with my skills and as an entrepreneur!

When I read *Think & Grow Rich* by Napoleon Hill, I was inspired by the chapter about "Specialized Knowledge." At the time, being new to the world of entrepreneurs, I relied on others to learn new skills for running a successful business. When I started my photography business, I got a partner, and her skills as an entrepreneur helped me to get started. Although she was great at business, her customer service skills could use improvement, which is where I excelled. My business was grown solely through referrals. Although I learned some great marketing skills from her, my skills in being of service to my clients proved to be more valuable when creating long-term clients. To this day, I still have clients from when I first started my photography. As I got better with my photography skills, I also got better at my marketing skills. I may not have received my college degree, but the cool thing about the internet is that now you could purchase Specialized Knowledge in the areas you need to improve. As the years went by, I went from doing everything to accepting that I needed to get help in the areas that I was not an expert in.

I purchased and took courses in improving my photography with newborns, maternity, family, and weddings. I took courses that helped me with marketing that taught me how to market to narrow down my target market.

As my business grew, my need to acquire more knowledge on how to run a successful business grew as well.

As time went on, accessing information needed to improve my business became easier. Also, I realized that I was great at other things besides just photography. I was great at helping women become very comfortable in front of the camera, and that came from who I was and I how made them feel.

The way I made women feel in front of the camera became my niche. As the years went by, businesses were popping up everywhere. Newborn photography became a very saturated industry and prices were very competitive.

I learned to leverage my networking skills. Getting familiar with others and their businesses helped me understand how I could hire others and their specialized skills to help me run my business more successfully. By 2016, I was running a thriving and prosperous photography business, specializing in maternity, newborn, family, and couples photography. I had built a well-established photography business, and was featured in websites and magazines for family and newborn photography. I enjoyed photography retreats with other high-end and well-known photographers all over the U.S., mingling and attending conventions such as WPPI hosted in my hometown of Las Vegas. It was beautiful and I had built this reputation and name for myself by being of service to others, with integrity, and coming always from a place of love. To show gratitude and to give back to the community, I chose three families a year to offer a free session to. I truly believe that when you serve others from your heart, which I enjoyed very much, it brings more abundance to your life.

In March of 2017, my husband and I decided to move to another state. At this point, I had a studio and a thriving business that would soon come to an end as moving meant closing the doors to my studio.

When we moved, I took a break from my photography business, which lead me temporarily in another direction. However, I never really gave up on my photography. It remained part of my life long after closing the doors to my studio.

This hiatus lead me to discover what my purpose as a photographer and healer was and how to serve others with my skills as a photographer with love. I was open to the idea of helping others show up as the best version of themselves in front of the camera. Showing up with a heart-centered love instead of ego. What I discovered was how to get my clients to fall in love with themselves in front of the camera by getting out their own way.

People have a preconceived idea of how they want to show up for their pictures, mainly due to something they have seen somewhere else, and most of the time they end up feeling disappointed by not getting the results that they were hoping for, because that awareness comes from a place of ego, and not self-love.

My Specialized Knowledge came from trusting my inner self and my ability to connect with others as I hold space for them to feel safe, a place to be seen, to be vulnerable, and fully self-expressed in child-like wonder and to help them feel like they come alive!

My experience throughout the years as a photographer has helped me develop a style that helps my clients feel at ease, safe, and confident in front of my camera, leaving the ego at home.

I connect with my clients by helping them make the shift in their state of consciousness from the ego to the heart, so they show up as their authentic selves.

As a Reiki Master and certified crystal healer, I have incorporated healing as a modality to help my clients experience opening energetically to the heart energy and allowing understanding, experience, and awareness to unfold. This allows them to experience self-compassion, as well as unconditional love for self, allowing them to show up authentically to allow me to capture the essence of their soul.

After a few years in California, I returned to photography full-time, pivoting my business to working with entrepreneurs. The pandemic changed life as we know it and now, more than ever, there are small businesses popping up everywhere. The only way to be noticed is to show up authentically, and I help my clients to do that energetically through my photography.

The road to success has not been easy, however when you are willing to invest in yourself and in others who are willing to help, it is well worth it!

FATIMA HURD

About Fatima Hurd: Fatima is a personal brand photographer and was featured in the special edition of Beauty & Lifestyle's mommy magazine. Fatima specializes in personal branding photography dedicated to helping influencers and entrepreneurs expand their reach online with strategic, creative, inspiring, and visual content. Owner of a digital consulting agency, Social Branding Photography', Fatima helps professionals with all their digital needs.

Fatima holds ten years of photography experience. An expert in her field, she helps teach photography to middle school students and she hosts workshops to teach anyone who wants to learn how to use and improve their skills with DSLR and on manual mode. Hurd is also a mother of three, wife, certified Reiki master, and certified crystal healer. She loves being out in nature, enjoys taking road trips with her family, and loves meditation and yoga on the beach.

Author's website: *www.FatimaHurd.com*
Book Series Website & Author's Bio: *www.The13StepsToRiches.com*

Frankie Fegurgur

DID SCHOOL RUIN YOUR EDUCATION?

Most people haven't cracked open a book since they left school. It's much easier to just zone out in front of the tv or scroll endlessly on our phones. Reading demands time, focus, and patience. And let's face it, most reading wasn't for enjoyment, it was mandatory for assignments that were forgotten shortly after completion. In college, I read 5-7 books a week per class, and the cost of the books plus the density of the subject matter made the desire to read nonexistent. The difference maker for me was that I had already worked for 6+ years and recently embarked on a journey of self-improvement through self-employment. I was disciplined with my coursework and deliberately enthusiastic about expanding my mindset. I needed to apply new information immediately because I had a family to take care of.

Deliberate enthusiasm has attracted volunteer opportunities where I speak with thousands of young adults each year. One of the most impactful recommendations I make to them is to treat every job as entrepreneurial. It doesn't matter where you start off, as evidenced two years ago by a young man who recognized me at a drive-thru window. His head shot out with a big smile on his face. He thanked me profusely, telling me how proud his family was of him. Just three months prior, he was in danger of not graduating from his continuation high school. I remember him sharing with me his dream to help create animated films, but he couldn't afford college and was too embarrassed to work a minimum-wage job. My advice to him was to take any honest work, including mopping floors. He should treat it seriously, imagining that he owned the building and overdeliver every day. Apparently, he took our talk to heart because he was the happiest person to ever work a fry station. And not only that, when I went to check on him the following summer, his manager said he had quit for another job that was helping pay his way through art school!

The path to that young man's dream career necessitates extensive Specialized Knowledge. He knows he is entering a highly-competitive field, and that he needs the best training to max out his abilities. He is an example of when personal responsibility meets a great attitude. Many of his peers will not enjoy the same good fortune, as ongoing world events mean that millions of people worldwide will become disenfranchised, from young adults to seasoned blue-collar workers. I'll be discussing the changing economy, the need to deploy Specialized Knowledge, and how to lead high-performing teams, regardless of your present career. First, I'll describe how our bureaucratic dinosaur of a school system is failing its students, while we barrel toward the largest wealth divide in history.

The pandemic recession revealed and accelerated the inequalities and inefficiencies of public school education. Schools scrambled to shift to virtual classrooms by distributing laptops with new software that teachers had to learn to navigate alongside their students. Students who weren't tech-savvy, or needed individualized education plans, or for whom English is a second language, fell quickly behind. It was common to see news clips of parents driving their kids around town to find free Wi-Fi just to complete their homework. These parents were often juggling multiple children and erratic work schedules or even layoffs. The strain on teachers continues, with burnout and a lack of freedom to utilize tools and approaches to which they've been accustomed. Our education system doesn't meet students where they are, and consequently doesn't prepare them for adult life.

The Great Resignation reflects the uncertainty and discontent in the economy. Workers across multiple sectors, especially in low-wage/unskilled roles, are leaving by the millions. Unsafe conditions, rude customers, and poor management, together with a lack of upward mobility are among the top reasons. I empathize with people who are undertrained, under-resourced, and underappreciated. The shortage of frontline and other blue-collar workers will lead to greater automation sooner than predicted. I remember that during the Great Recession, mass layoffs occurred, and certain jobs never returned. I believe that corporations, especially multinational ones, will adapt, just as they always have. I'll come back to why that is, but where does this leave the average person? The transition to digitization and automation for most manual labor has shown that not every demographic is carrying the burden of modernization equally. The downside of jobs that only require general knowledge and skills is that they are easily replaced, leaving people with few options.

If you desire financial independence, your greatest probability for success is in acquiring Specialized Knowledge. Choose a field that excites you. There are too many ways to earn money to be unhappy with your work. Consider your current industry. It's easier to establish independence in a field you are already knowledgeable about. You know much more than you think you do about how your employer bids on contracts, manages logistics, trains employees, etc. Now is not the time to be shy. Specialized Knowledge is reflected in the value and potentially decades of experience that you bring. Differentiate yourself with your unique approach and nuanced methodology earned through learning, teaching, and mastering skillsets. Degrees and professional designations will get attention, but not necessarily results. Before you invest the time and tears, know exactly how more schooling or certificates will accelerate the achievement of what you desire. Don't be blinded by vanity markers or hide behind titles and associations. Be kind to yourself. Sometimes you won't realize the expertise that you've attained until after the fact. Keep a brag sheet and use it as a reminder of how far you've come.

If your desire is to empower people and achieve financial independence on a greater scale, then it's time to build. Depending on your objectives, you may either leverage experts as needed, or assemble a full-time team. Business is a team sport. Individuals get sick, lose the faith, quit, or even try to sabotage the venture. Teams exceed what they would have otherwise done alone. Being the leader doesn't require you to be the utmost expert. In fact, for those wanting to transition from solo artist to team leader, the perfectionists always struggles the most. I see it often in sales environments. The top salesperson gets promoted to sales manager, but struggles because technical proficiency doesn't equate to leadership. They lack experience in coaching people, dealing with external issues, and balancing their workload. They are impatient when their employees struggle in areas that come naturally to the manager. One of the most important leadership skills I suggest in these situations is empathy. Don't lose sight of the person for the sake of the outcome. Leaders with higher EQ (emotional quotient) are not only more favorably perceived, but they also develop more resilient teams.

There are countless other benefits to collaborating with experts. Leveraging their expertise beats your own procrastination and lightens your workload. Focus on being an expert in your field, not everyone else's. An expert can help you know what you don't know. They can explain where to put your focus, revealing opportunities you would otherwise miss. This is the difference between the mediocre entrepreneur and the serial entrepreneur. They have almost a sixth sense to see what others aren't equipped to handle. They have the courage to follow through on calculated risks.

Confidence often comes from doing, and of course they act when others don't; they've already done what others won't! This is how multinational companies attract the top talent to work for them, enabling corporations to duplicate and scale exponentially.

Whether becoming an expert or leveraging them is the path you choose, it's common to feel isolated along the way, or like you've hit a barrier. Join or form a mastermind group. This concept will be headlined in a later volume by the awesome Mr. Erik Swanson. In the meantime, know that whatever challenge you're facing, there are entrepreneurs who have already been there or are currently going through the same struggles. Masterminds will expand your network and multiply your influence, with no limit to the resources you can access.

Despite the endless amount information at our fingertips, people still find themselves unprepared for the accelerated modernization of society. Our young people aren't taught how to think critically or how to acquire basic life skills. They become adults who shuffle from job to job, always lacking control over their financial future. There is hope for anyone willing to apply the timeless lessons of this series, regardless of their current circumstances. They can become a well-respected expert or lead a team of experts. Specialized Knowledge comes in various forms and is effective when exercised by lifelong learners with a passion for excellent work. In this new economy, we don't have to operate as islands. We can support each other and win for our families. If this discussion has sparked aspirations or even fears and self-doubt, I'd love to hear from you.

FRANKIE FEGURGUR

About Frankie Fegurgur: Frankie's "burning desire" is helping people retire with dignity. Frankie distills the lessons he has learned over the last 15 years and empowers our youth to make better financial decisions than the generation before them. This is a deeply personal mission for him—he was born to high-school-aged parents, and money was always a struggle. Frankie learned that hard work, alone, wasn't the key to financial freedom and sought a more fulfilling path. Now, he serves as the COO of a nonprofit financial association based in the San Francisco Bay Area, teaching money mindfulness. He, his wife, and their two children can be found exploring, volunteering, and building throughout their community.

Author's website: *www.FrankMoneyTalk.com*
Book Series Website & Author's Bio: *www.The13StepsToRiches.com*

Fred Moskowitz

HARNESS THE POWER OF YOUR SPECIALIZED KNOWLEDGE

When it comes to Specialized Knowledge, this concept can be broken down into two distinct categories: The Specialized Knowledge of other people, and the Specialized Knowledge that you possess.

1. The Specialized Knowledge of Others

The idea of leveraging the knowledge of other people, and especially the knowledge of the people you put yourself around. Napoleon Hill discussed this extensively in the context of creating mastermind groups where all participants are stronger together, leveraging the power of the collective knowledge of the mastermind.

Jim Rohn, who was the grandfather of personal development, taught us that we become the average of the five people we surround ourselves with.

When you are purposeful with regard to the people who you surround yourself with, and you strive to work together, now that will absolutely produce some amazing results in your life or your business! Consider that you are easily able to position yourself to experience and benefit from the power that comes from leveraging all of their specialized expertise and skills.

For anyone who is a business owner or an entrepreneur, one of the most important things to do is to go out and begin to assemble your all-star lineup. This includes your accountant or CPA, your attorney, your insurance agent, others with niche skill sets relevant to your business, as well as the vendors that support your business.

These are the people that have very specialized expertise where it would not make sense for you to hire them as a direct employee. You're going to work with them, you're going to hire their services, and lean on them for their expertise as you grow your business. This becomes your all-star team that you can lean on when you need that Specialized Knowledge.

As an example, when I was getting started with building up my rental real estate portfolio almost two decades ago, there was a very specific group of experts that I determined I needed to develop relationships with:

- Accountant/CPA, and ideally an accountant that has experience working with rental real estate portfolios
- Attorney
- Title agent and title company
- Realtors
- General contractor
- Building trade contractors (plumbing, HVAC, electrical, roofing, carpentry, painting, etc.)
- Property manager
- Mortgage and Banking/financing relationships
- Insurance agent

These were the first people who I began to meet, build relationships with, and to begin doing business with. In the beginning, it started out with just a couple of relationships. As time went on, I asked for referrals from the successful people that I was meeting, and as a result, my contact list grew and flourished.

Almost 20 years later, many of the people who were on my original all-star team continue to be some of my most trusted contacts. These are the people that I have on speed dial in my phone. They are the ones who I can reach out to any time that I have a difficult problem to solve or when I need an expert opinion.

When you align yourself with people who have deep expertise, you can quickly come to the conclusion that as an entrepreneur and business owner, you can't possibly wear all those hats and fill all of those roles. It is a good idea to take stock of your unique skills and abilities, and then you can determine what you're going to specifically focus on as you build your business. Stick to those few core competencies where you can truly excel, and hire out everything else that's needed for your business. As you progress with hiring out and outsourcing the services of others as needed, you align yourself with the right people, build those relationships, and that's one of the most important things to do, especially when you're starting out. You will actually find that those solid relationships will persist throughout your entire career.

When we read the *Think and Grow Rich* chapter on Specialized Knowledge, Napoleon Hill tells the story of Henry Ford being challenged about his knowledge in court. Ford found himself involved in a lawsuit, and he was called to the stand to testify as a witness. He proceeded to describe how he had his panel of experts available to him at any time, for whatever the pertinent topic was that he needed, to summon their expertise as needed. These men were ready to provide their input, opinions, and expertise at any time. Whether solving a problem or coming up with a new product or resolving a design issue, he had their Specialized Knowledge available to him on demand.

2. Your Own Specialized Knowledge

How do you go about developing your Specialized Knowledge? All it takes is to set the intention, and then to put in the focused and consistent effort on an ongoing basis. Think about how your knowledge can develop if you are able to improve just 1% every day, on a consistent basis!

Remember that no one else is going to do this for you. Motivational speaker Tony Robbins is well known for talking about the idea that if we are not growing, we are dying.

Recently, I heard a statistic that 33% of US high school graduates never read another book after they graduate from high school, and that 42% of college graduates never read another book after they graduate from college. I really like the idea about doing everything we can in order to not become a part of those statistics.

As someone who considers themselves to be a lifelong learner, I am always seeking to learn new skills, to develop my expertise in new areas, and to explore new and unique experiences.

I have come to the conclusion that those who are ready to put in the effort to learn new things end up developing diverse skills on so many levels. One of the best things that you can do for your own personal and professional growth is to develop new skills for your business or for your career. It does not matter whether they're directly associated with your line of work or not at all. In either case, the benefits can be tremendous. Even the learning of leisure activities or hobbies is very beneficial, because during the time you are focused on that activity, you are giving your conscious mind a break from focusing on work and business. Meanwhile, your subconscious mind is still hard at work solving those business and technical problems that are pending resolution back in the office.

In today's modern times, there is an abundance of educational content that has shifted to the internet and has become available to all of us. There are online courses, workshops, and lectures on just about every topic known to man, which can be watched and studied from the comfort of our own homes.

We now have access to very high-level experts in every field. Just about every notable person has made available their body of work in published and online formats. This content may be accessed for a reasonable cost, and sometimes even at no cost if the materials are placed into the public domain. If you desire, you can easily study and learn from the best of the best.

As an example, let's say that you desire to study the subject of negotiation and seek to improve your negotiating skills. Becoming a good negotiator can benefit just about everyone, no matter what business you are in. And where would you use this skill?

- Negotiating a business contract or agreement for goods and services.
- Negotiating the purchase or sale of a business or other substantial asset.
- Negotiating with your child about their bedtime.
- Negotiating with your spouse about where to go out for dinner, or about your next vacation destination.

Performing a cursory online search will show numerous options for courses and trainings on the subject of negotiation, and you could take up some online self-study. What if, perhaps, your budget and your time might allow for you to travel to attend a weekend-long workshop about negotiation, which is being presented by an individual who is a former top-FBI hostage negotiator? Think about what kind of skills and growth you would be able to come away with after attending an event like that.

The return on investment of your time and your money would be off the charts.

Summary

In this chapter, we have learned that there are two types of Specialized Knowledge that will benefit us: the Specialized Knowledge of others, and our own Specialized Knowledge. When we surround ourselves with a team of individuals that possess ultra-specialized skill sets, those skill sets become available to us and can be leveraged to solve problems, streamline operations, and achieve tremendous growth. When we focus on our own growth and the development of our Specialized Knowledge, this enables us to take on larger problems and challenges, and to achieve massive growth. There are even many options available for us to study and learn from the top experts in just about every field. I encourage you to focus on both of these types of Specialized Knowledge in your own lives and businesses, and then watch the amazing growth and results that will come to you.

FRED MOSKOWITZ

About Fred Moskowitz: Fred is a best-selling author, investment fund manager, and speaker who is on a personal mission to teach people about the power of investing in alternative asset classes, such as real estate and mortgage notes, showing them the way to diversify their capital into investments that are uncorrelated from Wall Street and the stock markets.

Through his body of work, he is teaching investors the strategies to build passive income and cash flow streams designed to flow into their bank accounts. He's a frequent event speaker and contributor to investment podcasts.

Fred is the author of The Little Green Book Of Note Investing: A Practical Guide For Getting Started With Investing In Mortgage Notes and contributing author in 1 Habit To Thrive in a Post-Covid World.

Author's Website: *www.FredMoskowitz.com*
Book Series Website & Author's Bio: *www.The13StepsToRiches.com*

Dr. Freeman Witherspoon

THE KEYS TO BECOMING A SPECIALIST

Knowledge is an imperative factor when it comes to achieving success and the accumulation of wealth. However, there has been so much misunderstanding of this. Many people think that knowledge is what makes one successful, but that is far from the truth or fact. What actually makes one successful is applied knowledge. The knowledge that is never applied is not knowledge at all. It is important that we understand this very important fact. Just as it has been believed that "knowledge is power," it is rather, applied knowledge is power. That is where the power within the knowledge is honed or harnessed.

If I am going to put it in a more illustrative way, knowledge has inherent power within. Or you can say that knowledge is potential power. When knowledge is therefore applied or organized, that is where the true power is unleashed.

Impactful author and coach, Napoleon Hill, in his book *Think and Grow Rich*, asserts that "There are two kinds of knowledge. One is general knowledge, the other is specialized. General knowledge, no matter how great in quantity or variety it may be, is of but little use when it comes to the accumulation of money." You can see insight from this assertion that the power within knowledge that produces results or success is when it is applied. It is not enough to just gather knowledge without using it. Unfortunately, our school systems today have done so much harm to us and society. You might be asking, "Freeman, how?" The reality is, we are taught to accumulate knowledge, but we are never taught how to use that knowledge in the ever-changing world today.

If you are being honest with yourself, you will discover that most of the things we learned in schools such as Algebra, Integration and Differentiation, and other things are not just applicable in life. As hard as this is to say, it is the reality. I didn't have so much the chance to go through the educational system, but I understand the power of knowledge. Later in my life, I joined the army, so I didn't go through the educational system very much. But that never stopped me from learning and improving myself. I am not in any way against formal education (my children and even grandchildren are going through it). It is important and we need it because it helps in our intellectual inclination. However, we should never be limited by that in life. We have to so we can develop in the area we are desiring to become skillful in.

Personally, I believe that what makes one a success is not formal education. I have had friends and I have watched people over the years, and I have come to see that people, mostly, who have gone through the formal educational ladder often didn't make much impact. They were limited by the college degree. Instead of them allowing that to become a motivation to grow and educate themselves personally, they were limited to the degree, thinking that is what matters in life. Hence, they stayed on the plains of average. When the government doesn't employ or give them jobs, then they become frustrated in life. Can you see the lines here?

Friend, apart from the formal education, we have to reach out within ourselves and educate ourselves on something we are good at or we are passionate about—passion is the signal of purpose. Develop yourself in the field to which there is so much passion within you because that is where increase and success is. Motivational speaker and coach Jim Rohn asserts that, "Formal education will make you a living, but personal education will make you a fortune." These words are thought-provoking and we have to consider them should we desire success and the accumulation of wealth. Personal education doesn't only make you a fortune, it makes you outstanding as well. Effectiveness and efficiency are birthed on this plain.

When I was in the army, I knew there was something else I was longing to do. I wanted to build generational wealth. Each day when I reported, I had this very motivation within and I kept the planning within. The more I thought about it, the more I had ideas on how to go about it. When I retired, I never gave up on that dream. I reached out to specialized teams. One of the teams that I joined which became a platform for growth and increase is Kingdom Men. These are groups of people who are burdened with the desire to make a difference and to ensure personal growth and success as well—and further the accumulation of kingdom wealth. The company of these men has made me see the world from a different perspective. It has been a challenging and also educative experience. (This is one of the ways to gain Specialized Knowledge—through cooperate groups)

We have had ourselves challenging one another to grow and become better. This has forced us to develop ourselves in certain fields. Through this group, virtues have been instilled; virtues that are an anchor to success and increase. For the like of consistency, dedication, discipline, desire, and integrity. We have been helped in many ways to build these within. What that has done is help us achieve the goals that we each have carried in life— the accumulation of wealth.

This is the same challenge I am putting before you today, friend. That you discover something you are passionate about and find people who are like-minded and begin to work around it. That is the best way to go. As you are doing that, you are harnessing what you could be. What you could be is in the discipline that you exercise.

You see, it takes discipline to learn something new. It takes commitment and consistency to become good or achieve incredible results in life.

Before one can reach the mark of greatness, one must go through the 10,000-hours rule. That is, whatever you commit 10,000 hours to you become a master at. This is why when a medical student goes to school, after these hours are completed, he can practice medicine. This is applicable as well when it comes to achieving success and the accumulation of wealth.

Looking at the examples of people who have achieved incredible results and have risen to increase and fortune, we can see one thing: the organization of knowledge. And also, we can see discipline to become outstanding. It takes giftedness and skill in a particular field and also the discipline to become successful and, above all, accumulate wealth. People like Henry Ford, Mike Tyson, Jack Welch, John Wanamaker, JP. Morgan, John D. Rockefeller, Clarence Darrow, Michael Jordan, and many others; we can see that they became specialized in a particular field. Before they achieved that specialized field, it took discipline, commitment, and self-accountability.

I want to challenge you for a moment. If you never had the chance to get through the formal educational system, that should never limit you from reaching the top. Just as I mentioned to you at the beginning of the chapter, (mostly, which is often the case) many people who have gone through the formal educational system have often remained at average. Average was their destination when that was not supposed to be so. However, when you look at people who never allowed themselves to be limited by the educational system, through developing their skill and potential, they achieved greatness and also accumulated wealth.

Solomon David, one of the wisest men in history, writes to us that, "Do you see a man diligent and skillful in his business? He will stand before kings; he will not stand before obscure men." (Proverbs 22:29, Amplified).

Whew! This is amazing! You see, what increases your skill and your giftedness is personal education. Personal education brings you to that place of Specialized Knowledge. When you educate yourself, you are increasing and bringing yourself that place where you can become special in your gift. And he makes us see the reward of that Specialized Knowledge or giftedness. He asserted you will stand before kings. That is talking about people of wealth and influence.

The way to become great and achieve incredible success is by learning this concept of Specialized Knowledge and maximizing the power thereof. No one has risen using the average ladder I have just shared with you. You, on the other hand, must learn to break free from that limitation and tap into the latent power of wealth that is within you so that you can become successful.

When I decided that I was going to become successful, it took so much pain and discipline until I became gifted at what I am doing now. All the businesses that are running for me now are a result of that discipline. Seeing the power within applied knowledge and the glory that organized knowledge can bring, I am therefore challenging you today to begin to organize and harness the knowledge that you have. After that, become committed to becoming a master in that craft. That is what is going to make you successful and then increase your value in the marketplace.

People are not going to give you money because you can speak nicely or articulately, but they will give you money because you are adding value to their lives. Money only comes when value is added. So what value are you adding today to someone? The more valuable you are, the more your financial fortunes are going to come as well. So, be challenged to become specialized in something. Know, organize, harness, and develop until you are a master at it. When that is the case, people are going to travel even from far to just gain an audience with you. That is the power of Specialized Knowledge!

Henry Ford has gone to be with the Lord, but people remember him for what he did. Whenever someone sees the Ford automobiles, they see a reflection of the personality of Henry Ford. That is what happens when you become a specialist at something. Long even after you are gone, people will still remember you for what you were good at. Be challenged today, friend, to become skillful at something. Just as Solomon David made us see the power of skillfulness and diligence, be encouraged to harness those virtues. It will get to a place where you will be able to even name your price for your services, and people will have no choice but to pay because you deliver nothing but the best.

FREEMAN WITHERSPOON

About Freeman Witherspoon: Freeman is a professional network marketer that manages several online businesses. He considers himself a late bloomer to network marketing. Prior to partnering with network marketing organizations, he served for over 20 years in the military. He has incorporated his many life experiences into managing successful business models.

Military service afforded him the opportunity to travel throughout the world. He has lived in Heidelberg, Germany, Seoul, South Korea, and many places throughout the United States. Freeman currently lives in Texas with his wife and three dogs; a Dachshund named Dutchess, a Yorkie named Boosie and a Pomchi (Pomeranian-Chihuahua mix) named Caesar.

Author's website: *www.FWitherspoonJr.com*
Book Series Website & Author's Bio: *www.The13StepsToRiches.com*

Gina Bacalski

FINDING THE DREAM TEAM

Real Estate is terrifying. Just think about it, real estate agents are literally responsible for guiding people through the process of making the largest financial purchases and sales of their lives. Mentally insert the gif of The Big Bang Theory's Sheldon, hyperventilating into a paper bag here.

After twenty years in the childcare industry, I knew I needed a change, I just never thought I'd do real estate because, to be honest, it was super intimidating and used to scare me. I've been in the real estate industry now for five years. Before taking the plunge and actually getting my real estate license, I was an assistant to two realtors. One in San Diego, and then I became the full-time assistant to an amazing realtor in Utah after I moved to the area.

It was only through the guidance and direction of the realtor that I was assisting at the time did I get my license and break out on my own and pursue real estate as an agent.

I learned a few things really quickly. #1: Real Estate License courses taught me things like what a bundle of rights were. When buying real property in the US, you own it all the way to the center of the earth and all the air rights "to infinity," (I want to write a sci-fi novel about this concept one day) and the mechanics of how to fill out a Real Estate Purchase Contract, which is useful knowledge that I am grateful for. #2: Real Estate

License classes did not teach me how to be a realtor, start a business, or anything else about how to run said business once you've started it. So when I finally passed all my exams and became licensed, I felt like I was drowning in all the unknowns that I didn't even know, but only knew I absolutely needed.

The brokerage I started out with did little to help with anything, either. So I joined a high performing all-male group which helped for a time, but overall wasn't the best fit. It wasn't until I met my current broker, Cathy Maxfield of Wise Choice Real Estate, did I really feel like I was home. Pun intended.

Cathy isn't like any of the other brokers that I had met before. Instead of having her own list of clients, her sole focus is on making sure the agents that are in her brokerage shine like the stars! The fact that there is a zero-commission split was very enticing as well, versus the 70/30 split at my last brokerage. The agents at Wise Choice Real Estate keep 100% of all commissions, we just pay a very reasonable yearly brokerage fee, which with all the support we're given, I sometimes feel like isn't enough.

When I say I love my broker and my brokerage, I mean it! Cathy helped me get my LLC, website, logo, database, signs, and literally everything my real estate business would need. She fosters an environment in the brokerage where all the agents sit down and talk about what's working and what's not. She'll give us her advice of what she has tried and what other agents have had success with. I can sit down with her and others, and hash out ideas and talk shop, whenever I need it. If there is any question I have about anything, I know she and her very knowledgeable staff are able to answer it right away, even if it's really late at night. Cathy is very much one of my realtor and business mentors, and I would not be the outstanding real estate agent I am today without that woman. I get teary-eyed thinking about how much I appreciate her and her ongoing support of my business and myself as a person.

I didn't know the name for what Cathy had set up before my networking days, but I do now; she created and cultivates an amazing real estate mastermind within the brokerage.

It was around this same time that I started networking and I ran into another key game changer for my business: None other than Mr. Jon Kovach Jr.

I first met Jon when he was running a networking mastermind group called Amplified Minds. The way he did networking was different, and I was totally all-in from day one. We built real relationships with real people and they helped in real-world and real-life situations. It was at Amplified Minds where I also met one of my other mentors, Levi McPhearson, whom I have mentioned before and will probably do so in the future. Levi's philosophies and trainings also came about through his mastermind group, Prosperity Gym, which partnered with Amplified Minds for a time.

Through the lessons and wisdom learned in the mastermind groups I was a part of, from Wise Choice, Prosperity Gym, Amplified Minds, and the mentorship from Cathy, Jon, and Levi, I was able see my business double and then triple as I applied their teachings, trainings, and guidance.

The wisdom I was fortunate enough to receive has helped others as well. I have had the privilege of helping other small businesses get started and find the resources they needed to solve their issues. A group of colleagues and I decided to start a coaching program where we helped mastermind with small business owners and had practical solutions to their issues. I fell in love with the process and with helping people and their businesses succeed. I only left because my real estate business was taking off and needed more of my time, but I still help individuals or small businesses that need it from time to time. Connecting people has long been a passion of mine.

It was also through the mentorship of Cathy and Levi that I decided to build my real estate team. Especially as a new agent, and even now, I know I needed to have people around me who I could lean on for various parts of the real estate transaction.

Having the incredible foundation of Wise Choice Real Estate as my brokerage, I was able to do so. At Wise Choice, I was introduced to the best loan officer I have ever worked with. Jason blew my socks off as well as every other client I have introduced to him. He's a numbers ninja and I will never work with another loan officer if I can help it. I know I can lean on him for all financial and numbers questions, and he is mind-blowing at exceeding deadlines and can make things happen faster than I have ever needed. Our synergy is out of this world and has made our clients' homebuyer experience a magical thing.

My title and escrow officer is equally amazing. I randomly met her through a church group activity, and now we will get pedicures together every month. She is thorough, extremely knowledgeable, reliable, and quick. I try to do all transactions with her. I know if I do, they go through smooth as butter and then some!

The transaction coordinator at Wise Choice Real Estate is another human I don't want to do business without. She is someone I can laugh and cry with, but she also keeps everyone on their toes and makes sure all the documents are where they need to go, when they need to be there. She crosses all my T's and dots all my I's and would not be as fabulous as I am without her.

While my loan officer, title officer, and transaction coordinators are the key players on my team, I am also bringing more people in my Gina B Homes tribe. I only work with the top and my clients know it. They know that if it's a person on my list, they will also trust them implicitly. I take that very seriously and that's the reason the people in my tribe are the very best at what they do. I have collected the industry-leading home stagers, photographers, cleaners, handymen, garage door repair companies, landscapers, and the like.

The point of all of this is that I was feeling so overwhelmed because I thought I had to be the subject-matter expert (or SME) in everything dealing with the real estate world. As it turns out, I don't. I have people for that. It was a lot of work to find those people, but it was absolutely worth it. And as it turns out, I'm the SME person for other people as well. As I let go of things I thought I needed to control and replaced that with great people that are experts already, I found myself being more productive and effective. All I needed was the right people around me. Do you have the right people around you?

GINA BACALSKI

About Gina Bacalski: Gina is a Real Estate Agent, licensed since June 2018. Her background is in Early Childhood Education where she received her Child Development Associate from the state of Utah and has an AS from BYU-Idaho. For the past seventeen years, Gina has thoroughly enjoyed her experience in the service industry helping families in the gifted community.

In 2019, Gina helped Jon Kovach Jr. launch Champion Circle and is now CEO of the organization. She brings her genuine love for people, high attention to detail, and strives to exceed client's expectations to the Real Estate industry and to Champion Circle.

Gina married the man of her dreams, Jay Bacalski, in San Diego, in 2013. The Bacalskis love entertaining friends and family, going on hikes, and attending movies and plays. When Gina isn't helping her clients navigate the real estate world, she will most often be found dancing and listening to BTS, watching KDramas and writing fantasy, sci-fi and romance novels.

Author's Website: *www.MyChampionCircle.com/Gina-Bacalski*
Book Series Website & Author's Bio: *www.The13StepstoRiches.com*

Griselda Beck

IT TAKES A VILLAGE!

Specialized Knowledge: Information not known to others; an area of expertise. There's something you know that someone else doesn't know. AND someone, somewhere, knows what you need to know too!

Many people interpret the words "specialized" and "expert" as needing to have a degree, certification, or license. While that may be true for some, it is not exclusive to those with such credentials. The reality is we all know something that is of value to someone else and can improve the lives of others, bringing them ease, joy, and success. We're always a step ahead of someone, and there are always people ahead of us. Remember this when it comes to your own Specialized Knowledge. Your contribution is priceless to those who need your gifts and expertise!

We all need support. No one can do it alone. All of the great thought leaders, even Oprah and Tony Robbins, have support. They have large teams that support them in every area of their business, counsel them in decision making, and support them in their journey.

Coaches, masterminds, accountability buddies, venture partners, professional advisors, and our support teams that help us execute our daily operations are all part of our "Village," our team. Who's on your team?

My Village

When I first started my business, I set a personal goal to focus on my own personal health and wellness in addition to launching and growing my business. I knew that I needed to surround myself with people who embodied the values and principles that aligned with the lifestyle I wanted to create for myself.

Support

I joined a few meetup groups, hiking and walking groups, and made friends with other fellow entrepreneurs in those groups. I even networked and became very close friends with entrepreneurs who were fitness enthusiasts at my church. We shared the same spiritual and entrepreneurial journeys and our desire to live healthy lives. This created an environment and support system around me in which I could learn, live, and practice habits that would bring me closer to my goals. Working out with people that were more fit than I helped me show up to the gym and improve my form and nutrition. Masterminding with people who were ahead of me helped me show up to networking events, and introduce myself and my business.

Here's something that might surprise you. I'm actually an introverted extrovert, and I do not like networking events. Smalltalk with strangers exhausts me. But guess what? Everyone that adds value to my life today was once a stranger. If I hadn't invested the time to get to know that person, I wouldn't have had the blessing to know the gem and treasure they are.

Hiring Out

I have also hired several coaches. One who supported me in putting together my first event, from the outline, timeline, venue selection, support team I would need during the event, promotion—all of it! A few coaches supported me in the early stages of navigating the key elements of online marketing for a personal brand. Today, I have a mindset transformation coach, relationship coach, business strategy coach, and am involved in a few masterminds.

I also have a few experts, consultants, and professionals I consult for advice on financial, legal, and other specialty matters, because I have ZERO plans to go to law school or become CPA certified. Hiring experts is especially supportive in identifying things I don't know that I don't know. It saves me time, money, and really supports me in creating successful outcomes while minimizing (not eliminating) expensive lessons.

I'll never forget reading Tim Ferris' story when he set out to have a NY Times bestseller. He had no idea how, but he knew that's where his book needed to be. So he went about hiring a publisher/agent who knew exactly how to make that happen. Specialized Knowledge can be hired out; you do not need to be an expert in everything. Tim is also where I learned about the blessing of hiring a virtual assistant and online business manager! Their skills and expertise are varied. You can hire out any specialty service you need: graphic design, web development, e-commerce expert, social media marketer, video editor, office admin, project manager, etc. Yes, it requires an investment. In this case, you either invest your time or money. The question is, which do you have more of?

Leveraging Relationships

Who do you know? Sharon Lechter speaks on the power of association. Here is how it has worked for me. Eleven months ago, I declared that I wanted to be a NY Times bestselling author. I started asking people I knew who knew authors for introductions. As I met more authors, publishers, writing coaches, and editors, I started to understand the steps required to reach that goal. It was through that networking within my network that I learned of this opportunity to collaborate with such celebrity authors associated with the Napoleon Hill Foundation. Seven months after that declaration, I became a bestselling author by leveraging the power of my relationships. You wouldn't be reading my words right now if I had not sat down to identify "Who do I know?" when this was only a dream!

I had a mentor once tell me that while I may have been cash poor at the time, I was relationship rich. That really struck me. Once the concept settled, I also realized that leveraging those relationships was an art form I hadn't quite mastered. So, I looked around to see "Who do I know?" Who is an amazing connector of people and always knows "somebody." I asked them for advice (support as discussed above) on how to network and collaborate with seemingly "untouchable" people. I also consulted books; Tim Ferris and Dale Carnegie wrote great guides on this. I also asked my coach for some specific feedback.

I have applied this to invite speakers to my summits, be featured on desired podcasts and media outlets, obtain tickets to a sold-out concert, paid and unpaid positions, client introductions, and even practitioner appointments on a booked calendar!

Next Steps

You have dreams and big goals. You wouldn't be reading this book if you didn't. Here are a few tips and questions to answer for yourself to get you started.

STEP 1: Clearly define what you want to achieve, and most importantly, WHY? What do you want to feel? Why is this important to you? What will happen if you don't do/become this? Why now? If you need further support on this, you can refer back to Volume 1 of this series titled, DESIRE, for plenty of examples.

STEP 2: Who do you know? Who in your current network could support you in creating a plan, being a sounding board, identifying key milestones and resources you will need, and lastly, introduce you to those resources.

STEP 3: Time/Benefit analysis for those resources. Some things are not worth spending the time to "figure it out" when you can pay someone a fee to do it for you in a fraction of the time and with much better quality. Graphic design and web development were definitely that for me. I know how to create a website and know my way around Canva, but I could not match the level of quality or speed that my designer/developer can do this! I was able to better utilize that time on things I could not hire out, and I'm happy to pay him for that service. Same with my LLC filing. I tinkered with it for days, feeling overwhelmed and eventually ended up sitting on it for months! My attorney got it filed in less than 24 hours. We still had to wait for it to be processed and approved, but I could not compare the amount of time for the prep work. It wasn't hard or complicated, I just hadn't done it before. I gladly paid him as well and would do it again!

In the early stages, budgets are tight, and entrepreneurs really do get a sense of satisfaction of "doing it all myself." PRO TIP: Make enough money as quickly as possible to hire support where you need it most! A business coach is a great initial investment, as they will support you in achieving this. Invest your early money into things that will support you in generating income.

As Oprah says, "You get in life what you have the courage to ask for." I live by this quote. No guru, CEO, or thought leader waited for those opportunities to show up. They went for it. They asked, hired, and leveraged. What are you waiting for? What is your next step? What do you need to know? Who do you know?

GRISELDA BECK

About Griselda Beck: Griselda Beck, M.B.A. is a powerhouse motivational speaker and coach who combines her executive expertise with transformational leadership, mindset, life coaching, and heart-centered divine feminine energy principles. Griselda empowers women across the globe to step into their power, authenticity, hearts, and sensuality, to create incredible success in their business and freedom in their lives. She creates confident CEOs.

Griselda's clients have experienced success in quitting their 9-5 jobs, tripling their rates, getting their first clients, launching their first products, and growing their businesses in a way that allows them to live the lifestyles and freedoms they want. She has been featured as a top expert on *FOX, ABC, NBC, CBS, MarketWatch, Telemundo*, and named on the Top 10 Business Coaches list by *Disrupt Magazine*.

Griselda is an executive with over 15 years of corporate experience, founder of Latina Boss Coach and Beck Consulting Group, and serves as president for the nonprofit organization MANA de North County San Diego. She also volunteers her time teaching empowerment mindset at her local homeless shelter, Operation Hope-North County.

Author's Website: *www.LatinaBossCoach.com*
Book Series Website & Author's Bio: *www.The13StepstoRiches.com*

Jason Curtis

SIMPLE TOOLS TO GAINING SPECIALIZED KNOWLEDGE

What is Specialized Knowledge?

In *Think and Grow Rich*, Napoleon Hill states, "Successful men, in all callings, never stop acquiring Specialized Knowledge related to their major purpose, business, or profession. Those who are not successful usually make the mistake of believing that the knowledge acquiring period ends when one finishes school. The truth is that schooling does but little more than to put one in the way of learning how to acquire practical knowledge."

As I have progressed into my entrepreneurial journey, I've come to learn that the more time I allocate to studying all aspects of business, I'm more confident in my life. From having a greater understanding in how to interact with others to having a greater genuine love and care for everyone. This has made my life sweeter with each interaction I have. It also makes me realize the rich blessings I have been given.

Repeat Intentions to Develop Specialized Knowledge

My best daily habits, that allow me to be successful in this principle of Specialized Knowledge is to have a set time and place for studying.

I make it a goal to read, at least 15 minutes daily, from a book that I have chosen to read for a particular month. I am part of a book club, through one of my business ventures, where I learn about very particular subjects in business and life.

What I have learned is that it is so important to have a set time and a place for optimal learning and flow. I recommend scheduling these sessions in places where you are getting lots of focus on productivity without distractions. This might be a place in your home, such as your kitchen table, a quiet corner somewhere in your house away from the typical distractions, or even a local library. For me, my favorite place is to curl up on a nice comfy chair in my daughter's room. It's a very inviting room and I feel at peace when I am on that chair.

Develop Specialized Knowledge While You Are Still Young

I didn't have that insatiable thirst or passion when I was younger, for learning. I found myself only really applying myself in certain subjects like social studies, history, and in music. I really didn't like subjects like math or English.

I wasn't a terrible student, but I wasn't really the best student, either. I really excelled in those classes I listed above, while just doing enough to squeak by in those subjects I didn't like.

The advice I'd give to my younger self would be to apply myself more in those subjects that I didn't really like. That intense focus could have had a profound impact later in my life, especially when it came to helping my daughters realize the importance of learning. I'm glad that I have such a wonderful wife who is always learning and helping me to be better in this.

Strategically Improving Your Specialized Knowledge

A few techniques and strategies I use to maintain my Specialized Knowledge is: Distributed Practice, Test Practice, and Retrieval Practice. I'll briefly summarize each below.

Distributed Practice is where you are supposed to distribute your learning sessions such that a considerable amount of time passes before you start learning again.

Test Practice is exactly what that means: practice taking a test. You're intentionally putting practice sessions or studying material away and challenging yourself to recall what you've learned without any aid.

Retrieval Practice is where you try to recall what you're learning after the studying or learning session. This challenges your mind to recover whatever information it has on the topic without an actual practice or testing environment.

Learn the Tricks To Your Trades

Just about any mentor I've ever had has stressed the importance of learning the tricks to YOUR trade. I say your trade, because to become the expert in your particular niche, you need to have that Specialized Knowledge.

I'm sure we have heard the phrase, "Jack of all trades" before. While it is important to have knowledge in many related fields, like construction and real estate, what will really enable you to stand out is to become really knowledgeable in a particular arena. For example, my good friend and mentor, Jon Kovach Jr., is really one of the best I know in the field of masterminds. Everything he does demonstrates his skills for masterminds and his passion to lead people through them.

Confidence Comes With More Specialized Knowledge

The biggest surprise in my journey has been the more I've learned, the more confident in my abilities I've become. Learning is power!

I tend to face adversity and obstacles head on. Being honest and upfront in tackling the hard things in life is particularly helpful in overcoming difficulties for me.

My secret weapon and advice is to become a life-long learner. Find that insatiable desire to read and then apply the principles you've learned into whatever particular subject you need to.

I would counsel anyone who wants to level up, to find a mentor or a person willing to teach you.

Another concept that can have an immediate impact is to surround yourself with others who will challenge you and help you emulate the qualities you want to have in your life.

Former North Carolina State head basketball coach, Jimmy Valvano, said it best, "If you think, you laugh, and you cry, that's a heckuva day." These very simple yet profound actions have had a great impact in my life and can impact yours, as well.

JASON CURTIS

About Jason Curits: Jason has been a serial entrepreneur for 15 years and has enjoyed serving and helping his fellow entrepreneurs build their businesses and win in this game of life—on purpose! Jason is an expert networker who knows how to turn connections into sales. Jason created On Purpose Coaching because he knew, through his life experiences, that he could create an impact in others. He focuses on helping his clients create better relationships with their customers. This fosters trust and rapport while generating customer loyalty. Jason is a #1 Best-Selling Author in the highly successful series *The 13 Steps To Riches*.

Jason is a Navy veteran of six years. He has sailed the seas and oceans in serving his God and country. Curtis and his wife, Brianna, have been married for eight years, and they have two children.

Author's Website: *www.JasonLaneCurtis.com*
Book Series Website & Author's Bio: *www.The13StepstoRiches.com*

Jeffrey Levine

TAX DAY WAS DOOM DAY

As a child growing up, I soon realized that April 15 was never a good day for my family. Each year, as the middle of April got ever closer, I could see my father's mood faltering. It was clear the whole situation filled him with tension. It was always the same: My father always owed the IRS money. Unfortunately, though, since my parents lived paycheck to paycheck, they rarely had the money to cover their IRS bills. They would borrow money and pinch pennies—never with any long-term plan.

This situation reared its ugly head each spring, and I saw my parents fill with dread over and over again. By the time I turned 18, their tax problem had escalated to a point where my parents could no longer pay the tax man. Instead, they had to sign an agreement to make monthly installments. Given their predicament of living paycheck to paycheck and being on a tight budget, another monthly bill turned what had been a challenge into more of a crisis. I suggested that my father approach his accountant and ask him for solutions to reduce his tax burden. When his accountant came back with the answer, "If you earn it, you must pay it," we were flummoxed. That wasn't the response we expected or wanted. Of course, ever pragmatic, I suggested my father find a different accountant, but to him that wasn't an option.

In college, I enrolled in a basic tax course. During the class, we covered the intricacies of the tax system and how people accrue and pay taxes. It was an eye-opening experience for me and allowed me to see why my father always owed on April 15. He was paying taxes on the dividends from his stock holdings. Even though he never received the dividends and, instead, reinvested with them, buying more shares, the dividends were still taxable.

I was exhilarated to learn why this way happening—and I knew there had to be some solution to my parents' tax woes. My next step was to reach out to my tax professor to discuss my father's situation. Seeing my eagerness at wanting to help my family, my professor suggested I apply to law school and enroll in as many tax courses as possible to increase my knowledge. I agreed that was a fantastic idea and applied to law school. My new mission was to learn how to help my father.

In my third year of law school, I took an advanced income-tax-planning course. My professor was fantastic, and that, combined with my enthusiasm for the subject, meant that I flourished. Mine was the best grade in the course at the end of the semester. I ran into the professor shortly after, and he suggested that I consider getting a Master of Laws in Taxation (LLM). It would require an additional year of law school during which to focus on tax courses, but knowing how much of a difference having an LLM had made in my professor's career, I took on the challenge and, thanks to his glowing recommendation and my good grades, I was accepted.

Once enrolled in my LLM, I found myself studying constantly. I was inspired to help my father, which made me insatiable about learning.

At the same time I was readying to graduate with my LLM, I received a panicked call from my father. He was being audited by the IRS and had received a bill for $20,000. Of course, he didn't have that kind of money, so he was worried about what to expect. Thankfully, I had much more knowledge at that point than I'd had in my younger years, so I worked with my father to prepare for the audit. I encouraged my father to avoid speaking with the auditor, telling him I would handle everything.

The auditor was surprised by our preparation. During our own pre-audit, we had discovered deductions my father had never taken advantage of in previous filings. In fact, following the official audit, it was discovered that not only did my father not owe $20,000 in liability, but the IRS issued him a $2,000 refund based on the deductions he had failed to file. My father was thrilled with that outcome and asked me to handle his tax returns from that point forward. He never again owed money to the IRS.

Following that stellar resolution, I embarked on my career and was accepted in a role at the top financial planning firm in the country. That experience was enlightening. With national clientele in my book, including CEOs of major corporations and successful business owners, I was at the right firm at the right time. I obtained far more knowledge than I had in college, including training in insurance, investments, retirement planning, and estate planning.

The knowledge I gained in my career enabled me to help my father—and others in the same situation—even more. After two years at that firm, I opened my own firm, with my first case being another audit. On that case, the stakes were even higher. Each of my clients, who were in the midst of a divorce, owed $100,000 in taxes. That was not money they had. To compound the issue, the IRS agent assigned to their case had a reputation of being extremely difficult to work with, so I knew I would be facing a challenge.

With the audit only one week away, I worked 10 hours a day in preparation. Thanks to my preparation and collaboration with my clients, each owed only $1,000 after the audit. They were thrilled with the outcome and started telling everyone about me. Seemingly instantly, I secured a number of referrals from them, which successfully launched my solo career.

Across my years of practice, I have been able to save clients tens of thousands of dollars in tax liability every year. And when they received refunds, I would encourage them to invest those funds for their future. These clients ended up saving hundreds of thousands of dollars more in retirement funds than they would have otherwise been able to do because of my guidance. My clients were then able to retire with more money than they needed.

During my childhood, my father had shared with me his theory on money: anytime you put money in your pocket, there is an invisible hole that takes a portion of it for bills and unexpected expenses, not to mention the money that is wasted. But because of my tax strategy that shifted refunds into investments, I was able to sew up that invisible hole and help my clients save more of the money they made.

Tax law is very complicated, and it's impossible for one person to know everything. Across my career, I have sought out the counsel of other experts to fill the gaps in my knowledge. Those go-to experts were a key strategy for me to successfully help my clients.

Henry Ford was a firm believer in the concept of having available experts on your team and at the ready to help. Although Ford was called "an ignorant pacifist" during the war, he was a shrewd businessman. He had a number of electric push buttons on his desk so that, at a literal "push of a button," he was able to reach the right person to help him with any challenge that arose.

Andrew Carnegie stated he knew nothing about the technical end of the steel business; however, he could get the Specialized Knowledge he needed from people in his mastermind group. These are just two examples of how successful people surround themselves with people who have different—and sometimes more—knowledge than they have. They can then leverage that brain trust to excel.

The same holds true for you. You don't need to know everything to be successful. You just need to know the person who has that knowledge. And with them on your team, you'll be unstoppable.

JEFFREY LEVINE

About Jeffrey Levine: Jeffrey is a highly skilled tax planner and business strategist, as well as a published author and sought-after speaker. He's been featured in national magazines, on the cover of *Influential People Magazine,* and is a frequent featured expert on radio, talk shows, and documentaries. Jeffrey attended the prestigious Albany Academy for high school and then went on to University of Hartford at Connecticut, University of Mississippi Law School, Boston University School of Law, and earned an L.L.M. in taxation. His accolades include features in *Kiplinger* and *Family Circle Magazine,* as well as a dedicated commentator for Channel 6 and 13 news shows, a contributor for the **Albany Business Review**, and an announcer for WGY Radio.

Jeffrey has accumulated more than 30 years of experience as a tax attorney and certified financial planner and has given in excess of 500 speeches nationally. Levine is the executive producer and cast member in the documentary ***Beyond the Secret: The Awakening.***

Levine's most current work, *Consistent Profitable Growth Map,* is a step-by-step workbook outlining easy-to-follow steps to convert consistent revenue growth to any business platform.

Author's Website: *www.JeffreyLevine.Solutions*
Book Series Website & Author's Bio: *www.The13StepstoRiches.com*

Lacey & Adam Platt

DO WHAT OTHERS WON'T, TO DO WHAT OTHERS CAN'T & GROUP VS MASTERMIND

Do What Others Won't, To Do What Others Can't

Learning should be a lifelong goal, not just while we are young and in school. Many people think that when they finish high school or college, they have learned all they will need to know to get them what they want in life. This just is not true. Sure, if you want to live a life of mediocrity that is true, but not if you want to excel in life.

There are a few examples in my life where I feel I really learned things that others were not willing to learn or try, and it has served me very well to create wealth for myself and my family.

When I was much younger, I got a job as a tile apprentice. I learned all the ins and outs of setting tile; best ways to lay out a room or how to set tile in a shower. I got very good at it over my time as a tile setter, and even after I left that profession, I always seemed to get a side job that someone needed done when my family needed extra money for Christmas or a bill that needed to be paid. How did that skill and knowledge serve me? Because many people don't know the first thing about laying tile or they have tried it, and it looked horrible. I was able to capitalize on that skill and knowledge for years to bring extra income to my family when we needed it most. I don't do much tile now, but I love that I have that skill and knowledge that has served me many times.

Another example, and probably one that illustrates my point, is in my professional career. I worked in the aerospace industry for more than 15 years. I wore many different hats in my career, but one job function proved to be more beneficial than all the others. You see, I worked as a production planner in the program office, but when I had the chance to learn how to be what is called a Program Master Scheduler, everything changed with how much money I was able to make.

If you don't know what a Program Master Scheduler is, I could bore you to death about what it is. In a nutshell, I create and maintain very complex high-level schedules for very complex programs that gives management information about when a program will finish, and if it will finish within budget. I had a coworker take me under his wing and teach me how to do this skill, and I remember when he was teaching me, he said if I could learn how to be a master scheduler and do it well, I would never be without a job that paid well. He was right! Why did I get paid well to be a Master Scheduler? Because I learned a skill that most people didn't want to learn or didn't understand and weren't willing to learn, therefore the skill has been a very sought-after skill indeed. It's all about learning and doing today what others won't, so tomorrow you can do what others can't.

So how do we learn these skills? We can learn them from continued education, home study, mentors, coaches, masterminds, and hands-on training. Learning specialized skills and information can be done easier today than ever before in history. Today, you have specialized schools, the internet, coaches, and mentors to help you learn what you want. After all, the definition of a coach comes from the stagecoaches back in the day that would take someone from point A to point B. That is the reason we get coaches and mentors, and I am a big fan of coaching. That's why I coach others today, to help them reach where they want to go. The thing is, a person must be willing to put in the effort, time, and energy to learn what they need so they can get to the next level of success in life.

So what are you going to learn today that others won't, so tomorrow you can do what others can't?

~ Adam Platt

Group vs Mastermind

To properly discuss the topic of Specialized Knowledge, I feel inclined to mention that there are two schools of the thought on this topic. The first is to go to school and work to obtain experiential Specialized Knowledge. The second is to surround yourself with the people who can answer the questions you don't know the answers to.

Let's talk about the first way. If you attend school, get a degree or two and then enter the work force, you are likely going to experience something referred to as teamwork. This is a popular way for schools and jobs to get people to create a group of people who can work with and off each other, to hopefully get the job done faster and more efficiently.

A mastermind is a harmonious group of people, who come together to bring forth a power of creativity and support initiated through their commitment to one another.

The difference between teamwork and a mastermind is that anyone can be a member of a team, and they might give their 100% to that team, if they pay them enough, even though they are not invested in the outcome of what the group is trying to accomplish.

On the other hand, a member of a Mastermind is very focused on creating and helping collectively accumulate the greatest outcome for each individual within the group. These people have Specialized Knowledge in similar fields so that they can help one another to problem solve and come up with the greatest solution. If you have ever been a member of a mastermind, you have seen how collectively one person builds upon the next, and this proceeds around the group until amazing outcomes are achieved for the problem presented.

Teamwork is more directed by one individual who steps up as the "leader" and presents the objective that needs to be completed by the group by a certain time and in a certain manner. Each person is then given a section of a task to complete, upon when coming back together, will hopefully create a solution to the objective. This, then, requires each individual within the group to come up with a solution to their portion of the task, and can end up with a result of scattered fragments of ideas that don't necessarily coordinate with one another, resulting in the least- effective outcome depending on the members of the group.

Whereas with a Mastermind, everyone is like-minded and specializes in the same type of knowledge, which helps easily build someone up as one person talks about their idea of how to solve the problem, and the next person is then able to deliver up a better solution based on what the previous person said. They build on that idea to create an even better idea.

The best way to determine if you're part of a mastermind or a team is to see if the members of this group share Specialized Knowledge. If all the members of the group are business owners, then they all share a Specialized Knowledge of how to run a business. If the members of a group work for the same business but within different departments of said business, they collectively have concern for this business to be successful. However, they have very different knowledge from one another to share. When this occurs, you have fragmented ideas from different points of view that are shared to accomplish one goal. Teams are usually created of individuals who are looking to have a benefit for themselves, individually. They will participate within this team if it means it will help them to get ahead. Masterminds are created with people who have the same agenda, a deep sense of mission and commitment to the same goal, and are comprised of the highest order of thinking—with the core value being the synergy of energy, motivation, and commitment, as well as the willingness to learn and grow together.

Do you see the difference in the types of people that create these two different groups?

The easiest and most sure way to know the answer to this question is, if when this group of people were together, did they build off one another, or merely just delegate tasks to get the job done faster, and maybe brainstorm for a bit or collaborate?

So the ultimate question is, Would you rather be a part of a Mastermind or a Group?

I think you can tell which one I am a part of! I will be talking more about masterminds in upcoming volumes of this book series, so stay tuned!!

~ Lacey Platt

LACEY & ADAM PLATT

About Lacey Platt: Lacey is an energetic, fun loving, super mom of five! She is an Achievement Coach, Speaker and new Bestselling Author who enjoys helping everyone she can by getting to know what their needs are and then loving on them in every way that she can. Her ripple effect and impact has touched the lives of so many and continues to reach more lives every single day. Allow Lacey to help you achieve your goals with proven techniques she has created and perfected over years of coaching. Lacey and her husband have built an amazing coaching business called Arise to Connect serving people all around the world.

About Adam Platt: Adam is an Achievement Coach, Speaker, Trainer, Podcast Host and now a Bestselling Author. Adam loves to help people overcome the things stopping them from having the life they really want. Adam owns and operates Arise to Connect. Adam believes that connection with yourself, others, and your higher power are the keys to achievement and greater success in life. He is impacting thousands of people's lives with his message and coaching. He lives in Utah with his wife, five daughters, and their dog, Max.

Author's Website: *www.AriseToConnect.com*
Book Series Website & Author's Bio: *www.The13StepstoRiches.com*

Louisa Jovanovich

YOU ARE LOVED AS YOU ARE

"How we do something is how we do everything."

I am a mindfulness and emotional intelligence coach and I LOVE what I do. Why? I get to work with amazing clients. Together we assess what exactly is standing in the way of success and together, we can achieve incredible breakthroughs. But it's not about getting to the finish line, it's HOW we get there. How we walk, talk, run, swim, fly; all along, on this journey. And if we steer this road together with GRACE and with LOVE, success is sure to be ours! That is my work!

Often when clients show up, they're (quite frankly) all over the place. And I love it. Deep down, they want so badly to achieve their dreams and become their best selves. But they are stuck in worry, and in overwhelm. I get it. I know what it's like to act from a state of panic, only to be worse off afterwards and afraid to take another step.

For me, it was my limiting beliefs that got in the way. Defeatist thoughts that played out in my head. I found myself thinking, "I'm not really good enough to raise my prices or ask for what I deserve. It's ok, I'll just take this. Maybe one day, I'll be worth more." Or, "I'm not sure I have what it takes to succeed! I have already tried it and I failed—I just don't want to fail again." Or even, "The life I have now is overwhelming. How will I handle something more?"

Simply put, success will not come if we don't DO THE WORK. And that means being uncomfortable. Stretching. Risking. And realizing no matter what, this is an amazing chance to learn; about ourselves, about our fear, and about our unstoppable will.

Most of us want to blame life's unfair twists and turns for the deep rut we have found ourselves in. We want to look outward for excuses. But what if our struggle has nothing to do with our circumstances? What if the real obstacle is our own destructive self-talk? What if we just don't have the right systems in place? What if change is really just small, daily shifts? What if it's that simple?

I know you have what it takes. I know you are capable.

I know you can do it, because I did.

We are not a stump in the ground. We're seeds! Buried deep in soil, in need of water and sunlight. For so long, we have simply let ourselves BELIEVE we are a chopped-down stump and not a seed. We fool ourselves out of growth.

So imagine, right now, in whatever situation you are in, that you are a seed—FULL OF POTENTIAL, growing into what you were meant to be.

Within each of us is an individualized knowledge base; a foundation within that we can deeply rely on, where we can root ourselves; and from here, we can GROW. I call these foundations our GENIUS ZONES. They help remind us who we are.

When we know who we are, we are free to grow.

My life once seemed so perfect. I believed I had a happy marriage. Happy kids. Happy job. But did I?

As years went on, I felt "OFF." Something wasn't right. I didn't like who I was anymore. I didn't like who I was becoming. I would start to feel this nudge inside me saying, CHANGE. WAKE UP.

During dinner, while I slept, during a fight, as I drove the car, I kept feeling like something was trying to wake me up. I had to listen to this part. I didn't want to. But it became louder than any other part. And honoring this part in me became the most important thing I've done. What I was doing, was listening to my INSTINCT, and feeling my COURAGE.

I had gotten so comfortable with what was familiar, with what was safe. Change felt scary and overwhelming. How could I leave a marriage? How could I do this to my kids? How would I find a different job in a different state? Everyone would judge me, hate me.

I stayed listening to myself, struggling, but listening.

I had to start small. I started by simply being grateful I was still alive. I am not a stump! I am a seed, I am still alive, I still have hope, potential. I can be so much more than what I have created so far.

I knew I needed to take action. I began my journey by remembering who I was: I, LOUISA, am a powerful girl who doesn't let anything get in her way!

I am a hairdresser of 23 years. I helped encourage so many lives with so much love. Everyone who leaves my chair shares how deeply I have inspired them to feel better and take action. I've combined these skills and work with professionals to level up their personal and professional lives. I use my intuition to see what is in others' ways. I help clients clear out their old stories that are holding them back.

Wait, this is good—I LIKE who I am.

I started to meditate. I started to journal. I started to ask myself powerful questions. I went deeper and deeper. My clients went deeper and deeper. I started to notice myself unlocking my superpower. My clients began to unlock their superpowers.

I began to take action. They began to take action.

And change happened.

The seeds of my life began to bear fruit.

Looking back, I realize that my ability to feel into others and understand their journey came from my babysitting days as a teenager. Most of all, I listened. I observed how others organized their homes, how parents operated as married couples, and how they kept their children safe and happy.

When I babysat, I had no idea I was sowing seeds of skills that would help me become a life coach. I thought that my babysitting skills would help me as a wife and mother, and they did, but those skills continued to help me even as I became a hairdresser, got divorced, and then became a life coach.

My meditation slowly began to teach me as well. It taught me that sometimes we can't see a solution when we are fixated on it. If you try to catch a dog by chasing after it, the dog will likely run away from you. But if you stop running and hold a treat out, the dog may return of its own free will. When our minds are focused on a persistent problem, the problem magnifies and looms larger than it really is. We must remain in the present moment, always. For that reason, a daily practice of meditation and journaling play a huge role in my practice with my clients.

Journaling, for me, began to reveal some wisdom; that we manifest the things we devote our energy toward. I would ask myself, "Is this the result I want?" If the answer was "no," I surrendered and trusted. I would listen more and go deeper. I would let my instinct rise up. I would realize that I can choose my own thoughts. That's so crazy!

I can choose my own thoughts. I am, indeed, a seed, full of potential.

Anyone can have what they want if they understand who they truly are. When we accept who we truly are, and when we root ourselves in our genius zones, we can create a definite plan of action. When we trust in our genius zones, then we are free to be ourselves. And as you grow in knowledge, so does your spirit.

Allow yourself to fall in love with who you are becoming. Check your attitude. Do you feel negatively about your fruit? Realize that you can choose to be more accepting of the fruit you are bearing. Take responsibility for what fruit is growing. And if you don't believe you are bearing fruit, or if your fruit hasn't ripened yet, that's not a problem. You're not stuck.

Before you do anything, write down (by hand) everything you want in life: from your relationships, to your health, to your career. This is the fruit you want to bear. Whether you end up bearing this fruit or not, you must start with the desire to bear fruit if you are going to bear any fruit at all. And stop digging in the dirt to see if your seed has sprouted roots. Trust the process.

If you know what you're passionate about and who you want to be, you can then behave like the person you want to become. Surround yourself with people who are doing what you want to do, and learn from them. Like a young tree leaning on a stake until it has the strength to stand on its own, give yourself a reference point.

Trust that you are a seed, and you will grow. You will bear fruit. Whatever you contribute to this beautiful world, stand tall and let the universe embrace you. The unique you. And know that you are loved, perfectly as you are.

LOUISA JOVANOVICH

About Louisa Jovanovich: Louisa is the founder of Connect with Source. She is a mindfulness and emotional intelligence coach. She enjoys helping others identify blind spots and create new beliefs which empower her clients to access a life they have never dreamed possible. She has completed 20 years of personal and transformational growth including Land-mark Forum, Gratitude Training, and is a Clarity Catalyst Certified trainer. She works with entrepreneurs who seek clarity and want to up-level their lives.

Her life experiences and school of hard knocks are what make her a knowledgeable and compassionate leader and enable her to help guide others through the process of looking for answers within in order to find success and breakthrough their limiting beliefs. Her unique coaching techniques help her clients see the truth behind the stories that are keeping them stuck in the reality they created.

Louisa is a single mother of two teenagers living in LA. Her love and compassion towards others are her superpowers, helping others reclaim their confidence, find their voice, and know their worth.

Author's Website: *ConnectWithSource.com*
Book Series Website & Author's Bio: *www.The13StepstoRiches.com*

Lynda Sunshine West

FOLLOW ONE COURSE UNTIL SUCCESSFUL

F.O.C.U.S. = Follow. One. Course. Until. Successful.

When I first heard that acronym, it sounded so easy.

As someone who has self-diagnosed herself with Squirrel Syndrome (a person who is easily distracted by shiny objects who allows themselves to get off track and forget what they were doing and has a hard time coming back to the task they were originally working on because another shiny object jumped in front of them and, of course, they got distracted by the new shiny object, then they have to ask themselves, "what was I doing?" in order to get back on task), this seemingly easy task of F.O.C.U.S. has proven to be much more difficult than I ever imagined.

As I trudged my way down the path of entrepreneurship, I found myself easily distracted with learning all the nuances of being a business owner: sales, marketing, website building, graphic designing, writing blogs, articles, social media posts, perfecting webinar and video skills, etc. Do ya feel me?

You see, I was in the corporate world for 36 years and had 49 jobs (by the way, I was never fired). The first 16 years of my working life was spent trying to figure out what I wanted to do with my life and mostly, how I could keep food on the table for my two kids. I spent most of that time in "survival mode." My actions were based on nothing more than paying the bills, having a roof over our heads, and food in our bellies.

In those first 16 years (and 42 jobs), I learned a lot of different skills and carried those skills to my next job and the next, and so on.

Job #43 is when I started tapping into what would become my Specialized Knowledge.

At job #42, I was working as a calendar clerk at a court reporting firm. It was a boring job, but it got me close to the people I needed to be close to in order to become a court reporter after I passed my court reporting exam (I wanted to be a court reporter so badly, but never got my speed fast enough to pass the mandated California State exam).

One morning, while at work, I heard a rumor that one of our "regular" attorneys had a secretary who that morning had quit her job and walked out on him. He didn't have the best reputation, but I was intrigued to learn more about what happened and decided to inquire about the position.

I saw him that morning walking down the hallway, jumped out of my chair, and ran over to him. Mind you, had I thought about this scenario before it happened, I would have talked myself out of it for fear of what he would think about me.

"Jonathan, I heard your secretary quit today. I would apply, but I'm not qualified."

"Can you type?"

"Yes, I type 120 words per minute."

"You're hired. I'll teach you the rest."

Yes, it was that easy.

Jonathan just lost his secretary (his fifth secretary to quit on him that year) and needed a replacement. Talk about being in the right place at the right time. I inquired. He hired.

That started my career as a legal secretary.

Jonathan didn't teach me how to do my job (he was a lawyer, not a secretary), but he paid for me to be trained. He tapped into someone else's Specialized Knowledge to teach me what I needed to learn in order to do my job.

I stuck my neck out and he stuck his neck out, and his trust in his own judgment about me turned out to be what I needed to propel me forward.

I worked for Jonathan for one and a half years and learned not only how to be a legal secretary, but also how to work with lawyers and how to run a legal office. I also became his personal assistant and learned how to negotiate real estate deals. He saw something in me that I didn't see in myself, and he taught me as much as I wanted to learn. And I was hungry to learn as much as possible.

After my time with Jonathan was done, I decided to move on to another firm, and another, and another.

I continued making my way up the legal ladder all the way up to working for the largest law firm in San Diego, California, working for two partners. I was good at my job and knew what I was doing. Ultimately, I landed a job working for the #2 judge in the Ninth Circuit Court of Appeals. I had "made" it. It was the penultimate job in my career, working for a judge in the Court of Appeals. But I was bored and burned out working in the legal field, and I hated what I was doing. I wasn't fulfilled and decided there had to be more to life—more to my life.

One day, at age 51, while driving to work, I decided to quit that job and become an entrepreneur, with no pension, no 401k, no retirement. "Wow! What a foolish move," you may be thinking, but it was necessary for my sanity.

Of course, I took all that knowledge I gained working as a legal secretary and started a business in the legal field, right? Nope. That's not what I did. Instead, I started a brand new journey of self-discovery and learning what "makes my heart sing." While I could have taken my Specialized Knowledge and turned that into a business, I wanted nothing to do with the legal field. It didn't feel good. It wasn't challenging. I was bored and I didn't want to start the next phase of my life being bored.

Through the ups and downs of entrepreneurship, I have gained knowledge in so many different fields. My Squirrel Syndrome, while at times can be a setback, at other times has helped me learn a lot more about myself and my gifts and has helped me gain more knowledge.

After six and a half years as an entrepreneur trying out different business ideas, from hosting food festivals, to running a women's mastermind program, from running destination races, to hosting hundreds of events, I finally settled on something I absolutely love and apply the skills I've learned on this journey.

I took my 36 years of organizational skills, my love for bringing people together, and my passion for helping people share their voice with the world and F.O.C.U.S. on creating collaboration books.

My journey of figuring out what I love doing and what I'm darn good at, and bringing them together as a business has had a lot of ups and downs, wins and losses, and has been the most exciting journey of my life. I wouldn't change any part of my journey because it is what has created who I am today.

What is your Specialized Knowledge? Are you using it to the best of your ability? Tap in and F.O.C.U.S.

LYNDA SUNSHINE WEST

About Lynda Sunshine West: Lynda is known as The Fear Buster. She's a Speaker, 10 Time Best-Selling Author, Book Publisher, Executive Film Producer, Red Carpet

Interviewer, and the Founder of Women Action Takers. At age 51 she faced one fear every day for an entire year. In doing so, she gained an exorbitant amount of confidence and uses what she learned by facing a fear every day to fulfill her mission of helping 5 million women entrepreneurs gain the confidence to share their voice with the world. Her collaboration books, mastermind, podcast, and many more opportunities give women from all over the world the opportunity to share their voice with the world. She believes in cooperation and collaboration and loves connecting with like-minded people.

Author's Website: *www.ActionTakersPublishing.com*
Book Series Website & Author's Bio: *www.The13StepstoRiches.com*

Maris Segal & Ken Ashby

WHO KNOWS?

When we pose this question, "Who Knows?" we open ourselves to the absolute possibility that we can bring our vision to life and support our dreams with "Specialized Knowledge," which is first, our own knowledge and second, the knowledge of others.

This little question, Who Knows? could be one of the most important questions you can ask. Whether you are expanding a business, creating a movement, need a digital app, seeking spiritual or medical guidance, or becoming a parent, Specialized Knowledge is the answer. What we are really saying when we use this two-word inquiry is the powerful secret to creating a life that is continually growing and expanding. Asking this question, whether in our professional or personal lives, also takes humility, courage, and leaving egos out of the mix. It's a recognition that to succeed, "it will take more than me."

Even bigger than that, we are opening ourselves to receive from, and give support to, a team to make an impact. American cultural anthropologist and writer Margaret Meade wrote, "Never doubt that a small group of thoughtful, committed people can change the world. Indeed, it is the only thing that ever has."

Our expertise as business relationship consultants, executive producers, and leadership coaches tells us that Specialized Knowledge fits into two main categories: formal education and experiential learning. While some may argue that one is more important than the other, neither stands alone. One offers specific skill building and learning gained from college, workshops, and trainings. The other centers on expertise and wisdom based on the insights from years of consistent experience.

So many monumental projects, historic movements, and innovative gadgets were all the result of someone with an idea, and someone who crafted its reality by Tactically Enrolling Acute Masterminds—TEAM. This simple TEAM principle, which drives collaboration, is the core concept behind Napoleon Hill's tenant of Specialized Knowledge. Who knows what I don't? Who knows how to design, manufacture, market, distribute, service, and scale my idea? Who knows how to get me in to the shark tank?

Since 1937, when Napoleon Hill wrote *Think and Grow Rich*, the world has changed by an exponential magnitude. In the field of technology alone, the idea of contemporary cell phones, computers, the internet, and all that accompanied those developments were primarily available in works of science fiction. Isaac Asimov called 1937 the "golden age of science fiction." At that time, the repository of Specialized Knowledge was available in libraries, not via searching Google. The TEAM principle is how the first Volkswagen Beetle, the copy machine, the sewing machine, and electric cars were built. All these creative endeavors designed to solve a problem, now commonplace in our everyday lives, would never have emerged unless someone asked the question, Who Knows? The answers to this question are in the powerful collaborations among people who have derived their Specialized Knowledge from formal education and/or experiential learning.

As entrepreneurs, we've been working together in our own company nearly as long as we have been together as a couple. Although working together was not our first thought, it became a bonus of experiential learning and passion. When we began dating, we never anticipated where it would lead. We realized very quickly that our shared commitment, to impact lives for the greater good, combined with similar backgrounds and Specialized Knowledge created amazing possibilities for our future. While we both had some college education, the globe became our classroom as we worked in over 30 countries with cross-cultural communities and leadership across the public and private sectors, giving a creative voice to issues, causes, and brands.

Like most people, before obtaining higher education, we began in our young careers as generalists and set out to build our skills to grow as professionals. How? We sought out experts, experiences, and collaborations that we could learn from. This soon led to opportunities where we were, ourselves, positioned as part of our clients' masterminds to offer them our Specialized Knowledge.

What is the power of utilizing the TEAM principle?

Most people possess a unique ability to do something unthought-of by following a dream with the aid and support of specialists. Too often, people fail to actualize a whopper of an idea because fear gets in the way, and they fail to ask Who Knows?

Tactically Enrolling Acute Masterminds drives collaboration and, ultimately, success. Collaborating liberates us from feeling overwhelmed when faced with a seemingly insurmountable project. Building a team with knowledge pertinent to the vision increases the probability of success. Surrounding ourselves with those trained in specific areas provides heightened confidence and empowerment. Increased optimism in the outcome brings a positive outlook for the project, and becomes an affirmation for our whole being.

Once the TEAM principle has been utilized, whether for grand or small scale, we follow these essential five steps in our creative process utilizing

Specialized Knowledge at every turn: *Inspiration, Visualization, Creation, Acknowledgement, Evaluation.* Skipping any of these steps can bring a great idea to a rapid demise. Too often, the owner of a whopper of an idea jumps from step one (Inspiration) straight to step five (Evaluation), before even starting. These phrases, (often only in the inspired-owner's mind) come up; "Oh, this has probably been done before," "There are others who know how to do this better than me," "It's probably too expensive," "Who am I to think I can do this." Do those phrases sound familiar?

The best practice is always to be curious and be willing to ask the question Who Knows how to support me in visualizing or designing this concept? Who Knows how to evaluate the creation with expertise? Prior to that last step of evaluation, although it may sound meaningless, it is crucially important to acknowledge with your mastermind every win and success along the way. Then, and only then, are you ready to evaluate so that all feel empowered to take the next steps.

A central word in our TEAM principle (tactically enrolling acute masterminds) is the word enrolling. In today's world, with such ease of locating those with the Specialized Knowledge, there may be several candidates who qualify. Choosing the right people can be both simple and challenging at the same time. Out of all the qualified prospects who possess the Specialized Knowledge required, it is important to engage the experts who align with your vision, your style, and the energy flow of your existing team (if one or more individuals are already in place). At the same time, it's important to gather a diverse group of formally trained and experientially trained individuals who will challenge your thinking in a positive way to ensure a 360-degree perspective.

Putting the TEAM principle to the test!

There are countless times in our lives, together and individually, when we have asked that simple question, Who Knows? Our company was hired for our Specialized Knowledge as executive producers for key signature programs commemorating America's 400th Anniversary, which took place in Virginia. The creative canvas included bringing this history to life with hundreds of staff, volunteers, performers, and thousands of participants and attendees. While we had produced many large-scale events, from Super Bowl halftimes to Papal visits, this one had more moving parts and partners critical to our success. From our first meeting with our client, we knew the weight of this monumental opportunity, and that we needed to build and lead a collaborative power team. Using the TEAM principle, a creative group was assembled with the Specialized Knowledge of logistics, operations, safety and sanitation, a production team with talent experience and equipment to mount a weather-safe, massive concert stage with lighting instruments and professional audio, just to name a few of the specialized connections we engaged to execute with required precision.

We certainly didn't have all the answers to manage crowd control for over twenty thousand people attending the final festival. We needed experts to create a four-foot by four-foot concrete cube, which would be the ultra-solid camera platform required by the White House for televising the appearance of then President George Bush.

We had designed a great experience, but until the expert team was in place, fully aligned in the vision, and taking action, it was just a design on paper. After a massive collaboration of experts, ultimately, America's 400th Anniversary was labeled the "gold standard" for future multi-cultured commemorations. Working closely with our client team, vendors, state, and federal officials, we were all proud to be part of this historic moment in time. We know that it could never have been possible without the Specialized Knowledge of so many amazing people.

Having a big idea means nothing until we actually take action to move the creative process forward. There is no guarantee that a team with the specific Specialized Knowledge will succeed at every turn in accomplishing the vision. It takes patience to build the right mastermind, and often, failed attempts offer great learnings! When a failure occurs, it is essential to recognize that each failure is a valuable discovery. This clears the way to explore an alternate possibility. Each missed shot is just a moment in time, not the end of the dream.

We inhabit a world that continues to evolve dramatically, decade by decade, moment by moment. This moment, now, is acutely different from the preceding moment. Each step of our journey toward the actualization of a vision can be enhanced by creating a TEAM with the desired Specialized Knowledge. Successful leaders are continually asking, Who Knows?

"Knowledge, like air, is vital to life. Like air, no one should be denied it." – Alan Moore

Reflections:

How are you using Specialized Knowledge in your life?

What steps are you taking to enhance "your" Specialized Knowledge?

What is your Specialized Knowledge?

MARIS SEGAL
& KEN ASHBY

About Maris Segal and Ken Ashby: Maris Segal and Ken Ashby have been bringing a creative collaborative voice to issues, causes and brands for over forty years. As strategists, producers, coaches, authors, speakers and trainers, their work with the public and private sectors unites diverse populations across a wide spectrum of business, policy, and social issues in the U.S. and abroad. Their leadership expertise in Business Relationship Marketing, Organizational Change & Cultural Inclusion, Personal Growth, Project Management, Public Affairs, Corporate Social Responsibility and Philanthropy Strategies has been called on to support a range of clients from classrooms and boardrooms to the world stage including; Olympic organizers, Super Bowls, Harvard Kennedy School, Papal visits, the White House, consumer brands, and celebrities across the arts and entertainment, sports and culinary genres.

Ken Ashby and Maris Segal recently launched Segal Leadership Global—a community of collaborative strategists, coaches and trainers creating global connections and possibilities in times of change and One Song—a creative music and song writing leadership workshop series designed as a collaboration team building tool.

Often referred to by their clients as "the connection couple," their philosophy is "our shared humanity unites us and when we lead with our hearts, our heads will follow."

Author's Website: *www.ProsodyCreativeServices.com*
Book Series Website & Author's Bio: *www.The13StepstoRiches.com*

Mel Mason

KEEP ONE DRAWER EMPTY

"What's this?" my friend asked. She was visiting my place for an evening and searching my kitchen drawers for a spoon to stir her tea when she opened my one empty drawer.

"That's my empty drawer," I responded matter-of-factly.

"What? Why would you do that?" my friend asked, perplexed.

I knew my friend had a tendency to keep closets full of clothes she never wore and drawers full of knick-knacks she never cleaned, so I was thrilled to have the opportunity to explain the philosophy behind my one empty drawer.

"I have an empty drawer," I answered, "because I need space for the important things. I keep what works, and discard what I don't need. I need space for learning, so I keep an empty drawer."

It can sound ridiculous to keep a physical location empty in order to have more mental space, but this philosophy is far from new. "Empty your cup" is an old Chinese saying that reminds us if our cup is full, we are full of ideas, but there's no more room for anything else. The Zen masters say, before I can teach you, empty your cup. And we can often facilitate this through physical acts of cleaning.

In my house, I always keep an empty drawer. I'm The Clutter Expert, so actively keeping that drawer empty is my way of ensuring I'm only holding onto the lessons of my past that I truly need. My empty drawer is synonymous with the empty cup I want to keep in my mind. Life has provided me with many lessons while I pursued passions related to martial arts and healing, as well as many traumas from abuse, failed relationships, and zany career ideas that never amounted to anything.

I used to be crammed full of experiences: the good, the bad, and the ugly. The ugly ones, in particular, seemed to take up a lot of space. So I emptied it all and began again. Only then did I find success—not just in my business, but in my personal life too.

Keeping an empty drawer (physically and mentally) is harder than most people think. By the time we become adults, we're so full of memories, stories, and assumptions that we can't hold much of anything new. We stop learning. We're closed off, filled to the brim, and perfectly content living in the mess. Even worse, we can't pull anything out of the drawer because all our stuff is too tightly packed in. Lessons from the past are almost impossible to wedge out of there, and our lives begin to feel stagnant.

Thankfully there's a way to get unstuck: education.

Education is the opposite of stagnation. The word "education" comes from the Latin roots "educare," which means to train or mold, and "educere," which means to lead out, draw, or pull from within yourself. Knowledge, therefore, comes from you, but it's embellished with the help of others.

I believe we are all one. We learn from contemporary experts, the masters who came before us, and others who share similar interests as ourselves. What we provide is our soul's passion and our Earthly purpose. In other words, if you want to gain knowledge in whatever you feel is your life's purpose, you need not do it alone. Education is a group activity. Gaining Specialized Knowledge is not a lonely gig—it's more of a group hug.

I don't believe competition serves anyone. When I want to learn something, I ask for help! I value other people's knowledge so much that I'm currently in multiple accountability pods, a mastermind group, and a group coaching program. And with a tv show, I've had to seek the help of masters to learn branding, promoting, and creating. I was not born with any of this knowledge. These resources might seem unattainable to most, but finding knowledge doesn't have to be elitist or expensive.

I believe that when we knock, doors open. When we ask, answers come. When the student is ready, the master arrives. And our teachers don't always have to be external. Mentorship can come from your higher self if you seek intuitive guidance. There isn't a day that goes by when I don't ask my guides from the other side what the heck I'm supposed to be doing. And they answer me every time. It's my job to suit up, show up, and keep my drawer open and ready for signs. Keeping your drawer open is listening for opportunity.

In my work, I see people with entrepreneurial spirits come up with ideas for businesses and websites all the time. The ones who keep an open drawer are the ones who succeed, because they are ready to receive new information and learn. They read books and articles, scour the internet, go to seminars, consult the masters, and seek out people who specialize in skills they aren't as good at, like accounting or web design.

I have a theory that people who do well in life have at least one empty drawer. This empty drawer allows them to remain wide open to the possibilities ahead of them. Andrew Carnegie had no practical understanding of steel when he entered the steel industry in its infancy. But because he was open to learning and receiving help, he was able to dedicate himself to acquiring knowledge, delegate tasks to people who already had expertise he could use, and persist through the uncertain stages of his business to become one of the richest men in American history. Rumor has it he didn't even know his own phone number, but he did know how to be wide open, and that helped him achieve great success.

So how do we create an open drawer? How do we clean out the clutter that is in our way? How do we address the hurt stories and suffering we unthinkingly repurpose into excuses not to fulfil our dreams?

When decluttering your life to gain Specialized Knowledge, the most important task is to sort through burns. Past experiences that feel enraging, frustrating, or even humiliating, are not wasted. No matter how tormenting the memories are, they help us understand what we really want to specialize in. We all have the potential to be fired up about something, and these burns help us zero in on what we're most passionate about. However, we have to remember to get help with this.

Sometimes we can get attached to burns that are not helpful. It is important to take the extra step of having healers, coaches, or mentors guide us through this process and help us understand which burns are helpful, and which ones can be discarded. Once we've discarded all the burns that we no longer need, there will be enough room to gather new knowledge that will help us grow in our clarified passion! Our next task will then be to organize this knowledge.

You can have all the knowledge in the world on starting a website, but if the knowledge is not organized, it can get in the way. Then it becomes wasted knowledge. It's useless, and it should be emptied from your drawer. Life isn't only about your career or how well you can hold a conversation. It's about gathering coping skills to deal with what comes with your path and your purpose. Once that gets into your psyche, life is easy breezy.

The hard part is accepting that all experiences are necessary in your life. It took me a long time to find what I wanted to learn. If I told you my whole story, you might think that I wasted time on detours, but I believe everything was meant to be. I always say, "Keep what you learned from the past, and empty out the rest to make room for new knowledge."

The fine print is that there are no wrong choices. Along the journey, all that doesn't work out still serves a purpose. Your ups and downs are not a wild goose chase. Every experience may not be what you want or expect it to be, but it was exactly what you needed because it's exactly what was. Whatever happens is exactly what was meant to happen. It couldn't have happened any other way. And everything is necessary for your growth.

For every detour and every wrong turn, I learned that there are bits and pieces that add to my Specialized Knowledge as The Clutter Expert. There's a plan for all of this. You just have to trust it. And believe me, I know this is easier said than done.

I recently lost my laptop. I had my whole business enterprise and what seemed like my entire life on that little computer. The old me would have freaked out and accused the first person I saw of stealing it. But I didn't. All the hardship I'd endured on my path of life was emptied from my drawer. All I had left in there were lessons on how to cope. I handled the crime scene like the Dalai Lama. My friend, who witnessed the whole fiasco, said, "Mel, you are so calm."

That was some compliment. I chalked that up as the result of learning my lessons. And I'm going to count that as a win. Oh, and I found my laptop under a pile of papers. Like I said, even as The Clutter Expert, I'm always learning.

When you choose to believe there are no mistakes in life, every endeavor takes just the right amount of time. If I didn't have the exact kind of traumatic childhood I had—if I wasn't put into a position where I needed to learn how to create order out of chaos for my survival—I wouldn't be who I am today with a background in energy healing and the ability hold a safe space for others who are learning to heal from the past and move forward with their life. If I didn't need to organize my own life first, how would I have learned that I could help others with a Specialized Knowledge of healing, discipline, and organization? There's always gain in the pain.

If you want to become more calm and grow closer to achieving your dreams, take this one small step: Keep one drawer empty. Then reach out to one person who has Specialized Knowledge in something you want to learn about and grow in. Take them out to lunch and fill up your drawer with what you learn.

MEL MASON

About Mel Mason: International Best-Selling Author Mel Mason is The Clutter Expert, and as a sexual abuse survivor, she grew up depressed, suicidal, and surrounded by clutter. What she realized after coming back from the brink of despair and getting through her own chaos was that the outside is just a mirror of the inside, and if you only address the outside without changing the inside, the clutter keeps coming back.

That set her on a mission to empower people around the world to get free from clutter inside and out, so they can experience happiness and abundance in every area of their lives.

She is the author of *Freedom from Clutter: The Guaranteed, Foolproof, Step-by-Step Process to Remove the Stuff That's Weighing You Down*

Author's website: *www.FreeGiftFromMel.com*
Book Series Website & Author's Bio: *www.The13StepsToRiches.com*

Miatta Hampton

MONETIZING YOUR KNOWLEDGE

You are filled with endless knowledge and experiences that are unique to you and you alone. There is not anything that you have gone through or encountered that was not designed specifically for you. It is not coincidence, but rather divine design. Every hardship, difficult spot, every up and every down was designed to get the best out of you. It was fashioned on purpose so that you could walk in purpose. These are lesson that you have gone through in life that taught you how resilient, how strong, and how courageous you are. These lessons are specific to you and are nothing more than Specialized Knowledge. You have gained specific wisdom and insights that you can use to get you to your next level. Have you tapped into your Specialized Knowledge?

As the youngest child, you get to see a lot of things, like the mistakes that your siblings make and vow to yourself that you will not make those same mistakes. By the time I made it to high school, I promised myself I would be the first high school graduate among my siblings. I did not have a road map on how to achieve that; all I had was the desire in my heart. I wanted to exceed people's expectations of me, who I was, and what I was capable of accomplishing. Not only did I graduate high school, but I earned a Doctorate in Nursing Practice. I understood at an early age that I did not want to be another statistic and that I had value. I didn't want to live a life of mediocrity or be subject to what one would consider a menial job. I had greatness inside of me and I was not going to follow the experiences that I had witnessed growing up. I learned what not to do by watching the mistakes of others. Being the youngest of five children, I always thought that I had it worse than my siblings. I felt my parents used me as their experiment kid. I started private school when I was in the fourth grade, and I absolutely hated it. I wanted to go to public school like my brothers and sisters. I mean, why did I have to be the one to go private school? It was stuffy and strict. This was my first experience of what it meant to invest in something on a high level. Not because you can, but because you realized it has value. My parents saw my worth, understood my value, and invested in me at a premium rate.

I remember the feeling I had the first time is invested in myself. I am not talking about some course for $19.99. I am talking about investing thousands of dollars into myself, into my business. I could not believe that I had paid such a large amount. The longer I thought about if I should do it, the more I was talking myself out of it. If I was ever going to find out if I had the capacity to go to the next level, I was going to have to take that leap. I was going to have to invest at the level of my thinking. My hands were sweating, my heart had dropped to the pit of my stomach, and I had a lump in my throat. I couldn't believe I was about to pull the trigger. I was excited, giddy, nervous, uneasy, standing there with a smile on my face. I could not believe I was about to invest that much into me and my business. But it was exhilarating. I no longer needed validation or affirmation from people, from a career, from a degree, from a title, or from a position. I was affirming myself and adding value to who I was, with all of my knowledge and my experiences. Investing at this level was giving me insight into how my ideal client would think and how they would feel. I was gaining knowledge into how high-ticket clients thought and what it felt like to invest at such a high level— all the objectives that someone who invests at a high-level feel, what they think.

I was able to narrow down who my ideal client was. She is a woman who has a career but knows she was built for more. She loves to be able to travel whenever she wants to. She drives a luxury car, and she loves handbags.

She wears cardigans and drinks Starbucks. My ideal client knows what she wants. She is a visionary, a strategist, and a planner. I was able to narrow down who I serve based off of my experiences.

Who is your ideal client?

How do you serve them?

What problem do you solve for them?

I had to learn to get out of my own way and to use my wisdom to create abundance. The wisdom that I had did not have anything to do with the degrees that I earned. Instead, it was about what life had taught me. What experiences has life taught you that you can create abundance and wealth with? It is about moving out of your own way and valuing who you are. There are three lessons that I learned when it comes to the knowledge that I have and my purpose:

1.) Free does not have value.

2.) If you pay a significant amount for the course you will finish.

3.) How to turn your knowledge into cash and market it.

I did not value my coaching because I did it for free. I coached everybody who would come to me with an issue. I would sit down with them and spend time coming up with solutions for their problems, for FREE. I would see the transformation in their lives based off conversations that we had. I would, at times, be frustrated when people would ask for advice and then not use it. That was my problem, not theirs, because I did not place a premium on the transformational experience that I was providing. People do not value free. If you don't believe this, pause for a second after reading this next line. Go to your kitchen and check your junk drawer. Yes, your junk drawer. That drawer where you keep those coupons that you refused to throw away that you were going to use one day. Or better yet, search your email for the digital coupon that says "FREE item if you do this" that you did not delete because you were going to use it one day. You either have currently or have had tons of expired coupons offering FREE items that you never used. You put it away and forgot all about because it had no value. It did not cost you anything.

Which brings me to my second lesson learned, if you pay a significant amount for the course you will finish. You have not been placing a premium on who you are, what you do, and the experience that you offer. You cannot continue to low-ball yourself and count other people's pockets. If it is of value to them, they will pay for it. There is a greater chance of commitment when there is a premium placed on your knowledge.

The third lesson I learned was how to monetize my knowledge and how to market it. I had coached and mentored for free for years and stood by as individuals used what I taught them to transform their lives. I was seeing the results of my expertise. The formula that only I had. And yes, at times it would bother me when I had spent hours solving someone's problem and they did not use what I had given them because they did not value my knowledge. I realized that I had no reason to be angry because I had not valued me, and that's why I had given so much free stuff away.

Settle it in your mind what you are worth. Be decisive and make up your mind what you are worth, because if you do not, people will determine it for you and pay you what they think you should have and not what you are worth. What value have you place on yourself, your time, your energy, and your experiences? You have been through some things that would have taken most people out (rejections, lack of support, hurt, and so much more). Sometimes we lose our self-worth due to our situation or circumstance, but what did those experiences teach you about you? What did you learn about your value, your self-worth and how can you use your experience to get you to the next level in life and in business?

DR. MIATTA HAMPTON

About Dr. Miatta Hampton: Dr. Miatta Hampton is a nurse leader, #1 best-selling author, speaker, coach, and minister. Miatta impacts others with her powerful, relatable messages of pursing purpose, and she empowers her audiences to live life on purpose and according to their dreams. She coaches and inspires women to turn chaos into cozy, pivot to success, and how to profit in adversity. Miatta provides tools and resources for personal, professional, and financial growth.

To book me as a speaker email info@drmiattaspeaks.com

Follow me on Instagram @drmiattahampton

Follow me on Clubhouse @drmiattahampton

Follow me on Facebook @drmiattahampton

Author's website: *www.DrMiattaSpeaks.com*

Book Series Website & Author's Bio: *www.The13StepsToRiches.com*

Michael D. Butler

SPECIALIZED KNOWLEDGE LEVERAGED FOR HUMANITY

"Give me a lever long enough and a place to stand and I can move the world." Archimedes, Circa 215 BC

The invention of the wheel, the discovery of fire, the law of lift the Wright brothers used to bring us the airplane are all examples of Specialized Knowledge applied to benefit humanity.

In my lifetime, the encyclopedia has been replaced by Google and knowledge is growing exponentially. Knowledge and access to that knowledge abounds, in fact doubling monthly in industries like nano technology and other sciences.

But the fact that knowledge is everywhere has not solved humanity's biggest problems.

It's hard to fathom that a third of the world still goes to bed hungry and half of the world doesn't have clean drinking water. These are treatable problems that can be all fixed in our lifetime.

Clearly, knowledge alone is not enough. We need Specialized Knowledge and the wisdom to apply it properly.

"Wisdom is the principal thing; therefore get wisdom, And in all your getting, get understanding." Proverbs 4:7 NKJV

George Washington Carver's discovery of three hundred uses for the peanut is a great example of Specialized Knowledge. Born into slavery, Carver became the first African American to earn a Bachelor of Science degree in 1894. He was recognized by President Franklin D. Roosevelt who signed legislation for Carver to receive his own monument, an honor previously only granted to presidents George Washington and Abraham Lincoln. The George Washington Carver National Monument now stands in Diamond, Missouri. Carver was also posthumously inducted into the National Inventors Hall of Fame.

From believing the world was flat, to sailing around the world without falling off, to believing we could run a 4-minute mile, to believing we could land on the moon, to now believing we can land on mars. Our beliefs change when our vision changes and our vision changes when someone is brave enough to apply Specialized Knowledge they have been taught.

Knowledge is not relative. It is fact.

You can disagree with gravity, but gravity demands you respect it or it will kill you.

You can disagree with the laws electrical current, but defying those laws will also kill you or bring you much pain if you ignore them.

The printing press is what brought the world out of the dark ages because it helped the common man and woman read books in their own language for the very first time. Getting one's information directly from the source without having to rely on the filter of the media, politicians or others historically improves human kind's well-being, wealth and health in the world and translates into longer life spans.

I grew up in a small farm town in Oklahoma. We had 3 TV channels picked up through our antenna and since I was the youngest child, I got volunteered to be the human-auxiliary-antenna, holding the aluminum foil at just the right angle so the family could see the nightly programming clearly.

So for me, it wasn't television but books that became my favorite entertainment. And this was evident to my family with me maxing out my library card at our local library and since the maximum number of books I could check out at any one time was 10, many times I'd also borrow my brother's library card to max his out too. We've gone from those 3 analog channels that signed off the air after the news nightly at 10:30 pm to thousands of channels of content streaming 24/7 on every topic you can imagine.

The Dewey Decimal system has been replaced by google and kids are graduating college at earlier and earlier ages. The number of patents and trademarks are up globally and will only continue to multiply.

The greatest benefit of applying Specialized Knowledge in my life and business has been through the wise application of team building. We've seen our company grow exponentially when we get the right team members on board complementing each other's strengths and weaknesses to work around a shared mission.

Academia many times falls short because they merely showcase knowledge and don't apply it in the real world of life and business. Real problems can be solved and are being solved on a daily basis when teams of people work toward a common goal and complement each other's strengths to improve the world.

My call to action for this chapter is, keep acquiring Specialized Knowledge to help humanity, but don't stop there—share it, use it and teach it so others can pick up where we leave off and keep moving humanity forward.

MICHAEL D. BUTLER

About Michael D. Butler: As a global book publisher and speaker Butler is a recognized authority in the book publishing space. Helping authors and speakers evolve and create platforms of influence in an ever-changing marketplace.

The CEO of The Mark Victor Hansen Library with over 80 New York Times Bestselling titles, global distribution and sales with over half a billion books sold.

Founder at BeyondPublishing.net his authors have spoken in fitty countries and on six continents. He's most proud of his four grown sons and two grandsons.

Author's Website: *www.MichaelDButler.com*
Book Series Website & Author's Bio: *www.The13StepstoRiches.com*

Michelle Cameron Coulter & Al Coulter

BECOMING THE BEST IN THE WORLD

What was a huge part of the magic to becoming the best in the World?

Surrounding ourselves with the best.

As a little girl, totally afraid of the water and failing my first level of swimming lessons FOUR times, who would ever guess I would go on to be the best in the world in an aquatic sport?

When I started the sport of synchronized swimming at the age of 13, I was told I was too old to start the sport at that age. For me, when I look back, it was such an advantage. It was so new to me and I was so keen. All my teammates and fellow swimmers had been swimming five or six years already. That could have been a big disadvantage, however, to me, I looked at it as such an advantage. Even though it was scary entering into that space, I was surrounded with so many who had so much experience I could learn from.

The biggest bonus and gift was that I had the World Champion in our club. I used to watch her to see how she would do things. I would watch half-above the water and half-below and then I would work towards doing what she did.

I would come to practice early or stay late. If we had to do a drill five times, I would do it six times. That was one of the secrets to stacking the foundation to build towards being the best I could be. It is crazy when I share that I never tried to beat any of my teammates, I would just focus on every day doing something better than I did the day before. It was constant and never-ending improvement. The results started to come and I started moving up the ranks: to make the senior "B" team; then to the "A" team; then the National team; then to be invited to be one of the five pairs in Canada for the first-ever Olympic Trials for our sport. Synchronized swimming's Olympic debut was 1984 in Los Angeles.

I remember thinking at that time, what an honor it was to even try out for the Olympics. I knew I was not good enough at that time to make it, however being that close to even thinking about it, after that my mind switched to, "Ok then, what will it take to actually Do it for next time?"

After the '84 Olympics, I was paired up with the strongest, most successful swimmer in our country. She had won the Olympic Silver in '84.

We had swam together on our national team for years. Now we were working towards being not only the best pair in our country, but in the world.

We were training 6-8 hours a day. We went on to win our first World Championships against all odds; swimming against identical twins who had been swimming together as a pair for 16 years, and swimming in their hometown.

Our competitors made us stronger, constantly stretching and pushing us to take our craft to the next level. We went on to win three consecutive World Championship titles in pairs/duet, capping off with the pinnacle Olympic Gold.

What made us the Best?

Having a coach who had a big vision, and who was relentless to learn and expand the horizons in becoming the best.

She knew and always asked how we can do this better, surround ourselves with the best, go outside of what has been done before.

She brought in experts in other fields who could help us stretch and grow to new heights, to do things that had never been done before in the pursuit of excellence.

Back in my day of training in the mid-80s, no one was really using sport psychologists. It was thought that if you didn't have your head together or needed help in that area, then you didn't have what it took to be a champion. If you needed a "psychologist" then it was looked at as a weakness.

The fact is, it really is 90% our thoughts and what we focus on, when it comes down to game day or competition day and how we perform.

Our coach knew that having a strong mental mindset would be a difference maker. She brought in the best of the best, and we were one of the first teams to work with a "Sport Psychologist"—who specialized in mindset and maximizing our power of thought, visualizing, and mental rehearsal for peak performance.

She sourced the best exercise physiologist to understand more how far we could push our bodies, would test our maximum oxygen consumption, lactic acid levels, track when we could push harder, or when our bodies needed to rest or recover. We were grateful to find out this information, as there were times I would pass out at practices, and the test showed our bodies actually needed rest. Pushing harder at those times actually didn't push us to the next level. It was understanding when we need rest or a "taper" to then be able to take it to the next level.

It allowed us to train to a much higher level and capacity. We were world-renowned for having the most intense, longest underwater sequence with the highest difficulty in the world. Our Olympic Gold medal routine started with one minute underwater covering 30 meters and all double-leg maneuvers. Our entire 4-minute routine was 70% underwater.

Mentorship was also massive. Who we surround ourselves with, who had the experience and expertise, who had fine-tuned and mastered what it took to be the best in their field.

As synchronized swimmers, one of the closest sports to us creatively was figure skating. We wanted to increase the amount of the pool we would cover in a routine, have the sense of flow and speed through the water, and expand our creative expression. We ended up working with one of the world's best choreographers.

We expanded our potential in new directions by bringing in specialist in different arenas who could help us expand and create even more unique moves and strengths.

Surrounding ourselves with the best, or those who have spent years specializing and fine-tuning their skills, supports us in bringing our level of performance up much faster, which has the opportunity to open huge potential and shortens the learning curve.

When we bring our gifts together, and surround ourselves with the best, the sum of the parts have the potential to be magic—even Golden.

~ Michelle Cameron Coulter

When I look back on my playing career, I realize that I had many gifts buried inside of me, and it took many specialized coaches, trainers, psychologists, doctors, and more to bring out the best in me. It reminds me of the saying, "It takes a village to raise a child."

When I joined the National Volleyball team as a young 19-year-old way back on September 27, 1979, I had to fly 2,000 miles away from home and start a whole new life.

The first person who started to mold me was our head coach, Ken Maeda, from Japan. He was difficult to understand but believed in a hard work ethic and respect.

Next was the assistant coach, Bob Harrison, who was a university coach. He took on the challenge of smoothing the communication between the coach and all the players. We always laughed as Bob would talk similarly to Ken so he would feel better about his broken English.

Then we had our trainer, who looked after all of our injuries and taping to recover or prevent injuries. I saw him a lot as having one of the highest verticals on the team at 42". I was always the last one to land and numerous time landed on other people's feet, and would sprain my ankles. Over my 13-year tenure with the team, I had 32 major ankle sprains.

Our physical fitness trainer, Dr. Death (David Smith), loved to push us further than we ever thought we could go. By 1984, we were in the best shape of any team in the world. Dr. Death came up with so many ways to push our endurance and strength. We would ride the stationary bike for 45 minutes, barely being able to push the pedals, wondering if we could ever get our breath. If you have ever done a VO2 max, you know they are nasty and we had to do one each month to see how we were doing.

The team technical director helped book all the gyms, trips, and functions, and was best known for handing out the team gear. It was always the best day when uniforms, shoes, sweat socks, kneepads, and travel gear arrived. That was like Christmas as a little kid. We would get so excited.

We also had a psychologist that would come in and work with us weekly on visualization. Back then, it was ground-breaking work.

We also had a team dentist and an eye doctor.

I look back at the lessons I learned over my 13 years on the National team and I feel they hold true today. It is so difficult to do it by yourself.

Who are you missing on your team? What is the hidden talent inside of you that you need someone's support to bring it out and unlock that next level?

~ Allan Coulter

MICHELLE CAMERON COULTER & AL COULTER

About Michelle Cameron Coulter: Michelle is an Olympic gold medalist, entrepreneur, mother of four, community leader raising millions of dollars for charities, global inspirational leader, and founder and CEO of Inspiring Possibilities.

About Al Coulter: Al is a two-time Olympian in volleyball, captain of Team Canada, world record holder in matches representing one's country in any sport, with over 735 matches, entrepreneur, father of four, and personal best coach, specializing in relationships, team, and resilience.

Michelle and Al are the embodiment of today's leaders. Strong and empowering, they embraced life's challenges with strength and courage. They bring insight, compassion, depth, and inspiration to the table with multiple world championships, three Olympics, an Olympic gold medal, marriage, and four children.

They are sought-after inspirational leaders. Through their speaking, workshops, and retreats, their gift and passion is to inspire possibilities and support people to embrace their greatness in a real, authentic, healthy, and vibrant way—creating thriving community, connection, and one's own gold medal results.

Author's website: *www.MichelleCameronCoulter.com*
Book Series Website & Author's Bio: *www.The13StepsToRiches.com*

Michelle Mras

RECALL. RETRIEVE. REUSE.

"Knowledge is power." - School House Rock

Have you ever witnessed a child being born? Before the birth, there are high levels of fear, anxiety, and chaos, intermixed with periods of such intense quiet among the high activity. So much so that the mother wonders, "Is my baby alright?" When the mother experiences unfathomable pain and wants to give up, that is the moment the new life makes the grand entrance. The prize comes after the painful experience.

This is when our foundation of Specialized Knowledge lessons begin. I believe we learn while in the womb. I remember my children responding and reacting to my activities, what I listened to, and what I ate while I carried them within me for nine months. Regardless, let's focus on the lessons we learn outside of the womb.

Imagine a newborn. Helpless, yes. Unaware, not so much. I view newborn babies as highly com-plex computers that rapidly acquire information with unlimited storage capabilities. When a baby takes its first breath, opens its eyes, and takes in the shocking changes of light, temperature, pres-sure, and security, it cries out in distress. Their little minds are computing the new stimuli and categorizing it. "What is going on?" "This is new!" "I am not comfortable!" "Put me back!" The baby does all this because it is removed from its comfort zone and becomes stressed. Sound familiar?

Most challenges you face as an adult have been seen or experienced on some level throughout your lifetime. As infants, we learn to distinguish sounds and smells. For instance, which voice feeds us, what they smell like, who doesn't feed us, and the different noises, i.e., doorbell, pets, music box, television, etc. We begin to learn this information within the first hours after birth. In every aspect of our developmental process, we are learning, adapting, and adjusting our programing. We have our highly complex computer brains acquiring information at a fast pace, processing and storing.

How often have you found yourself in a new situation, new job, a group of unfamiliar people, or something as simple as an elevator? The awkwardness is practically overwhelming. Why? We were taught at birth that anything outside of our normal (womb comfort zone) is scary.

The next set of tools we learn as we age are the skills around learning to use our muscles, pull up, stand, and eventually walk. Our super-computer brain now must collect all the information it gathered as we were born and has observed from our backs and bellies. The vast amount of data gathered, recalled, retrieved, and reused on a moment-to-moment basis is astronomical. Now, apply it to learning how to use these weird appendages. We grasp objects, faces, and eventually any solid object we can grip. We learn to move our legs under us to push up onto our hands and knees, and eventually manipulate them in sequence move to our bodies. We test the stability of objects near us to eventually pull up into a standing position and use the flexibility of our knees. We learn to bounce and test the strength and bend of our knees.

We move our feet to begin to walk while steadying ourselves on an object. Eventually, we let it go. We release what creates stability to venture into the unknown. We fall onto our knees, some-times straight onto our faces. We cry in pain and frustration, but find a way to pull back up, hold our secure object for support, and again, release it to walk solo. Over and over again, we fall and get back up until one day, we walk without falling. Success! Our computer mind has now taken in thousands of data points, recalled variations, retrieved the best data for the task of getting up, walking, and reused it to keep us moving forward.

These basic Specialized Knowledge examples are fundamental to success. What helps you get up when another stays down? How do two people face similar life challenges and come out on the other side completely different; one more hopeful and the other full of doubt? Specialized Knowledge is the key to resilience and success. You owe it to yourself and society to discover your core skills not learned from an institution or formal training. Get back to your roots. That is where you will find the strength, willpower, and determination to be successful in whatever you choose to do.

We learned the core skills of success by surviving our first years of life:

1. Be cognizant of your surroundings.

2. Recognize who and what can be trusted.

3. Know when you feel unsafe.

4. Pursue your hunger/goals.

5. Reach up.

6. To reach your goal, sometime you will fall.

7. Falling hurts.

8. Getting back up is fulfilling.

9. Baby steps add up to great strides.

10. If you don't succeed, do it again with slight adjustments.

Change is not easy. Change is not butterflies in a field of daisies. It's scary. It's uncomfortable. The beauty of change is in the possibilities. This is the basis of much of my professional speaking and coaching material. My examples are derived from my life and the experiences shared by my clients. Unbeknownst to many, we each have vast knowledge stored within us. It's helpful to have a guide, mentor, or coach to guide the recall, retrieval, and reuse process to help us navigate through our challenges and toward our goals. Because, "We can't see the forest for the trees." - John Heywood

No one can do the mathematical calculations necessary to catch a baseball in real time. Yet, through years of practice and experience, a player can catch a ball moving at high velocity without performing the calculations. It is a perfect example of Specialized Knowledge.

Think of the major lessons you have learned throughout your life. What are they? My challenge to you is to list them out. Then, list all the less-significant lessons you learned in order to reach the major lesson. Those minor lessons are just as important as the major lessons. Take note of the minor lessons, because from those we can develop the foundation of resilience. The sub-data acquired is where the Specialized Knowledge building blocks lay. The importance of this sub list is immense because they are what we need to increase the success ratio when addressing a challenge. The ability to quickly adapt to recall, retrieve, and reuse old data is what sets you apart from the pack of others addressing the same issue. Remember, each of us has a unique processing code. This is our unique way of problem solving. This is the first of our Specialized Knowledge.

Throughout my travels in coaching, a common theme among the people I meet is that they are seeking something outside of themselves to reach the next level of success. All you need is inside your master computer. Learn how to access that knowledge, trust yourself, and be willing to fall. Multitudes of degrees, certifications, and the like are helpful for opening doors, but what actually lands the opportunity and secures the position is your personality: how you adapt to new environments, and your ability to learn new skills quickly. Where do those soft skills develop? Where do they stem from? Specialized Knowledge is how we recall, adapt, and reuse old information processed through our life experiences. This is how we are designed. Trust the toddler instinct within you, steady yourself, take that step, be ready to fall, and most importantly, get back up.

Just as a mother gives birth to a child, your ideas, goals, and breakthroughs in business and in life will come to fruition just beyond what you believe is your breaking point. Keep pushing through whatever seems to be in your way. Do it afraid. Being afraid means you care about the outcome. That's good! Complacency does not lead to success. Give your best efforts in all you do. Find your lessons. As long as you learn, you succeed.

Be the best version of you, unapologetically.

ABOUT MICHELLE MRAS

About Michelle Mras: Michelle is an International TEDx Speaker, Communication Trainer, Success Coach, co-Host of the Denim & Pearls podcast, the Author of *Eat, Drink and Be Mary: A Glimpse Into a Life Well Lived and It's Not Luck: Overcoming You,* and Host of the *MentalShift show on The New Channel* (TNC), Philippines.

Michelle is a survivor of multiple life challenges to include a Traumatic Brain Injury and her current battle with Breast Cancer. She guides her clients to recognize the innate gifts within them, to stop apologizing for what they are not and step into who they truly are. She accomplishes this through one-on-one and group coaching, Training events, Keynote talks, her books, Podcasts and MentalShift television show.

Awarded the Inspirational Women of Excellence Award from the Women Economic Forum, New Delhi, India; the John Maxwell Team Culture Award for Positive Attitude; has been featured on hundreds of Podcasts, radio programs, several magazines, and lends her voice to audiobooks and has a habit of breaking out into song.

Michelle's driving thought is that every day is a gift. Tomorrow is never promised. Every moment is an opportunity to be the best version of you... Unapologetically!

Author's Website: *www.MichelleMras.com*
Book Series Website & Author's Bio: *www.The13StepstoRiches.com*

Mickey Stewart

THE DRUMMER AND THE PUSSYCAT DOLL

In 2008, I hit a breaking point in my career. I was a stressed-out, overworked, exhausted musician and teacher, running the drum programs at two private schools in Scotland, and teaching bodhrán on the weekends through the Royal Scottish Academy of Music and Drama. Although I was doing what I loved for a living, and was in high demand for my services, I was stretching myself way too thin. I was teaching so much that I developed polyps on my vocal cords and could barely speak. I was losing my voice and was told I might need surgery. According to my speech therapist, I was "abusing my voice."

Teaching is my superpower. It's what I was put on this earth to do. How do I know that? Because when I'm teaching, information that I didn't know even existed manages to pour out of my mouth, as if something, or someone, is speaking through me. And every time this happens, I'm left with an overwhelming feeling of, "Wow, I didn't even know I knew that, but that's REALLY clever!" It's like I'm not doing it alone.

I know teaching is my calling, just like I know my son is my son. It's just the truth. So the thought of no longer being able to teach scared the bejeebies out of me. However, my severe voice issues ended up being one of the biggest gifts I could have ever received, forcing me to ask myself: "HOW CAN I CONTINUE TO TEACH WHEN I CAN BARELY SPEAK?"

The answer came to me almost instantly. "MAKE VIDEOS! Record something once that can be watched repeatedly by thousands, or even millions of people!" It was indeed an "AHA!" moment for me.

This one question kicked my imagination into overdrive. It birthed the idea of cloning myself through video, something that would not have happened if it weren't for my vocal issues.

In an effort to rest my voice, I decided to cut back on my local, in-person teaching, and did everything my speech therapist advised. Then I immediately began my journey to learn everything possible about creating online videos. This meant not only just watching YouTube videos on how to make YouTube videos, I needed to become specialized in this area! So I invested in a video marketing mentor, saving myself years of trying to figure it out on my own.

Knowledge itself, however, is of no real value unless it can be implemented. It must be APPLIED rather than merely CONSUMED. As I began creating my own online bodhrán course and applying the new skills I was learning, I started to bridge the gap between knowing and doing. Because I was spending so much time and money learning how to create/edit/host videos, how to organize them into a comprehensive online program, and how to market my new program, I did everything my teacher told me to do—to the letter.

In order to share my drumming expertise on a global scale, and deliver it while I slept, I still needed more Specialized Knowledge; specifically, specialized "technical" knowledge.

While I could have outsourced the million new tasks that were now on my to-do list, I felt a need to personally possess this Specialized Knowledge, to understand how to do it for myself. Editing felt like a new way to artistically express myself. Creating something from nothing, whether it's a tutorial video or a sales page, can be extremely satisfying if you're passionate about it.

In March of 2010, while in the process of getting my feet wet making drum tutorial videos on YouTube, I found myself re-reading *Think and Grow Rich* by Napoleon Hill. In his chapter on Desire, Hill instructs his readers to create a Definite Chief Aim. So, in keeping with following my mentors to the letter, I typed out my Definite Chief Aim. It read:

"By my 39th birthday, May 19th, 2010, I have reached my goal of a £10,000 launch. I know I am giving my BEST material and I am helping thousands of people learn bodhrán. I have listened to what my students wanted and sold my DVD as a hard copy and downloadable version. AND it was all easier than I ever could have imagined."

I laminated my Definite Chief Aim and used it as a bookmark as I continued to read *Think and Grow Rich*. This meant I read my Definite Chief Aim daily. And, since I'm a very slow reader, it also meant I got to physically hold, see, and read my bookmark A LOT! This exercise provided my subconscious mind with constant, repeated instructions while I continued my way through the book.

Since this was my first time creating a Definite Chief Aim, and also the first time I ever created and launched an online course, I thought I was truly aiming for the stars with my £10,000 goal. I continued to read my Definite Chief Aim bookmark every day with child-like enthusiasm.

As soon as we begin to feel and believe autosuggestions (such our Definite Chief Aims) to be TRUE, they become comparable to super-charged magnets; magnets that inspire us to TAKE ACTION. Once we start taking action toward our goal, things start falling into place, like perfectly-lined-up dominos. While we can't physically SEE the magnetic power, we can WITNESS its invisible ability.

I could literally feel the momentum building each of the ten months leading up to my first launch. It was as if the Universe was bending to my will! When I thought of things I needed, they seemed to magically appear.

Not long after realizing I should have promotional photos for my new website and upcoming bodhrán course, a local photographer contacted me (out of the blue!) and asked if he could do a photoshoot with me. He also asked if he could use me as a subject in his portfolio. A completely free-of-charge photoshoot. Check!

Two months prior to launching, I had the thought, "I could really do with a week off to just work on my course." The very next week, Scotland was hit with enough snow to shut everything down for a week. (And we never get snowed in!)

The end result? My May 2010 deadline came and went, and my £10,000 launch didn't happen. But eight months after my deadline passed, I finally launched my online bodhrán course and ended up ALMOST DOUBLING my financial goal, making more money in ten days than I had earned teaching full-time the year before. Later that year during my second launch, I had my first $20,000 day, teaching a type of drum most people had never even heard of.

In the words of Napoleon Hill, "When riches begin to come, they come so quickly, in such great abundance, that one wonders where they have been hiding during all those lean years."

I particularly liked when Hill explained, in his Specialized Knowledge chapter, how starting a "step up" can place you not just where you can see opportunity, but where OPPORTUNITY can now SEE YOU!

Video teaching opened up my classroom to a global audience through my online bodhrán courses and today, my YouTube videos are viewed in every single country in the world. My voice-scare detour also benefited others. If each of my 15,500 YouTube subscribers wanted a private one-hour Zoom lesson with me, I'd have to teach thirty-five hours a week for thirty-eight weeks of the year for almost TWELVE YEARS before I could then begin hosting second lessons with each of them. Cloning myself through video provides my students an opportunity to access hundreds of hours of lessons with me "on-demand."

The act of writing my Definite Chief Aim (and reading it daily) ignited my imagination and attracted new ideas to help me create my online bodhrán course. Hiring a video marketing mentor provided me the Specialized Knowledge I needed to execute my Definite Chief Aim. It also saved me years of having to figure it out on my own.

"Idea is the main thing. Specialized Knowledge may be found just around the corner – any corner! But imagination is the catalyst that unites a good idea with the Specialized Knowledge required to translate it into success." – Napoleon Hill

If you haven't written your Definite Chief Aim yet, I highly recommend doing so!

If you're able to find (or hire) a mentor to gain Specialized Knowledge in a particular field, I highly recommend doing so!

Ten months after writing my Definite Chief Aim, and a few weeks after that first big launch of my new online bodhrán course, I found myself in Los Angeles as a guest speaker at my video marketing mentor's event, being introduced on stage by one of the Pussycat Dolls. Before the co-producer of the Blair Witch Project made his keynote speech, I opened Day Two of the event with a drum solo that brought a room filled of online marketers to their feet, dancing around at 9 a.m. in the morning like it was the coolest thing they'd ever heard.

MICKEY STEWART

About Mickey Stewart: Born in Cape Breton, Canada, Mickey Stewart is a musician, coach, and author who has been a player and instructor of the snare drum and bodhrán for forty years.

Responsible for heading up the drum program at Ardvreck School in Perthshire, Scotland since 2002, Mickey is in high demand to teach throughout the U.K. and North America.

Creator and founder of BodhránExpert.com, her YouTube videos have received more than two million views from students and fans from every country throughout the world.

Over the past eight years, she's been involved in the TV and film industry as a supporting artist. Even more recently, she's begun following her newest passion, which is teaching others how to share their talents with the world.

Stewart lives in Crieff, Scotland with her husband of twenty-four years, Scottish musician and composer Mark Stewart, along with their 16-year-old son, Cameron, who is also a piper.

Author's Website: *www.MickeyStewart.com*
Book Series Website & Author's Bio: *www.The13StepstoRiches.com*

Natalie Susi

THE MAGIC OF KNOWLEDGE

The 15th century philosopher, Sir Bacon, famously stated, "Knowledge is power." This is an accurate statement, but he missed one very important word. What he should have said is, "Specialized Knowledge is power." It is this kind of knowledge over general knowledge that actually produces tangible results, happiness and fulfillment, and financial gain.

Let me bring this to life a bit more by sharing a personal story.

When I turned 30, I was broke, exhausted, and confused. I had been running a business in the food and beverage industry for 8 years, and I was becoming more and more clear that this business and this way of living was completely out of alignment with my purpose on the planet. At this point, I had acquired a lot of general knowledge about a lot of business topics. I learned how to create, market and sell a brand. I learned how to turn an idea in my head into a tangible product. I learned how to be the marketing team, the sales team, the delivery person, and the visionary—all at the same time. I was wealthy in general knowledge and poor in business success and financial gain. I was confused about how I had worked this hard to be this broke, and I knew something needed to change.

Once I realized that my work was not in alignment with my purpose, I sold the business so I could get back to my true passion of teaching. I had a master's degree in English Literature, and I loved working with students. When I had initially traded the classroom for the boardroom, it was due to a combination of two factors that included California budget cuts making it hard to find a job and genuine curiosity around building a business. I was excited to start this next version of my life, but I knew that stepping back into teaching needed to look much different this time around. My entrepreneurial life had taught me so much, and had also ignited a deep fascination for the study of human behavior and psychology. I realized that I didn't want to teach writing skills. I wanted to teach life skills. I wanted to explore concepts that helped people uncover their triggers, patterns, and stuck points, so they could feel happier, healthier, and more in alignment.

Once I got clear on the desire to acquire a deeper understanding of this kind of Specialized Knowledge, I started researching the best names in the human-transformation space. I went down the personal development rabbit hole and studied people like Jack Canfield, Tony Robbins, and Dr. Joe Dispenza, and modalities like Meditating, EFT Tapping, and many others. I was healthily obsessed with learning about why people do what they do, and I wanted to learn as much as I could about how we develop limiting beliefs and how to overcome them.

I used the principles from our previous books around faith, desire, and autosuggestion to manifest the ideal teaching position. Within three months, UCSD offered me a position teaching a writing and communications course called, "The Pursuit of Happiness." It was exactly what I had asked for; the perfect combination of writing skills and life lessons from my business experience and my studies around human development. I organized the curriculum using a framework I called "The 9 Pillars of Happiness." The nine pillars are: Live from Love not Fear | Be Choosy | Be Grateful | Be Giving | Be Present | Be in Flow | Be Accepting of Yourself & Others | Behave from Love not Fear | Be a Conscious Communicator.

I continued to study, implement, and expand my Specialized Knowledge on these topics. I read the newest books from my most impactful teachers. I attended 2 to 3 week-long seminars per year. I wrote multiple blog posts and spoke on radio shows and podcasts. I also joined masterminds and book clubs where I connected with people who were focused on enhancing their skill sets around these topics too. These group settings create a safe space for like-minded people to hold each other accountable, navigate challenges together, and further develop the practical skills to learn and grow. I intentionally built my personal and professional network with people who embraced this lifestyle, and I built my lifestyle around habits and practices that perpetuate my continual growth and commitment to these ways of thinking and being.

In addition to teaching students, I also started coaching people and fellow entrepreneurs on how to implement these concepts into their lives and their businesses. As I increased my study and practical use of this Specialized Knowledge, I increased my bank account, as well. I was beginning to generate the income I had always desired, and the work actually felt fun, valuable, and in alignment with my purpose on the planet.

As I continued to grow as a teacher and as a coach, I started to hone this Specialized Knowledge even further. I moved away from teaching all nine pillars, and I focused on just the one titled "Be a Conscious Communicator." When people hear that I teach a course called, "The Pursuit of Happiness," they invariably ask me some form of the follow up question, "What is the secret to happiness?" or "What can I do to feel happier?" I always answer with the following explanation. "Your level of happiness is largely dependent on the quality of your relationship with yourself and with others, and the quality of your relationship is reliant on the quality of your communication with yourself and others. Every happy moment and almost every unhappy moment can be traced back to a moment in time where communication went seamlessly or communication went sideways. Communication is literally the key ingredient in the recipe for happiness." That is why it is the most important concept to learn, study, and become brilliant at utilizing.

Internal communication with yourself is where it starts. Once you start positively shaping the way you speak and the way you listen to yourself and your own needs, you can then begin to start shifting the way you communicate externally with the people and situations in your life. I teach Specialized Knowledge around how to build these skills, and I define "Conscious Communication" as the ability to authentically and genuinely communicate from a place of love instead of fear with everyone, in all areas of your life. I add, "When you communicate in this way, you create a space where everyone feels seen, valued, heard, and understood." People who can do this create deep connections with the people around them, and they inevitably make more money, have more fun, and create more happiness and freedom for themselves. This is the concept I have the most Specialized Knowledge in, and the one area I will continue to be healthily obsessed with studying, exploring, and enhancing my skills in.

What area comes to mind when you read that last sentence? Check out the below questions to help you uncover or expand on the topics you'd like to learn more Specialized Knowledge about, so you can create a life of being on purpose and in alignment in your personal and professional life as well.

Brainstorming Exercises:

What is the subject that you love to learn Specialized Knowledge about?

Why is this subject important to you? What personal connection do you have with it?

How does this subject connect with what you already do on the planet, or is it indicative of something you'd like to do at some point?

Will studying this Specialized Knowledge help you increase your bank account and your financial goals? Is it something you can build your professional career around?

If yes to the above question, how will you keep pushing yourself to expand this knowledge and build your wealth with it? If no to the above question, how can you create space for this topic you are passionate about in your current career, so you can begin to build wealth around a topic you are fascinated by?

NATALIE SUSI

About Natalie Susi: Natalie has more than 14 years of experience as a teacher, speaker, entrepreneur and mentor. Currently she's a 5-year UCSD professor focusing on communications and the Pursuit of Happiness. As an entrepreneur, she founded and grew Bare Organic Mixers beverage company for 8 years resulting in an acquisition in 2014.

After selling the company, Natalie combined her educational background as a teacher and her experience as an entrepreneur to provide personal development coaching and consulting to individuals, businesses, and creative entrepreneurs. She developed a program called Conscious Conversations and utilizes a step-by-step process called The Alignment Method to support leaders in cultivating conscious teams and businesses through a process of self-reflection, self-discovery, and self-ascension that ultimately increases profits, productivity, and the growth of the individuals personally and professionally.

Author's website: *www.NatalieSusi.com*
Book Series Website & Author's Bio: *www.The13StepsToRiches.com*

Nita Patel

PEOPLE

I'm writing this chapter in-flight as I head back home from New York City. I've come to New York many times, and I've met many new people in the city each time. But this trip felt far more fulfilling than any other trip to New York. As I reflected on this, I realized it was because of the people I met on this trip. Not only that, but there was a strong sense of connectedness between all of us. We exchanged laughter and joy with a deep sense of respect and appreciation. And the appreciation came from understanding each person's journey.

Understanding people is a ticket to success. When you understand people, you will be successful in any industry, in any role, anywhere in the world. Building relationships with emotional intelligence is the most important thing you can do for yourself regardless of your career. Why? Because whether you work in sales and marketing, or run an artificial intelligence firm, we all work with people. If you work for someone else, you have a boss. If you work for yourself, your boss is your client. Even in the industry of robots, people are still the priority. While we all have our expertise, we all still need to navigate and work with people.

Knowing how to connect with people will help you in your professional life and bring you joy in your personal life because you will have mastered the art of relationships. Often, family is the biggest source of our happiness or pain. When we celebrate, we celebrate with family. When you're in conflict with your parent or children, you can't quit and find a new parent or a child. It's not like walking away from a boss or a job you don't like to find a new one. Having the ability to resolve conflict and find harmony with our loved ones quickly makes life far more joyous and peaceful.

Why do we choose to specialize our knowledge in technical aspects only when most of our life revolves around people? Yes, people can be difficult to deal with. They're difficult to please. They're demanding. They have opinions and make judgments you may or may not agree with. It's easier to avoid all the conflict by not engaging with people at all. But how does life feel when you're disconnected from people?

The bigger question is, how does it feel when you're in harmony with your favorite people? How does it feel when you're in harmony with your boss or coworkers? It's a beautiful place. You are more authentic, your exchange is genuine, and it brings you true joy and peace of mind. Life is good in that moment. Despite all the other challenges in the background, knowing how to connect with people eases the pain of those challenges.

I recently realized that having a sense of connectedness was one of my core values. From the moment I made this decision, I have connected with the most brilliant, successful, loving, and authentic people in the world. Not just connected with them, but I've been able to build a relationship with them. It has led to new opportunities, allowed me to serve others through my expertise, and allowed me to be a bridge between incredible collaborators.

Here is my simple formula to a successful relationship: listen, respect, reward (or appreciate), and compromise:

How to Listen

Put your thoughts on the shelf and step away from them to give someone the attention they need and deserve. Your response will be more insightful, holistic, and powerful when you listen with all your attention.

Respect starts from within

When you respect yourself, others will respect you. When you respect yourself, you know how to respect others.

Take time to know people

Even if you just met them, you could learn a lot about a person in how they introduce themselves and what they share in the first five minutes of conversation. Listen to know how to appreciate others.

Compromise

And finally, compromise means doing something you may not want to do and not expecting anything in return for it. In business, it means to negotiate but with good intentions. When you give and receive with balance, harmony is created in that exchange. It helps further strengthen your relationship with someone.

Being in a successful relationship with anyone, whether it's your barista, your boss, or a family member, requires you to be selfless. No ulterior motives! A pure, authentic exchange will only amplify the goodness. The emotions you put out towards someone always come back to you. Ask yourself every day, "How do I want to be treated?"

I love people. I love learning about people. They're fascinating. Their behaviors, why they do what they do, why they make the decisions they do, how they learn and grow, why they believe in themselves or not, what makes one person know that we can live on Mars, while the next person doesn't believe in their ability to survive a fractured pinky—it's all so fascinating.

Human beings are complex beings, yet there's simplicity in each of us. We complicate what happiness means to us by defining it through our careers, power, and possessions, yet we forget that a cup of tea can make us happier in the moment than the thought of a perfect life or successful career.

To experience connectedness is to experience life.

NITA PATEL

About Nita Patel: Nita is a best-selling author, speaker, and artist who believes in modern etiquette as a path to becoming our best selves.

Through her professional years, Ms. Patel has 25 years of demonstrated technology leadership experience in various industries specifically with a concentrated focus in health care for 14 of those 20+ years. She's shown her art across the world to include the Louvre in Paris. She's a best-selling author and performance coach, pursuing her master's in industrial organizational (I-O) psychology at Harvard. Her investment in psychology theory and practice is what led her to a deep interest in helping others. She has become deeply and passionately devoted to nurturing others and in building their confidence and brand through speaking and consultative practices.

Author's Website: *www.Nita-Patel.com*
Book Series Website & Author's Bio: *www.The13StepstoRiches.com*

Olga Geidane

YOU KNOW SOMETHING
I DON'T KNOW

You know something I don't know. THAT knowledge is exactly what someone is looking for. They search for that on Google, YouTube, Bing, and other platforms. They are ready to pay for that. They are ready to buy if from you.

Are you ready to sell it?

"Who? Me?" You might think to yourself right this moment.

Yes, you! The one who holds this book and sits with their bum on the pool of UNUSED, UN-gifted, UN-disclosed knowledge and expertise!

I know you don't believe that you know something that others are willing to buy. I didn't believe it, either. Why? Because the more we learn about something, the more obvious it becomes to us and then it turns into the "normality". Just like right now, you are reading these words in 'Engilsh and you totaly undertand them' despite the fact that I swapped some of the letters in them. Your brain remembered the meaning of the words at the time when you were reading those letter-by- letter. Your brain focused on the details and you felt like it was hard and difficult to read until it became "normal" for you to read out-loud fast enough.

Exactly the same happens with the knowledge you and I have.

Let me share with you my story to illustrate what this chapter is about.

When I was 15, I stood at the bus stop surrounded by people waiting for their buses too. Back then, there were no smartphones, so we couldn't "socialize" among ourselves on Facebook or Instagram, so we were talking. I know to some of you it might sound weird: TALKING to strangers, but others will say, "Oh yes, those good old days!"

It was a grey cold day, everyone was dressed up in dark and black, and there I was in my bright red hat. I ALWAYS loved red!

A middle-aged looking lady complimented me on wearing something so bright on this dull day and the conversation started. She told me about her challenging relationship, how different she was from her husband and how difficult her life was. I shared my opinion and thoughts, and just asked a few questions, and here she went quiet on me. And then a few minutes later, she gave me this verbal vomit, this unstoppable-like-a-gun, talk about what she is going to do differently and how she will tell him right away about how amazing he was as a husband and how she will from now on prioritize herself and… My bus was approaching, so I just had to stop this emotional woman. She quickly asked me my age and was shocked to find out about it. She said, "I don't know what happened to you and HOW you managed to learn so much at such a young age, but I will never forget meeting you. I am 45 and no one in my life so far made me think the way you did. You inspired me!"

That truly surprised me. So far, I was only hearing that people liked talking to me. That they felt good after speaking with me. THIS woman made ME think now. So on that bus, on the way back home while I was sitting on the left by the window, I was reflecting back on my life:

At the age of 13, I wanted to commit suicide.

I didn't feel I belong or fit in.

I was bullied a lot at school because my family was poor and I was way too skinny and way too tall.

I was still trying to forget and process the abuse at the age of 11 by my first stepfather, and now I am getting used to my second stepfather and the youngest stepsister.

I was hating being the oldest of all four and looking after them. I didn't want to be responsible for them and to look after them.

I wanted to be free.

I wanted to play.

But my childhood was taken away.

So when I was dealing with all of that, by a total chance and coincidence (we all know there are NO coincidences!), I came across a book called *Transformations of an Orange Donkey* by Norbekov. That book challenged my thinking and perception of myself. That book was the beginning of my journey as a coach because it showed me the world of knowledge. The knowledge and understanding of human behavior and thinking actions and reactions. That was my first step to who I am now. After reading that book, I started learning more and more. And I am talking about the time when we had to go to the library, you know! There was no YouTube or even internet available for me. I was getting books at the library, I was rewriting the most important quotes and paragraphs (I still keep them!) and I was getting another one.

As time went by and I started working, I finally had access to the internet and I was finding PDFs of books on personal development and secretly printing them out. I still keep them, too, because they remind me of the hunger I had back then towards knowledge.

Fast forward many years, I transform people's lives based on ALL that knowledge I gathered across decades. Now, I speak and deliver workshops, all thanks to what I managed to accumulate and practice myself.

What are you doing with the knowledge you have gathered so far? How are YOU going to make sure you deliver what you came to this planet with?

When are you going to stop robbing other people of the knowledge they could be receiving from you?

I know it is challenging for you to recognize what you do actually know that others don't know, and therefore I will share with you a few tips on how you can discover your Specialized Knowledge:

Start with writing down what you are passionate about. If there are a few subjects, then pay attention to the one which you are very, very passionate about and can talk about forever! It doesn't have to be some earth-shaking thing. Start simple. Maybe it's cooking or healthy living or sport or cars, etc.

Then, write down all the topics that people usually ask you for advice on. Something that your friends, maybe even family and co-workers are regularly consulting you on.

Now see if there are any similarities between the first list and the second list.

And now, see if there is anyone else in the world speaking and selling something that YOU are often asked about and that you are actually passionate about.

Think of the impact you will create once you share what you know. Will you transform or inform? Will you educate or motivate? How many people can benefit from what you know?

Believe in your own value, and see your own value for others to start noticing it, too. If you don't believe in having something special within you, then others won't see that, either. Practice noticing that you can create your "I was recognized for knowing..." list. In this list, you write down all the wonderful things people praise you for that you know, despite you sometimes answering to them "Thank you, but that's obvious." Or, "Thank you, thank you, but that's nothing special." Or, "Thank you, but that's so basic." Those "Thank you, but..." statements are LIMITING YOU!

So what are YOU going to do with the knowledge you have?

Remember, there are people who need your knowledge, expertise and point of view.

So stop hiding it and shine it bright, share it with the world!

OLGA GEIDANE

About Olga Geidane: Olga is an International Speaker, an Event MC/Host, Facilitator, Mindset Coach, a Best-Selling Author, and a Regional President of the Professional Speaking Association in the UK. She is a host of Olga's Show and A World-Traveler.

Olga helps ambitious people to unlock their extraordinary performance and their true, authentic side. She is passionate about helping people to live their best lives. Olga knows how tough it is to be broke and unfulfilled in life: at the age of 24, just after her divorce, Olga came to the UK from Latvia with no spoken English, with just £100 in her pocket and a 2.5-year-old son. Olga is a very inspirational survivor: she went through abuse, betrayal, cheating, financial loss and emotional breakdown. Matt Black (Business Model Innovation & Disruption Consultant - Snr. Advisor to CEO CSO CCO COO - Author & International Public Speaker) said: "Olga really takes it up a notch beyond anything I have seen before. She is one of the bravest people I have ever seen on stage. If you are looking to book a speaker or attend a talk that will be inspiring, challenging and leave you wanting to take action... She is perfect."

Author's Website: *www.OlgaGeidane.com*
Book Series Website & Author's Bio: *www.The13StepstoRiches.com*

Paul Andrés

THE POWER OF THE INQUISITIVE MIND

For anyone looking to achieve a goal, proper planning and foresight is often important as the first step toward that goal. In his book *Think and Grow Rich*, Napoleon Hill talks about how to become rich and successful using 13 steps toward that goal. These steps toward riches and success include things like desire, such as a desire to achieve your goal, having faith in yourself that you can achieve it, having imagination to grow your goals, having support, among other things, and of course, having Specialized Knowledge about the goal that you are trying to attain. I'm going to share about Specialized Knowledge, what that truly means, and how it differs from other kinds of knowledge that you may know about. It is so much more than just knowing about something; it's actually having a deep-rooted understanding of its workings.

In his book *Think and Grow Rich*, Hill talks about the difference between two types of knowledge—general knowledge and Specialized Knowledge.

When talking about professors, as an example, Hill mentions that they have a general knowledge, not a Specialized Knowledge. Hill explains that professors know how to do certain things and perhaps the steps to complete a certain task or goal, but they may actually lack the ability to achieve them. Rather than having a general knowledge of a subject, having a Specialized Knowledge is a much more focused thing, is much more difficult to achieve, but is ultimately paramount if you want to gain wealth and achieve your goals.

One thing that Hill makes sure to point out is that as you acquire knowledge over time, you have to do something specific with that knowledge. According to Hill, that knowledge should be put into use for a definite purpose through practical plans. In fact, organized planning is one of the other steps that Hill talks extensively about. In this step, you want to take your goals and create step-by-step processes to help you work toward them. It's not surprising then, to find out that people who have a Specialized Knowledge about a topic often make more than people who have a general knowledge about the topic.

Say, for example, you are having some tightness in your chest, maybe even some slight pain and you decide that you need to go to the doctor. If you found out that you needed to have heart surgery, you would go to a specialist for that, not a general practitioner. A heart surgeon has gone through much more specialized training to acquire their knowledge and skills, thus being the expert you would choose for this surgery, and they would be able to charge far more for this procedure because of their pedigree and Specialized Knowledge.

In my own life, I have come to greatly understand the power of Specialized Knowledge over general knowledge. When I first got into real estate, I made it my job to fully understand the real estate market in the area in which I lived. I spent countless hours poring over books, online resources, and talking to other experts to truly understand how to be successful in my area as a realtor. Similarly, when I then started my own design business, I became a Specialized Knowledge expert in all things interior design. This meant countless hours researching the latest trends, understanding different design principles, like Feng Shui, for example, and spending time in the field with other professionals to learn the many tips and tricks of the trade, so that I could apply them to my own business.

This is a never-ending process, as it's important to continue to grow your Specialized Knowledge over time, even after you reach your initial goals and set out to accomplish new ones. Like any expert would eagerly share, the learning never stops. Obtaining Specialized Knowledge is a living skill that should always be invested in and applied to, if you truly want to experience the fruits of your labor.

To truly understand how this might apply in your own life, imagine that you drive an electric car. Of course, if you have an issue with it, you would take it to a mechanic. Most frequently, car mechanics have a general knowledge of the inner workings of gas-powered vehicles, and less knowledge about electric vehicles. In this case, you would want to seek out a mechanic who has Specialized Knowledge about electric vehicles and how to repair your electric car, rather than taking it to a car mechanic who maybe has not worked specifically with electric vehicles. Choosing the mechanic with the Specialized Knowledge will ensure a smooth outcome that will most likely include less issues and possibly a more cost-effective approach with the chances of mistakes being minuscule.

Now, when you go to start your own business, or set out to achieve a personal goal, you will want to make sure that you have a Specialized Knowledge about the topic or goal that you are trying to achieve. Having a general knowledge is great, but true success will come from having a deep, Specialized Knowledge about the topic.

If you look at some of the most successful people in the world, whether they are successful in business or in life, they are always seeking out new knowledge and filling in what may be gaps in their understanding about their own chosen field. The old adage goes, "You don't know what you don't know," and this is especially true when it comes to Specialized Knowledge and being able to achieve your goals. If you constantly come from a place of desiring more knowledge and a deeper understanding of the world around you, in your goals and your chosen field, you will be able to grow and become more successful over time, attaining the goals you set out for yourself and also setting the course to work toward greater goals in your life.

PAUL ANDRÉS

About Paul Andrés: Paul is an award-winning conscious entrepreneur, visual storyteller, and intuitive coach. From digital and interior design, to business clarity and personal growth coaching, to social justice advocacy and volunteering, Andrés is proof that aligning your passions with your purpose is the true magic to success. He currently devotes his time to helping awakened entrepreneurs and heart-centered creatives design the life they deserve through personal and professional coaching and consulting, as well as shedding light on uncomfortable topics that bring awareness to the social justice issues of today as the host of his video podcast, In Your Mind. Andrés is also a two-time #1 best-selling author. You can catch him as a featured guest speaker at events across the country.

"Home is so many things, but ultimately, it's where life happens. It's where we sleep and grow a family, it's where we play and grow professionally, and it's where we learn and grow within. Each home plays a key role in helping us design a whole life—the life we all deserve." — Paul Andrés

Author's Website: *www.PaulAndres.com*
Purchase Book Online: *www.The13StepstoRiches.com*

Paul Capozio

BUILDING YOUR PIÈCE DE RÉSISTANCE

I'm going to approach this chapter with one of my strange analogies. What I'm not going to do is recap the difference between generalized knowledge and Specialized Knowledge, but they are relevant. Let's together focus on the importance on "putting knowledge into action." Napoleon Hill's thoughts on Specialized Knowledge was simply the ability to make money with it.

The ability to call upon knowledge when necessary and have it in an organized fashion is what I call operational recall. Many times, opportunities or circumstances arise when we must call upon such knowledge and it must be second nature. It is also at such times when some of us come to realize that we are lacking this knowledge or have what is referred to as unconscious incompetence. We don't even realize we missed an opportunity. We didn't even see it.

When we are in awe of someone and can't quite duplicate their success, that is precisely when we need to realize we are missing certain Specialized Knowledge. Remember these moments. They are the universe cluing you in to what you don't know. Organized Specialized Knowledge gives us the ability to function in real time. Opportunities show themselves at their own pace, so we must be ready. Specialized Knowledge access is critical in times of high stress, matters of high importance, life and death situations, ever changing deals, renegotiations, etc.

My son, Nicholas, was born with a heart defect. Our ordeal ended in NYC Columbia Presbyterian hospital. We were fortunate enough to have one of the greatest surgeons at the time perform his surgery (law of attraction). While we were there, he was in the most comprehensive neonatal ICU in the world. We met other families who had troubled babies, some with happy endings, some not so happy, and this is a story of the latter. There was a couple whose son was born with a significant heart defect. We would see the baby in his incubator each day while visiting my son.

One day, I arrived and the incubator was no longer there, nor were the worried parents. Of course, when I asked, I was given the bad news. But I overheard the conversation of the surgeon and the nursing staff, and I'll never forget it.

You see, the surgeon who performed the surgery on my son left for vacation. A lesser-experienced surgeon performed this other child's operation. I overheard him say that when he opened the child's chest, the heart was seriously malformed, and when he attempted a reconstruction, the bleeding was profuse and things went downhill fast. He said, "I wish Dr. Michler was here. That poor kid's chest was a mess and maybe he would have had a chance. I was in over my head." I haven't thought about that day in a long time, but what that young surgeon was really saying was that he lacked the Specialized Knowledge that Michler had. He held Specialized Knowledge accumulated over numerous surgeries and I am sure, numerous failures. But the point is he had collected that knowledge and if the situation arose, he would have been able to call upon that knowledge and experience while under severe stress or pressure. So the story is twofold: One, we were very lucky in timing to have been there one day earlier, and the second is to be the beneficiary of Specialized Knowledge and its implementation.

NOW GO RUN HOME TO MOMMA

When I get questions about what the most important aspect of business and specifically sales could possibly be, and if I only could give one bit of advice, I would say it's an implementation technique that I strategized about 25 years ago when I first started helping people make the invisible visible.

It's called the Momma Syndrome. What is Momma syndrome? We all know when we are little kids and we skin our knees, we would run home to Momma. Why? She would clean out the wound and put a band aid on it, kiss it, and we would feel better, right? We had a comfortable place that we knew we could run to. We might even get a lollipop. Well, that response still exists in all of us to this very day. Think of areas of Specialized Knowledge as your momma. In this universe, you will have many moms and stepmoms who all love you and you love them. What it means is that most of us have at least one good area of Specialized Knowledge of our particular product or service that we provide that we're really comfortable talking about or use. Our go-to.

The danger of a small collection of such knowledge is that every pitch that we do, or every explanation about our product or service, is going to work its way back to that area that we feel most comfortable with.

Let's say you're a car salesperson and you have extensive engine knowledge or drivetrain knowledge, but maybe you're a little lacking on the electronics of the car, like cruise control, self-parking, or whatever. Those other features, you don't know so well. It's interesting to observe this in action when you understand the Momma syndrome and you're listening to someone else. You can hear them when the questions start coming up about areas that they are not as comfortable with, and because they want to present in a polished fashion, it's amazing how their technique will allow them to steer that conversation back to the first Momma (which would be drivetrain) and stop talking about the stereo.

You need to start focusing on the areas of your product or service that you are least comfortable with and get comfortable in those areas you need or don't even know you need. I promise, you will see your closing ratio go up dramatically. I happen to be involved with a company right now with a few blockbuster products. I'm in product sales right now and have a very large sales organization where I train people constantly. I avoid training on the product, because there's so much data, so many testimonials, and so many things about the product that every time I sit down with someone and do some one-on-one sales training or even in large groups, I never talk about the product or its results because that information is just flooding the marketplace.

What I do is talk about is everything other than that to build up their Specialized Knowledge in the areas that they're lacking in, and I see the numbers grow exponentially. So, here is your call to action. I want you to now pick a feature of your service or product that you're not comfortable with, and I want you get proficient with it.

Focus on that. I want you to get it down. I want you to start incorporating it into your quiver of Specialized Knowledge arrows. In fact, if you really want to do this exercise correctly, I want you to start off there.

Don't open with your encore!

No great band opens up with their encore number. They're always opening up with a number that is going to get you excited but is not the pièce de résistance

They don't open with their encore, so you shouldn't, either. Exercise the areas of Specialized Knowledge you have collected so you can bring them out as unconscious competence. You know, that you know, that you know!

YOU'VE GOT THIS!

PAUL CAPOZIO

About Paul Capozio: Paul Capozio was born in Hoboken, New Jersey and grew up on the streets of Hudson County. At 35, he was recruited to be the President of Sales and Marketing for a 350-million-dollar human resources firm. In 7 years, he drove the top line revenue of that firm to over 1.5 billion.

Capozio owns and operates Capco Capital, Inc., an investment and consulting firm. The majority of Capco's holdings are of manufacturers and distributors of health and wellness products and human resources firms. Capco provides sales consulting and training, helping companies increase sales through traditional and direct sales disciplines. Making the invisible visible and simplifying the complex is his stock and trade.

A dynamic public speaker, he provides motivation and "meat and potatoes" skills to those in the health and wellness field who do not consider themselves "salespeople," allowing their voices to be heard above the "noise."

He is a husband of 32 years to his wife, Linda. He is also a father and grandfather.

Author's Website: *PaulCapozio.com*
Purchase Book Online: www.*The13StepstoRiches.com*

Phillip McClure

SPECIALIZED KNOWLEDGE WILL SAVE LIVES

Tanks and Soldiers were missing. "Well, let's go get our boys back!" the Battalion Commander roared. "Where are they and what's their situation?" The missing tanks were last seen scattered, many burning, and almost all were trapped behind enemy lines.

My grandfather, Corporal Taylor, was selected along with just a few other men for the rescue mission. The mission required a small group to infiltrate behind enemy lines using stealth and speed to reach the objective undetected. They could not take heavy armored vehicles with them as they would draw too much attention. The team was made up of battlefield tank mechanics. Their job was to get the tanks operational again while in active combat, if needed. The small team of soldiers, armed only with their weapons, toolboxes, and their Specialized Knowledge set out into the darkness to find their brothers-in-arms.

Survivors were found, many wounded and unable to move, and every tank was down. Quickly, toolboxes and first-aid bags flew open and they went to work. After locating the most intact tanks, they started ripping off broken parts and replaced them with operational parts from some of the surrounding hulks of cold steel that rested in the wake of the battle. Once they repaired all that could be repaired and loaded up the wounded, they had to then do the test. They needed to break the silence and make a lot of noise to find out if the engines would even start. Was everything put back together correctly in the dark? Would the salvaged parts from the wreckage actually work?

It did work and the tanks started! With big puffs of thick smoke and the roar of the engines, the tanks came to life and the race was on. Could they reach friendly territory before being found, and would the quick repairs hold up? Racing fully-loaded towards friendly forces in the dark, overloaded with their personnel and the wounded all riding on top of the tanks, they were discovered by an enemy patrol. The fight was upon them. American tanks found some cover by an old farmhouse to get the wounded off the tanks. They positioned themselves for the fight of their lives, and the lives of their wounded brothers. Meanwhile, the Nazi German patrol maneuvered around the adjacent barn, preparing for combat themselves. This needed to be over quickly as they had no reinforcements in the area and could be outnumbered and surrounded by the Nazi's very quickly.

The young men pressed the attack and ferociously fought their way through opposition. Being low on ammunition, with the sun beginning to crest the hills, they had no time to waste. The wounded were once again loaded on the tanks, and they were on the move again. Once they finally made it back to safety, one of Corporal Taylor's friends stuck his finger through my grandfather's uniform and laughed. A bullet had been so close to striking him that it went in part of his shirt and out another without touching his skin. The Bronze Star was awarded to each of those tank mechanics for their acts of bravery and heroism demonstrated that night.

That is an example of what Specialized Knowledge can do. Without being proficient in daytime and nighttime repairs in a highly-stressed environment, compounded with soldiering skills, that mission would never have been possible. Acts like that are what helped sons and fathers come home and what created the next generation. I would not be here today if he had not been proficient in his skills. Continually learning and training yourself for maximum proficiency does give you the advantage. You are simply able to perform acts that others cannot do. It is your ability to be a subject-matter expert, one to be looked at to lead, one to be listened to, and the one that makes sure the job is done.

This shows what you can do not only when you get into the flow-state as an individual, but as part of a team, where everyone possesses trained and Specialized Knowledge and it compounds with each other's skills. People often look at a great athlete or political/business leader and think, "If I was only as good as them, I could have what they have."

The fact is, many people can, but most simply will not try as hard, work as hard, and sacrifice to have the knowledge to bring their dreams into reality. They simply go for just good enough to pass. Being just good enough to pass will never align with goal attainment. It will keep you off the radar of a supervisor, but that's about it. Align yourself with others who possess the Specialized Knowledge you do not possess. Together, you will overcome challenges faster and more efficiently. Find your reason for your goals and then learn what must be known to accomplish it. Ten minutes a day, start with just that, ten minutes, anyone can find that sometime throughout the day. You will most likely find yourself spending more time than that, but at least keep your word to yourself and do your ten minutes, minimum. Once starting this, you will find yourself improving and better equipped, and you will be adding tools to your toolbox of knowledge that you can pull out when needed. Next-level attainment requires self-discipline, confidence in your field, and the ability to find and incorporate the knowledge required to satisfy your thirst for greatness.

I must admit that a few times, I had to wipe the tears from my eyes while I wrote this story about him. I am also a soldier and I have faced these fears and walked into the darkness myself to protect the ones I love. I never got to meet him, but we are from the same cloth, and I understand. He is a hero.

I cannot verify that the entirety of this story is true, but I have seen his Bronze Star medal. I have read the citation written when this was awarded to him, and listened to this amazing story passed down to his son, my uncle.

PHILLIP D. MCCLURE

About Phillip D. McClure: Phillip is married to the love of his life, Maaike McClure, and is a very proud father of two exciting kids. He was raised in the Great state of Montana before moving to Utah. Phil lives life to the fullest. His accomplishments consist completing a full Ironman, deploying four times with the Army, earning multiple decorations along the way. Including two Utah crosses! Which makes him the only soldier in history to receive that medal twice. Currently, Phil is the Owner of NorthStar Coins, Events by NorthStar, the co-owner of P.B. Fast cars and recruits pilots for the Army Aviation program. It was during his last deployment that he accidentally created his first mastermind and it has forever changed his life as well as the others involved. He mentors and coaches in self-improvement and physical fitness.

Phil is an exotic-car enthusiast who spends as much time behind the wheel as possible, whether it is carving through canyons, ripping around the racetrack, or coaching others to see their potential. Competitive driving is the best therapy in the world.

Live life to the fullest and have fun while doing it. You don't get a rewind in life so take mistakes as the lessons they are and improve, don't make the same mistakes twice.

Live in flow, not with the flow.

Authors website: *NorthStarCoins.com*
Book Series Website & Author's Bio: *www.The13StepsToRiches.com*

Robyn Scott

LEARNERS VERSUS LOSERS

There are 2 types of people in this world, learners and losers.

That's right, I said it. Now, before you go get your undies in a bunch, just take a breather. Hear me out on this concept. When I say "losers," I mean the loss of your power. When you're in "loser mode" you are really in a victimhood mentality. You are suffering from a perceived problem that is stealing all your power and your ability to solve that problem. Being trapped in this mindset comes at a very high cost and positions you as a loser.

I also like to use this term intentionally so that it stings a bit. I know that you know it hurts you in your life to be trapped in victim mode. Unless you face the real impact, you may never choose to finally get out of your own way. So please, consider this my formal invitation to do so.

"If you don't use it, you lose it."

The "it" referred to in the above quote is your power. Your access to your power is a key factor not only in life, but in event planning. When you lose your power, you lose your momentum. You lose your progress and things can unravel quickly.

Have you ever had that happen to you? Everything is upside down and inside out. In the middle of it all, you want to just throw your hands up in the air and simply ask, "What else can go wrong!?" In the next moment, the universe answers you and shows you what else, in fact, can go wrong.

I choose to point out the difference between Learners and Losers so that you can choose to be a Learner on purpose. You can practice that quick rebound rate and get right back in the game.

A concept that I would like to share in this chapter is emotional momentum.

Emotional momentum relates to the topic I was sharing in chapter three about pessimism versus optimism. When you come from pessimism, it will catch momentum filled with negativity. It will steamroll and snowball so big that it rolls right over you and pulls you in with it.

It's no fun. It's exhausting. It's frustrating. It will shine light on your true colors, and this could be right in the middle of an event or with your team while planning. You are the leader that everyone looks to for guidance.

You are a learner with the potential to choose to be a loser. Now, I say this to you because I've experienced it. I, too, have been caught in the dip or been caught off guard. I get tired, frustrated, or distracted. I've overplanned or underprepared. I've had the loser mindset. Let me tell you, I've lost in that arena. There really are no winners there.

So take on being a Learner. One of my favorite parts of being a learner is being willing to grow. You start by admitting that you don't know it all and you don't have it all together. We try to pretend like we do know it all. When things go crazy, we will be quickly revealed in how little we do know.

It's quite a humbling experience. I invite you to simply take on the approach that you are a Learner and you're learning every step of the way. Be willing to grow and go with what feels best. This helps in industry and in life. When you can go with what feels best, you can trust that you are doing what's best for you, the event, and the people you will be serving. This will empower you to be open to new ideas and stay flexible in your approach.

As a Learner, you receive new ideas with gladness and allow others to contribute to your success. We are leaders in our own right. We love to lead. We love facilitating events because we love to lead! Whether you like standing on stage or in the back of the room, serving others as an event coordinator gives you the satisfaction of leading and causing something to happen. The downside of this characteristic is that we often want to be the focus of the show. This can sometimes prevent us from allowing others to step into their leadership or letting them help us when we can't see the way.

There are going to be times in your life when you throw your hands up and shout out, "I'm a Loser and I want to be a Learner!" Give up your ego and take it from there.

One way to take it from there is to admit that you are not at level ten in your development. You are not where you want to be and that is okay! We spend a whole lot of time being upset about not feeling like we have "made it" to the place we envision in our careers, relationships, and lives.

Evaluate your event planning prowess on a scale of zero to ten. At a zero, you are clueless, and this is your 1st event. At a ten, you're basically the Tony Robbins of event coordinating. Most of us fall somewhere in the middle of the scale of zero to ten. Where do you fall on the scale? Where in your personal and professional development are you?

You may consider yourself a level five event planner. You may be halfway to where you see yourself going and that is just fine. If you are at level five, be the best gosh-darn five that you can, and recruit help as needed. This will make you a great event planner, whatever your level!

Humility when you need help will set you free from your struggles. We are not designed to do things alone. Learners position themselves light-years ahead of the pretenders. Those people pretend to know it all and refuse help and contributions from others.

Now that you have placed yourself on the scale, you can progress from there. Learners willingly ascend through the levels. Every event will take you up on this scale. Every meeting, every agenda, and every execution will move you up the scale in your progress. Have faith!

If you want to get to ten sooner, host more events. I know that you know this. I am simply here to put words to it. I'm here to put it on paper so that you can see that you are not alone in your growth process. We all go through it. We all get there. And you will get there.

To help you in your level ascension process, I have compiled a list to help you get clear on when you are being a Learner and when you're being a Loser.

Loser:

- Resistant
- Resentful
- Resigned
- Crabby
- Doubtful
- Defeated

- Pessimistic
- Judge harshly
- Critical
- Distant
- Disconnected
- Frustrated and frustrating
- Selfish
- Self-absorbed

Learner:

- Humble
- Open minded
- Assertive
- Willing
- Flexible
- Adaptable
- Powerful
- Curious
- Expansive
- Playful
- Joyful
- Present
- Connected
- Attentive
- Compassionate

Persistent When you are a Learner, there is a certain amount of humility that you have that can cause you to shy away from being all your power. We tend to think that it is arrogant of us to know how great we are at something. We consciously do not show off all our brilliance for fear of seeming too good for others. Our life-long conditioning prevents us from putting our excellence on full display. This is the opposite effect of not feeling good enough, and the tendencies often look the same. We hide out and use self-sabotage.

I would love to wrap up this chapter by sharing an idea to help you keep your head in the game. I want you to remember and use "The Room."

You belong in the room. YOU belong in the room. Stay in the room. Work the room and rock the room! If you take on being a Learner, I want you to understand that you belong in the room, any room. The conference room, the concert hall, your house, the stage, or wherever you dream of being. If you have a fear or an inadequacy, it's okay.

Throwing events can truly be intimidating at times, but I want you to remember that you belong in the room. And once you get in there, stay in there! Stay in the room when it gets scary, when all is going crazy, and when you have no one to turn to. Stay in the room! You will have success because once you stay in the room, you can actually work the room.

This may be as simple as connecting and networking with everybody in attendance. This could mean running back-and-forth, making sure everything's rockin' and rollin'. It could mean being the one up on stage shining your light beams all over the place! As the event coordinator, it is your job to work the room. If you do that like the rock star you are, you will totally rock the room!

Of course, this doesn't mean that you have to have both hands up above your head screaming, dancing, and doing cheesy icebreakers. It means that your presence is known. When you show up, the energy shifts. When people see you, they know you planned this thing. Show confidence so high that of course you would rock the room. You arrive with your chin up, shoulders back, and chest out as you let people know that this is your event. You are here to make it the best gathering they've ever been to.

"Our deepest fear is not that we are inadequate. Our deepest fear is that we are powerful beyond measure. It is our light, not our darkness, that most frightens us. We ask ourselves, 'Who am I to be brilliant, gorgeous, talented, fabulous?' Actually, who are you not to be? You are a child of God. Your playing small does not serve the world. There is nothing enlightened about shrinking so that other people won't feel insecure around you. We are all meant to shine, as children do. We were born to make manifest the glory of God that is within us. It's not just in some of us; it's in everyone. And as we let our own light shine, we unconsciously give other people permission to do the same. As we are liberated from our own fear, our presence automatically liberates others." -Marianne Williamson (Excerpt from *Bringing People Together: Rediscovering the Lost Art of Face to Face Connecting, Collaborating and Creating*)

ROBYN SCOTT

About Robyn Scott: Robyn is the Chief Relationship Officer for Champion Circle. She manages the prospecting program for Divinely Driven Results. Scott is a Habit Finder Coach and has worked closely with the president, Paul Blanchard, at the Og Mandino Group. She is also a certified Master Your Emotions Coach, through Inscape World. Scott is commonly known in professional communities as the Queen of Connection and Princess of Play. She has been working hard for the past 9 years to hone her skills as a mentor and coach.

Scott strives to teach people to annihilate judgements, embrace their own stories, and empower themselves to rediscover who they truly are. Scott is an international speaker and also teaches how to present yourself on stage.

Her first book, *Bringing People Together: Rediscovering the Lost Art of Face-to-Face Connecting, Collaborating, and Creating* was released in August of 2019 and was a bestseller in seven categories.

Author's website: *www.MyChampionCircle.com/Robyn-Scott*
Book Series Website & Author's Bio: *www.The13StepsToRiches.com*

Shannon Whittington

TOO GOOD TO BE IGNORED

When I was working as a nurse in New York City, I had a patient named Freddy who was an engineer for UPS. Freddy didn't have a college degree in engineering, and he didn't have a high school diploma. In fact, he didn't even graduate from elementary school. So I asked this wise man, "How did you become an engineer?"

"Well, kid," he said, "It works like this: You see a machine, but of course you don't know how to work it. So you learn. You learn from someone else or you teach yourself. That's what I did; I taught myself. I went to the library and checked out books about those machines. I read them cover-to-cover and then I showed up to work and I fixed them. I read so much; I could fix any machine in that building. And the engineers who worked there (those guys with highfalutin college degrees in suits and ties), they'd come to me to solve their problems because I was the only one there who knew how. Whatever you wanna know kid, go read a book."

Freddy had what we refer to as "Specialized Knowledge." In short, it means to be an expert in your industry; to have such distinctive competence in your field that people have to come to you for help. Nearly every successful person has something about them that sets them apart from everyone else. It is up to us to discover what that is. When people try to achieve success, they'll often think they need to be a "Jack or Jill of all trades," someone who knows how to do a little of this and a little of that. I used to think that, too. When I decided to become a speaker, I thought, "I can speak about this, and this, and this..." And even though I had received my certification in servant leadership from the John Maxwell team, that alone did not get me any speaking gigs. I soon discovered that there were thousands of people with this certification, and if I was going to be successful, I would have to set myself apart.

In his book *Own Your Industry*, Peter Krueger speaks specifically to this fact. He says that the person who stops studying merely because they've finished high school or college is forever hopelessly doomed to mediocrity. I have to admit, at one time, this was me. I stopped learning and, trust me, it didn't serve me very well. Fortunately, I soon discovered that if I wanted more, I had to reach above mediocrity. The first thing I had to do, and one of the hardest, was to admit to myself that I had knowledge deficits in certain areas. I thought, mistakenly, that since I'm gay, I knew what I was talking about when it came to providing healthcare to the LGBTQ+ community. But I didn't. There are members of this community, particularly those who are transgender or nonbinary, who have healthcare needs and lived experiences that I was very ignorant about. And as much as this truth hurt, I needed to face that I wasn't as knowledgeable as I thought I was.

So what did I do? I went back to school and received my Masters of Nursing in Leadership and Management. After receiving my master's, I went back to school for a one-year certification in LGBTQ+ health. And I knew, even then, that I still needed to learn more. So today, I'm back in school, yet again, earning my doctorate. In fact, my thesis is: Nurse Competence in Care of the Transgender and Nonbinary Patient. I realized just how important it is for clinicians and healthcare providers to know about cultural competencies in the LGBTQ+ population, and I decided that I would become the expert to teach them.

As you can probably imagine, all of this education has come with a huge personal sacrifice. I no longer have free mornings, evenings, or weekends.

I spend this time studying so that I can be seen as the industry expert. I want to transform how healthcare is delivered to LGBTQ+ people and I want to transform how organizations can provide workplace inclusion for my community. When someone needs a speaker or a consultant about affirming care for transgender and nonbinary patients or post-operative gender-affirming surgeries (a very niche topic), I want them to think of me. I have spent many years with the goal of becoming "too good to be ignored," as Krueger states.

This might seem daunting, particularly to those of us who may not have a master's degree or a doctorate, but the reality is that you don't always need to have years of formal education to be an industry expert. We can all become a Freddy. Here's another example: Growing up, one of my neighbors cut grass. As a teenager, this was how he spent all of his free time. While we were out having fun, he was out cutting grass. He could've spent it playing basketball with his friends, hanging out, but no, he cut grass for everybody. He did this all through high school, and he kept learning more and more about how to provide top-level lawn service.

Today, this man has his own company. My mom hires him to mow her lawn every season. He always shows up right on time with three employees. The next thing you know, there's all of this lawn equipment scattered about and they literally cut my mom's grass in less than 20 minutes. Because he dedicated so much of his time to learning Specialized Knowledge, he has tons of clients and lives in a mansion. All because he spent his free time cutting grass. You'd never know it by the looks of him, though. He shows up in a raggedy truck. He's sweaty, with grass clippings on his clothes. But in the evenings, he drives that clunky pickup straight to his mansion. How beautiful is that?

Because of my Specialized Knowledge, I get to earn a living giving speeches about LGBTQ+ health and LGBTQ+ workplace inclusion. Whenever I get on stage or go on podcasts and people throw all kinds of random questions at me, I no longer have to say, "Wait a minute, let me look that up." I instantly know how to answer them. I certainly don't know everything and still have a lot to learn (hence my latest doctorate adventure), but it feels incredible to have this Specialized Knowledge and to be seen as the "go-to person."

Specialized Knowledge also means, unfortunately, that you'll face criticism, particularly from people who may not have the courage to pursue their dream. I've received emails and LinkedIn direct messages from people spouting homophobic and transphobic rhetoric at me, telling me to "shut up" and to stop doing what I do. My response? "This is the reason why I do what I do. To make the world a more understanding place for all of us." When you hold yourself up in the face of weaponized ignorance, when you keep your sight on the bigger picture instead of the static of those doing insignificantly, you will be destined for success.

I believe more than anything that each of us has an individual purpose. Some of us know that purpose in preschool, some of us don't realize it until we're much older. But no matter when we do, that realization shapes not just our career paths, but who we are as special and beautiful souls. Attaining Specialized Knowledge means honoring that unique spark in each of us by focusing on it, shaping it, studying tenaciously, and using it to achieve things beyond our wildest dreams. It's worth the sacrifice. It's worth the late nights and the study-packed weekends. Because when you begin to see the individualized fruits of your labor, it's going to feel so good that it will make you hungry for more.

SHANNON WHITTINGTON

About Shannon Whittington: Shannon (she/her) is a speaker, author, consultant, and clinical nurse educator. Her area of expertise is LGBTQ+ inclusion in the workplace. Whittington has a passion for transgender health where she educates clinicians in how to care for transgender individuals after undergoing gender-affirming surgeries.

Whittington was honored to receive the Quality and Innovation Award from the Home Care Association of New York for her work with the transgender population. She was recently awarded the Notable LGBTQ+ Leaders & Executives award by Crain's New York Business, as well as the International Association of Professionals Nurse of the Year award. Whittington is a city and state lobbyist for transgender equality.

To date, Whittington has presented virtually and in person at various organizations and conferences across the nation, delivering extremely well-received presentations. Her forthcoming books include *LGBTQ+: ABC's For Grownups* and *Kindergarten for Leaders: 9 Essential Tips For Grownup Success.*

Author's Website: *www.linkedin.com/in/shannonwhittington and on YouTube at ShannonWhittingtonConsulting-for 101 LGBTQ videos*
Book Series Website & Author's Bio: *www.The13StepsToRiches.com*

Soraiya Vasanji

THE THREE GIFTS OF GOING DEEP

It is a gift to know and speak into a diverse set of topics, but it is entirely a different kind of success to specialize in an area and apply it for wealth and personal satisfaction. In many instances, it's important to research an area deeply to understand it and see it from all the various angles. While growing up, many of us watched television shows like The Cosby Show, Saved by the Bell, and Full House, where they reinforced the importance of school, and a focus on learning to acquire skills to get a good job and take care of our families. What they did not necessarily emphasize is specializing uniquely and keenly in one area, and then identifying how to capitalize on the information for personal satisfaction, gain, resourcefulness, and monetization.

My father played an important role in teaching me the value of specializing in one concentration, and then applying that in another setting. Additionally, he showed me how prudently choosing a variety of skills can set you up as a strong candidate for promotions and upward movement. The way you think in one industry, when applied to another industry, can lead to amazing findings that the general way of thinking just doesn't lend itself to. My dad emphasized this growing up, and it helped carve my trajectory from sales to marketing research to marketing, as well as spanning national and global responsibilities and across diverse therapeutic areas.

Applying my biopsychology and science background, I joined Abbott Laboratories (now AbbVie), a pharmaceutical company, after graduating from college. I worked in the US nephrology specialty sales force for two years, and later supported the global market research oncology team. Moving teams and picking up skills in these different areas allowed me to better set myself up to join a marketing team because I had skills in sales and research. Additionally, when you specialize in a certain field or in a type of task, you become known as the go-to expert or resident expert in that area. Once you achieve this status where people come to you for support, then you know with certainty you have gone deep enough into the myriad of complexities in that field.

As the youngest specialty pharmaceutical sales representative in the Nephrology sales force, I quickly established myself as the disease-state expert, and read countless journal articles, studies and data to better understand in order to then teach my peers. Instead of assuming I understood something, I would ask questions, and then more questions, and then even more questions on top of those. A highly-esteemed Endocrinologist at Rush University once asked me if I wrote out my questions in advance because it always seemed like a ton of them ready to go in rapid fire succession! In truth, I was just listening intently to everything being said. He shared that I was more skilled than his residents and my ego definitely smiled! But the valuable lesson here is to not "over-speak" someone else by word dumping all that you know. Asking these questions proved more to him that I knew the complexities of the kidneys by the way I asked my questions. Moreover, when you truly go deep enough, you discover the first gift: that acquiring intricate Specialized Knowledge in an area of interest discerns you as the "expert".

Will Durant, a historian and philosopher said:

> "Science is organized knowledge.
> Wisdom is organized life."

Yes! I couldn't agree more! When we draw wisdom from our experiences and combine that with our learned knowledge, we generate power and impact.

This brings to mind the skill of being able to "action your knowledge." What I mean by this is intentionally putting your learning into place, into use, or into a strategy that creates the results you want to achieve. It also takes courage and trust to know you will do what it takes or what is needed in that moment and to rely on the knowledge you have within. In my life, I knew I wanted to create the successes my father had, and was continuing to create. I saw how following a path that allowed for diversification in my skills in sales, market research, and marketing, and spending quality time in each allowed me to wear multiple hats and think from all perspectives in a situation. This level of empathy and insightful purview helped me to get promoted faster than my peers.

Additionally, I was able to take everything I learned in this sector of my life and apply it as an entrepreneur to my Leadership Coaching business. To really understand a patient, client, or customer's challenges and needs as if they are my own on the deepest of levels, makes a difference. For example, when I was marketing a product for Multiple Sclerosis, I didn't just speak with patients to understand how they felt on a day-to-day basis. Instead, we took these learnings and created a simulation for our company to go through "A Day in the Life of Living with Multiple Sclerosis." We set up interactive stations like wearing a lead coat and trying to walk from a bed to the bathroom, while having something over your eyes that blocks out part of the view, symbolizing the vision and heaviness some of our patients shared with us. My favorite experience (which created deep empathy) was when we put plastic dish gloves on and then tried to perform a highly dexterous activity like trying to open a necklace clasp—entirely impossible. The dexterity loss, numbness, and tingling from trying to do something with your hands meticulously without being able to feel a thing is mind-blowing. These experiences allowed me, my team, and my company to truly understand what some of our patients live with, and it made it all the more important for us to succeed in the programs we were creating for them.

The second gift of Specialized Knowledge is when you harness your understanding to create deep connection with a shared group in an unparalleled way.

Where having Specialized Knowledge has truly supported me in my life is while going through the fertility and procreation process. I married my soulmate in my mid-twenties, and wanted to achieve a certain level in my career before having children, so we waited a few years before we thought about expanding our family. When the time came for the green light on kids, the universe gave us a red light. It was not an easy, straightforward road for us.

Looking back, I applied the same thought processes to acquire information and skills in my career to my fertility journey. I researched, I asked questions, I followed protocols and reflected on what worked and what didn't work. I did more research on analogous subjects and the impact they have on fertility, such as nutrition, lifestyle, exercise, supplementation, medications, healing modalities, emotional stress, and mindset. All my pharmaceutical, leadership, and coaching experiences were being put to the test. What I learned quickly was that in order to understand what was not working in our cycles, I needed to acquire more knowledge to be able to ask the right questions. It is important to note that everyone's experience is different, and simultaneously there is a lot that is known about infertility and there is a lot that is unknown. This was where I experienced a personal, pivotal breakthrough moment in my life of appreciating and acknowledging the power of medicine and also seeing its limitations, which was where the power of the mind and body comes to play. After neonatal loss, unsuccessful embryo transfers, successful egg retrievals, a successful IVF pregnancy, and more unsuccessful egg retrievals, I truly understood the yo-yo of the mind and body in this process to create my dream family.

We all have a picture etched on our heart of what we wish our family looks like, and when everything you do brings you short of that picture; well, I truly understand that feeling. I live it. Being in this process for over a decade has taken its tolls and yet the biggest gift is that I get to share is a deep connection with others whose journey resembles bits and pieces of my puzzle.

The third and most amazing gift of Specialized Knowledge is that now as a mindset coach to those creating the families they envision, I get to give away all my knowledge to better others' lives, so they can find comfort, acceptance, information to ask their doctors, and a safe space to share their deepest pains, frustrations, wishes, and gifts.

Specialized Knowledge allows us a multitude of successes, three of which are: being seen as an expert in that area, creating deep connection in a purposeful and valued way, and then giving away this knowledge to support others in creating their best lives, too!

SORAIYA VASANJI

About Soraiya Vasanji: Soraiya is a Certified Professional Coach (CPC), Energy Leadership Index Master Practitioner (ELI-MP), and has a Master's in Business Administration (MBA) from Kellogg University. She inspires women to be present, not perfect, ditch what doesn't serve them, and create their best messy life now. She loves sharing her wisdom on mindset, the power of language, self-love, self-worth, and leadership principles. She is the founder of the Mommy Mindset Summit series, where she interviews experts on topics that interest moms, so they can create a life of authenticity, abundance, and joy—and show their kids how to have it all, too.

Soraiya is married to her soulmate, has a four-year-old daughter, and lives in Toronto, Canada. She is a foodie and a jetsetter, and she loves collecting unique crafting and stationery products!

Author's Website: *www.SoraiyaVasanji.com*
Book Series Website & Author's Bio: *www.The13StepstoRiches.com*

Stacey Ross Cohen

KNOWLEDGE IS THE NEW CURRENCY

According to Napoleon Hill, there are two types of knowledge: general and specialized. Individuals with general knowledge are a "jack of all trades'" with a broad scope of knowledge widely applicable to a range of industries. Alternatively, individuals with Specialized Knowledge have a more narrow, but deeper, well of expertise. Whereas generalization is acquired through conventional education, specialization is attained through specific education programs, mentoring or experience, making it more expensive and difficult to obtain.

Indeed, Specialized Knowledge gives individuals a competitive edge in the workplace, because in-depth expertise can solve more complicated problems. For instance, surgeons receive one of the highest-paying salaries in healthcare, in no small part because of eight years of medical school plus specialized training.

My husband, Bruce, has Specialized Knowledge in residential real estate law in New York. He is particularly in high demand for his legal knowledge of co-op and condominium transactions, a direct result of his experience with more than 2,500 transactions through the years. Bruce's work is truly granular: changing real estate regulations, co-op boards, tax implications, and more. In fact it's so granular, it's limited by state. When a client asks him to handle a Florida transaction, he can't take it on. But he is incredibly resourceful and will find his clients an attorney that practices in Florida.

Becoming a Specialist

So how does one acquire Specialized Knowledge? There are essentially three steps:

1. Determine your major life purpose and decide what type of knowledge is required. What do you want to be known for? What area do you want to achieve success in?

2. Identify relevant sources of knowledge. This could entail certificate programs, graduate degrees, mentorships, online courses, and more. Surround yourself with people you can learn from, and take advantage of a mentor or coach. Also, consider creating a personal board of directors made up of individuals with different competencies. And as you grow in your profession, remember that you will need to find new sources of knowledge.

3. Focus on precision. The methodical implementation of Specialized Knowledge, like finding the right career path, leads to success. Create action steps to achieve your goals, get very granular, and hold yourself accountable.

As you pursue these steps, don't fall for an old cliché. It's often said that "knowledge is power," but this is not so according to Napoleon Hill. Knowledge is merely potential power. Even if you have Specialized Knowledge, you must couple that knowledge with intention, and develop and implement a strategic action plan.

Change is the Constant

Acquiring Specialized Knowledge isn't a one-time act. You need to learn everything about your field, which will constantly be changing.

My mantra is that if you keep doing the same thing, you will not get the same result, but instead you will be stuck in reverse. The new competitive advantage is about change and innovation. Is your skill set still relevant? If not, you may need to reset and acquire new skills or even a new career path where broader opportunities are available. At the end of the day, you must stay relevant and routinely update your knowledge base.

In short: Prepare yourself for a lifetime of learning. Commitment to education is non-negotiable.

Think Big with Thought Leadership

I like to consider myself the thought leader of thought leadership, and strongly believe this concept is key to specialization. So what exactly is a thought leader? And how can it benefit you?

A thought leader is an authority on a particular subject matter or industry. They don't keep their Specialized Knowledge to themselves. They share their insights and ideas with audiences through speaking engagements, media interviews, and content development. Thought leaders have a truly distinct (and sometimes disruptive) perspective which inspires innovative thinking in others. Establishing yourself as a thought leader in your field gives you a competitive edge. When done correctly, you can reap many benefits, including career advancement, higher salary, rewarding partnerships, new clients/business opportunities, and revenue growth.

Indeed, people make decisions based on an emotional connection with a brand or individual. In order for someone to engage with your knowledge or to buy what you're selling, they need to know, like, and trust you. And thought leadership can achieve just that.

Below are five strategies to become a thought leader in your industry:

1. Define your brand. Building a personal brand is the first step to achieving thought-leader status. Identify your purpose, strengths, values, and passion. This exercise is not about me, me, me; it's about your value to others. You need to understand your target audience as well as your competition. What's important to your audience? How can you solve their needs better than your competitors? Only then can you crystallize your expertise or niche and put your stake in the ground.

2. Create a strategic roadmap. It's tempting to jump into the tactics of thought leadership, like creating a blog. But you need to be intentional, proactive, and have a well-informed strategy. When I work with a new client to build thought leadership, I insist on starting with a plan which details objectives, target audiences, messaging, tactics, and a 6–12 month timeline.

3. Develop relevant content. Thought leaders need to produce content regularly. And good content is not enough. You need to create great content to capture your audience. Whether you develop articles, blog posts, e-books, news releases, white papers or videos, make certain the content speaks directly to your audience. It is also important to be bold, share your point of view, and make industry predictions. Lastly, showcase your value with a "wow" portfolio of client testimonials, achievements, success stories, and a professional bio/profile with headshot. And remember, nothing matches the power of earned media to build thought leadership. I work closely with thought leaders to secure high-level media coverage in broadcast, print, and online.

4. Become your own news channel. Once you have great content, you need to deliver it through a multi-channel approach: websites, speaking engagements, social media, blogs, e-newsletters, podcasts, and more. Select channels that are in sync with who you are and that reach your audience, since you can't be everywhere. Speaking, in particular, is a top tool to build thought leadership. Record your speaking engagements and make sure to publish them on your website and social channels. Create a speaker's bio and/or sizzle reel to further grow your opportunities within the speaking realm.

5. Grow your network. It's been said that, "Your network is your net worth," and that's spot-on. Networking is one of the most important investments you can make. Engage and build relationships with mentors, influencers, and industry leaders. And rather than focus on how many people you meet networking, focus on meeting the right people. Be social and attend networking events (virtual and live), and be sure to reconnect with your new contacts promptly via LinkedIn and other platforms. Seek out professional groups within your industry and invest time in engaging with that community and building authentic relationships. Also, consider joining a board or committee (both professional and community).

A great example of a thought leader is Elizabeth Gilbert, author of *Eat, Pray, Love*. Gilbert gave an inspiring TED Talk (which I've watched half a dozen times) called Your Elusive Creative Genius. She talks about creativity in a disruptive way, contradicting the predominant view that creativity is a rare gift. Instead, she contends that all of us have a genius within us. She shares her own personal creative journey and challenges her audience to find their own creativity. Her thought leadership status is well-deserved. She is insightful, visionary and a sought-after authority and speaker on creativity. She also regularly delivers thought-provoking content through social channels, and has a podcast in which she interviews famous creatives.

As you pursue success, don't lose sight of the importance of knowledge in your quest. Make sure you're developing a specialized skill set, make sure you're always learning in order to keep that skill set current, and make sure you're broadcasting your expertise to the world.

STACEY ROSS COHEN

About Stacey Ross Cohen: In the world of branding, few experts possess the savvy and instinct of Stacey. An award-winning brand professional who earned her stripes on Madison Avenue and major television networks before launching her own agency, Stacey specializes in cultivating and amplifying brands.

Stacey is CEO of Co-Communications, a marketing agency headquartered in New York. She coaches businesses and individuals across a range of industries, from real estate to healthcare and education, and expertly positions their narratives in fiercely competitive markets.

A TEDx speaker, Stacey is a sought-after keynote at industry conferences and author in the realm of branding, PR, and marketing. She is a contributor at *Huffington Post* and *Thrive Global*, and has been featured in *Forbes, Entrepreneur, Crain's* and a suite of other media outlets. She holds a B.S. from Syracuse University, MBA from Fordham University and a certificate in Media, Technology and Entertainment from NYU Stern School of Business.

Author's website: *www.StaceyRossCohen.com*
Book Series Website & author's Bio: *www.The13StepsToRiches.com*

Teresa Cundiff

KEEP SPECIALIZING YOUR KNOWLEDGE UNTIL YOU FIND YOUR POWER

One of the things I loved most about college is that everyone who was there wanted to be there! Here's my reasoning: up until college, the 12-13 years spent in school (depending on how many years of preschool one may have attended), you basically had to be there. The transition from high school to college leaves behind all those who are not interested in specializing what I'll call their formal "book" education.

For me, going to college got rid of all the people who bullied me and made fun of me for one reason or another. And whatever the reason was for their not being in college (at least, at my college), I didn't care. I was off on the grand adventure of furthering my education, which I now understand from Napoleon Hill's 4th principle was Specializing my Knowledge. And that was perpetuated by the ever-popular question asked of all freshmen, "What's your major?" And so, it began.

I submit to you, however, that specializing our knowledge is an ongoing endeavor! It's something that we keep doing and niching down over the course of our entire lifetimes until we find our power. Isn't that why we join masterminds, hire coaches, take courses? Of course it is! We seek to improve ourselves and develop our Specialized Knowledge. And why? Because we seek to be an expert in our field. We desire to be the expert others seek out!

It is the expert who commands the highest salary. Think about the medical field, for example. There is the General Practitioner and then there is the Specialist. How about Dr. Ben Carson? The world-renowned pediatric neurosurgeon! He kept specializing his knowledge until he found his power. He niched his education down to a finely-tuned specialty and the world beat a path to his doorway, much like the old saying about building a better mousetrap (look it up!).

So, if you aren't making the money you want in your specialty, you must ask yourself some pointed, soul-searching, thought-provoking questions. Are you in the right specialty? Have you exhausted all the education available to you in said specialty? Have you surrounded yourself with people who support you in your efforts to become proficient in your specialty? Let's break these questions down, one at a time.

Are you in the right specialty? This question must be answered with all honesty and sobriety because everything you are doing hinges on this. It's like watching American Idol back in the day when people would tell Simon Cowell that singing was their dream when they clearly couldn't sing. They had only been put through the rounds so Simon could insult them, yet they had been led to believe they had a shot. It's a travesty that someone who truly loved them didn't sit down with them and tell them honestly that they couldn't sing and to stop the madness before they were shattered and mocked on national TV. Do you know in your heart of hearts, in that secret place deep down inside, that you are doing what you are called to do?

Do you have some third-party confirmation from various people that you are doing the right thing? Meaning lots of people have told you, "You know, you should be a life coach?" or, "You have such a knack for lifting people up. Have you ever thought of being a speaker?" I'm just sitting here asking you to honestly assess that you are pursuing the field that God has for you. Don't shoot the messenger!

Secondly, have you exhausted all the education available to you in your specialty? In my example of Dr. Carson, he had to go through many years of schooling to achieve his goal. Maybe you need some courses that will earn you certifications to get the job you want, or maybe you need to take some trainings to learn how to develop your own course to get it running and marketed. Or maybe there's an area you want to strengthen within your calling, so you seek out resources to do that. The question really is, are you always moving forward to improve your skills?

Way back in the day when I was in college, I earned my B.S. in Information Systems. Now, that degree is completely different in 2021 than it was in, ahem, 1986! Did I continue to specialize in that field? No, I didn't. I went to graduate school for my MBA which is a different type of specializing. Then, did I work using my that education? Not exactly. I worked in a magazine printing plant in several different departments and then married a US Army officer. And, as I have explained in previous chapters in the earlier volumes of this series, I specialized in raising amazing young men who now contribute in a great way to society. Proud momma!

I am practicing what I am preaching to you here though, so there is no hypocrisy on my side of the street. I am also a professional freelance proofreader, so I am always taking courses to make sure my skills are sharp for my clients. So, regarding that field, I have Specialized Knowledge with a fine point on it. I have great confidence in my abilities and know that I know what I'm doing when it comes to grammar, punctuation, sentence structure, etc., and can deliver for my clients. In fact, I'm so confident, my tagline is, "I know where the commas go!" A thought that I think makes the average person shudder.

If you can speak like that about your field of specialty, then you have chosen the right field. You have fully educated yourself in your field and are probably smart enough to keep your education at a very high level by keeping yourself abreast of any developments in your industry.

Now, when it comes to hosting my TV show, Teresa Talks, I am still a newcomer to the small screen and seek out those who are wiser than me to learn from their wisdom and expertise. I am still specializing my knowledge in that field.

This brings us to the third question. Have you surrounded yourself with people who support you in your efforts to become proficient in your specialty? I'm not talking about your friends and family here, even though they are very important. I'm talking first about a mastermind group (since it was Napoleon Hill who introduced the concept). A mastermind group can be so valuable to your growth and development toward specializing your knowledge. A group of this sort is also a wealth of resources and connections that are priceless. You often don't know who you are in the room with! You meet with them on a Zoom call and you have the connection, but it could lead to amazing relationships that grow into friendships.

If you think you want to hire a life coach, then hire a life coach, but make certain you do your research to find the one who is the best fit for you. Ask for recommendations and interview the names who land on your short list. You are looking for the person who will help you to specialize your knowledge all the way down to the place where you can feel powerful in your field. Where YOU are an expert! Where YOU are the person now being sought out because YOU are highly specialized!

I submit to you that the key is to never stop seeking Specialized Knowledge, even when you have arrived. If you are at the top of your field, you want to stay there. And if you're at the top of your field, share your Specialized Knowledge and bring folks along with you. Your course will make you a fortune! But having a heart that is giving and willing to share will earn you a reputation that is priceless.

Another thought I want to touch on is that I am of the mindset that we will probably change our field of specialty a few times during the course of our lifetimes. Give yourself permission to do so. I worked a whole bunch of different part-time jobs while my boys where in school that allowed me to get them on and off the bus. Life takes twists and turns. Mine certainly did, since I was a military wife and we moved around. It wasn't until last year when I found proofreading and finally found the one thing that I knew was my perfect fit for a side gig! And then the TV show came along, and that was another perfect fit. One of my funny mantras is, "I never met a camera I didn't love!" LOL! Plus, I love to talk and read, so interviewing authors was perfect for me.

If you have your specialty, specialize your knowledge to a fine point because there is where you will find your power. You will be the expert others seek for your Specialized Knowledge. Seek out the people who will make you better in your field and be your biggest cheerleaders! Here's to your success!

TERESA CUNDIFF

About Teresa Cundiff: Teresa hosts an interview digital TV show called Teresa Talks on Legrity TV. On the show, she interviews authors who are published and unpublished— and that just means those authors haven't put their books on paper yet. The show provides a platform for authors to have a global reach with their message. Teresa Talks is produced by Wordy Nerds Media Inc., of which Cundiff is the CEO.

Cundiff is also a freelance proofreader with the tagline, "I know where the commas go!," Teresa makes her clients' work shine with her knowledge of grammar, punctuation, and sentence structure.

Teresa is a two-time International Best-Selling Contributing Author of *1 Habit for Entrepreneurial Success and 1 Habit to Thrive in a Post-COVID World.* She is also a best-selling contributing author of *The Art of Connection; 365 Days of Networking Quotes,* which has been placed in the Library of Congress.

Author's Website: *www.TeresaTalksTV.com*
Book Series Website & Author's Bio: *www.The13StepsToRiches.com*

Vera Thomas

GREEN AND GROWING OR RIPE AND ROTTING?

Are you green and growing
Or ripe and rotten?
Holding on to past knowledge
Too soon forgotten.
Every day we can learn something new
To stay green, daily learning is a must do
Knowledge is power
That cannot be denied or
taken away
Knowledge plus wisdom
As we live each day
Touching other lives along the way
Vera Thomas, 11/4/21

I have met twelve- and thirteen-year-olds who are ripe and rotten. I have met sixty-seventy-eighty- and ninety-year-olds who are green and growing. It has nothing to do with age, it is all about an attitude of learning and growing not only in your chosen field of expertise, but learning and growing in every area of life. We so often get stuck in our ways, our thoughts, and our behaviors that are not only detrimental to ourselves, but also detrimental to our society and well-being.

Book One in this series is on Desire. "Desire without knowledge is not good, and whoever makes haste with his feet misses his way." (Proverbs 19:2 ESV). The Thirteen Steps to Riches must include knowledge.

Specialized training in the areas of one's expertise is essential for sustaining and maintaining credibility. To be a continual life-learner is to be one who does not take living for granted. As we live, we learn. We move forward or back. There is no such thing as standing still. The very air we breathe is moving and changing. If not, we would die. Water, when it stands still, becomes stagnate and will stink. Learning and growing is no different. In fact, there are 109 references in the Bible regarding knowledge and wisdom, with 84 related to study. The Word is the focus of this chapter so that we understand how knowledge and wisdom are imperative to a life of success and riches. If knowledge and wisdom were not essential to our being, why are they mentioned so many times in the Bible, which is a "Lamp Unto My Feet and Light Unto My Path?" (Psalm 119:105).

"Keep hold of instruction; do not let go; guard her, for she is your life." (Proverbs 4:13-17 ESV).

Proverbs 4:20-26

20 My son, pay attention to what I say; turn your ear to my words.

21 Do not let them out of your sight, keep them within your heart;

22 for they are life to those who find them and health to one's whole body.

23 Above all else, guard your heart, for everything you do flows from it.

24 Keep your mouth free of perversity; keep corrupt talk far from your lips.

25 Let your eyes look straight ahead; fix your gaze directly before you.

26 Give careful thought to the[a] paths for your feet and be steadfast in all your ways.

Scriptures says, "Study to show thyself approved unto God, a workman that need not to be ashamed, rightly dividing the word of truth." (2 Timothy 2:15). Experts in their fields understand that ongoing learning and seeking of knowledge is not only important, it is necessary. We cannot teach what we do not know, and we cannot give what we do not have.

Proverbs 12:1 ESV, "Whoever loves discipline loves knowledge." To acquire knowledge requires discipline. Finding the time to read, study, and engage in activities that will enhance knowledge in a given field is a no-brainer. "A worker's appetite works for him; his mouth urges him on." (Proverbs 16:26). The appetite for knowledge and a thirst for wisdom will lead us to the path of success!

"My people are destroyed for lack of knowledge." (Hosea 4:6). Knowledge is power. It seems in today's society, knowledge has taken a back seat to the dumbing-down of our nation. There is such a focus on perversion and knowledge is lacking.

Yes, it is imperative we study in our chosen field of profession, however, knowledge and wisdom must permeate our whole being. "The proverbs of Solomon, son of David, king of Israel: To know wisdom and instruction, to understand words of insight, to receive instruction in wise dealing, in righteousness, justice, and equity; to give prudence to the simple, knowledge and discretion to the youth—Let the wise hear and increase in learning, and the one who understands obtain guidance." (Proverbs 1:1-33).

"For the protection of wisdom is like the protection of money, and the advantage of knowledge is that wisdom preserves the life of him who has it." (Ecclesiastes 7:12). Again, knowledge and wisdom go hand in hand.

"For wisdom will come into your heart, and knowledge will be pleasant to your soul; discretion will watch over you, understanding will guard you." (Proverbs 2:10-11).

"There is gold and abundance of costly stones, but the lips of knowledge are a precious jewel." (Proverbs 20:15).

"For this very reason, make every effort to supplement your faith with virtue, and virtue with knowledge." (2 Peter 1:5 ESV).

King Solomon knew the power of wisdom and knowledge. "In that night God appeared to Solomon, and said to him, "Ask what I shall give you." And Solomon said to God, "You have shown great and steadfast love to David my father and have made me king in his place. O LORD God, let your word to David my father be now fulfilled, for you have made me king over a people as numerous as the dust of the earth. Give me now wisdom and knowledge to go out and come in before this people, for who can govern this people of yours, which is so great?" God answered Solomon, "Because this was in your heart, and you have not asked possessions, wealth, honor, or the life of those who hate you, and have not even asked long life, but have asked wisdom and knowledge for yourself that you may govern my people over whom I have made you king." (2 Chronicles 1:7-12 ESV).

"A scoffer seeks wisdom in vain, but knowledge is easy for a man of understanding." (Proverbs 14:6 ESV). "But as you excel in everything— in faith, in speech, in knowledge, in all earnestness, and in our love for you—see that you excel in this act of grace also." (2 Corinthians 8:7).

One of the scriptures I stand on daily, "If any of you lacks wisdom, let him ask God, who gives generously to all without reproach, and it will be given him." I truly stand on this before making any moves, including writing this chapter. Knowledge we acquire through study. Wisdom is acquired through the power of the Holy Spirit. We only have to ask.

"Who is wise and understanding among you? By his good conduct let him show his works in the meekness of wisdom. But if you have bitter jealousy and selfish ambition in your hearts, do not boast and be false to the truth. This is not the wisdom that comes down from above, but is earthly, unspiritual, demonic. For where jealousy and selfish ambition exist, there will be disorder and every vile practice. But the wisdom from above is first pure, then peaceable, gentle, open to reason, full of mercy and good fruits, impartial and sincere." (James 3:13-18).

"And if I have prophetic powers, and understand all mysteries and all knowledge, and if I have all faith, so as to remove mountains, but have not love, I am nothing." (1 Corinthians 13:2 ESV).

In conclusion, know that knowledge and wisdom are one of the most important keys to success. Without it, our desires may go untapped, our faith may waver, and our dreams and goals may go unrealized. "For the moment all discipline seems painful rather than pleasant, but later it yields the peaceful fruit of righteousness to those who have been trained by it." (Hebrews 12:11 ESV).

"An intelligent heart acquires knowledge, and the ear of the wise seeks knowledge." (Proverbs 18:15 ESV).

Based on the importance of knowledge and wisdom that we have outlined here according to God's Word, let me ask again, are you green and growing, or ripe and rotting?

VERA THOMAS

About Vera Thomas: Life Coach, Speaker, Trainer, Mediator, Poet, and Producer of a weekly podcast/radio show called "The Vera Thomas Show." Vera has worked with companies, non-profit organizations, schools, and churches customizing and delivering training and leadership programs.

Enduring physical, emotional, and mental abuse as a child, rape, homelessness and surviving as a battered wife leaving her husband when her son was only 6 months old, Vera has organized a program called the "Father's Walk!" This program would focus on fathers walking their child to school on a specific date. Impacting over 10,000 fathers who took part in the program, it allowed the movement to change systemic attitudes and behaviors towards fathers in family court, child support, and children services.

Author's Website: *www.VeraThomasCoaching.com*
Book Series Website & Author's Bio: *www.The13StepstoRiches.com*

Yuri Choi

CREATIVE OUTPUT OF KNOWLEDGE & INSPIRED ACTION CREATE ABUNDANCE

Did you know that Elon Musk read all the books at his local library in his childhood because he was a shy, quiet kid and he just wanted to learn a lot? He read books on various different subjects, a number of different industries, from many different perspectives. He read fictional stories about traveling time, and he read books about physics. He read books about spirituality, and he read books about business and finance. And he is also now the wealthiest human on Earth. Today, his net worth is over 286 billion dollars in the most recent Google search. So more knowledge and reading equals magnificent levels of wealth, right?

Actually, I am here to let you know the opposite of that - that reading and learning have no value until it is translated into a valuable and meaningful contribution to the world. It wasn't the reading alone that got him wildly successful. You see, reading and learning a lot are a part of the equation, but it is an incomplete equation with that part alone. Knowledge alone isn't power. Knowledge is just potential power. Knowledge can become powerful, bring about abundance and success when it is translated into inspired, courageous and continuous actions. If Elon Musk read all those books as a kid and as an adult, but never created and founded these amazing innovative companies such as the Boring Company, Tesla, PayPal, SpaceX and more, he wouldn't be the wealthiest man today. It was what he did with that knowledge, and infusing it with his personal magic, that it became what it is today.

To understand this better, I'll share one of my personal stories when this distinction was made for me which drastically changed the way I create my reality. One of the things my first coach ever told me on our first coaching call was "to stop reading books so much for a bit." I was signed up for a journey of self-discovery and growth, and I was utterly confused. Isn't reading and learning, putting things into my brain how I grow and become successful?

This really threw me off at the time. Here was a mentor that I had just hired to help me grow, and yet he was telling me not to do the one thing that I thought would help me build my business and become a better coach. I had been conditioned to think for many years in school that the only way to be "successful" is to get good grades by reading, learning and memorizing more and more things. But this knowledge wasn't really helping me build the life and business of my dreams yet at the time. Why was that? Even though initially I was triggered by his "weird" advice, I was starting to think maybe he was onto something.

Later, I realized the deeper meaning behind this rather odd advice to stop reading as much as I was for a bit. At the time, I was hiding behind books and the mere "activity" of learning, and wasn't doing the very thing that would translate my knowledge into actual contribution in the world. Here's the thing. We often forget our true purpose to be on this Earth, which is to be not forever just consumers of information, but to be divine creators of new creations. When we create, we expand the world. When we create, it is sacred. Of course, input of knowledge and technical skills into the brains of the creators is a crucial step of the process, initially. However, notice that the only reason we would learn is so that we can take that knowledge and actually turn into creations, that would actually instigate powerful shifts in this reality. So when we are in the flow of creating, this is how we remember who we really are.

This process of human creation that infuses our unique flavor of our soul with knowledge, and yielding unique ideas, products, services, art, and music out into the world is where energies of abundance and prosperity like to play. Yet in our society, so many of us are taught that knowledge is power. And from my own experience, as well as in *Think and Grow Rich*, we are reminded that knowledge alone isn't power. Education and general knowledge are potential power. What allows potential power to fully actualize into authentic personal power and amazing valuable creations into the world is through courageous, inspired, action and application of the knowledge. It is when knowledge moves through the human body machine, gets entangled and gets infused with a unique soul and its divine wisdom, that it becomes something extremely new and valuable for the world.

For instance, Elon Musk was able to utilize all his gifts, education, skills, and knowledge to invent a self-driving, solar powered, sustainable car, such as Tesla. It is because of his unique (and very broad array) of knowledge that he was able to create and birth new inventions and products into the world in a way that's never existed before by infusing it with his own Elon Musk energy and passion. Teslas are great cars, and they are even more incredible in the sense that it is an accumulation of so many of Elon Musks' passions, knowledge, and creativity, such as his engineering skills that actually engineered many parts of the car, his passion for sustaining the Earth's health for as long as it can by using less gas (before we find a way out to Mars), his interest in solar powered and renewable energy, and so on. He is passionate about helping humanity evolve and advance in massive and meaningful ways. Tesla is a culmination of many Musk's passions, soul, knowledge, and creativity all fused into one company.

Human Creativity, Emotions and Consciousness: Next Era of Specialized Knowledge for Abundance

There are traditional ways to explain Specialized Knowledge, which suggests that the difference of value between general knowledge and Specialized Knowledge is the difference between going to a general doctor and going to a specialized surgeon for your brain. One has broad knowledge when it comes to helping patients, and the neurosurgeon has very specialized set of skills and knowledge that allows him to operate on a human's brain. And yes, it is true that this type of Specialized Knowledge is what builds wealth and invites abundance, compared to wide arrange of general knowledge.

And I want to also broaden this idea of Specialized Knowledge as I believe that the climate of our reality has changed vastly since the publication of *Think and Grow Rich.*

Today, especially with technology advancing as fast as it is, and talks of AI and robots becoming more and more mainstream, I propose that the future's Specialized Knowledge (that will also be hugely responsible for creating and attracting abundance) will no longer be just highly specialized skills and knowledge. Despite the huge advancement in technology, there is something that our understanding and application of AI and robots have not tapped into yet; and that is human emotions, consciousness, and creativity.

In fact, nowadays, there are robots that are being created to operate very highly-technical and difficult surgeries and tasks, that humans before were getting paid a lot to do. One day, I don't think the traditional concept of Specialized Knowledge being the most profitable type of knowledge will continue to hold true.

Speaking of Elon Musk, in a recent interview on the Joe Rogan Experience podcast, he discussed that he is currently working on his newest, most innovative creation yet called Neuralink. This is a device that is potentially going to enter into a human's skull, so that the human has access to the infinite amount of knowledge, even Specialized Knowledge, that is available in the world. It might actually be that one day, this technology would allow any human, or even a robot, to be plugged into a system that allows them to operate on a human's skull because it can download a large amount of technical, even what was once considered Specialized Knowledge.

Even with the amazing advancement in technology, the few things that will either never be fully figured out or not figured out for a long, long time are: human emotions, consciousness, and creativity.

And this is exactly why I believe these are some of the most important concepts for humanity to learn and grasp a better understanding of, in order to attract abundance in the future.

Trends and findings are already emerging around this. For instance, it was found that emotional intelligence is now considered one of the top factors into better leadership for executives, CEOs, and managers in organizations. There has also been a huge movement towards people wanting to tap into their own consciousness through meditation and various other mediums, more than ever before. Also, more than ever, creativity is becoming more and more valuable than ever before. For instance, NFT's are a newer trend among the technologically savvy entrepreneurs and leaders. NFT stands for non-fungible tokens, and essentially it allows people to create digital artwork and assets, and each of them can be tracked individually through blockchain technology—forever.

So for instance, while there are many copies of the Mona Lisa painting, there is only one unique owner of the original. More than ever, authentic creativity and unique art in all forms are being valued and celebrated. Today, the NFT industry holds value of over 1.05 trillion dollars, and this is just the beginning. While AI and robots might be able to create new digital art, at least as of now, art created by humans is more valuable and celebrated. And it is no surprise when you think of creativity in this way. Creativity is the process of infusing humans' unique emotions and soul, and returning something that's never existed before.

Today, I want to ask, especially as we prepare for the new era, what are you doing to cultivate, celebrate, utilize, and learn about human emotions, consciousness, and creativity? How can you allow these to become your competitive advantage in this modern, technologically innovative world?

Journaling Questions:

Do you believe that the way we understand Specialized Knowledge will change in the upcoming decades?

In what ways have you found that creativity, consciousness, or human emotions have already played a role as a form of Specialized Knowledge for you in your own life?

YURI CHOI

About Yuri Choi: Yuri is the Founder of Yuri Choi Coaching. Yuri is a performance coach for entrepreneurs and high achievers. She helps them create and stay in a powerful, abundant, unstoppable mindset to achieve their goals by helping them gain clarity and understanding, leverage their emotional states, and create empowering habits and language patterns.

She is a speaker, writer, creator, connector, YouTuber, and the author of *Creating Your Own Happiness.* Yuri is passionate about spreading the messages about meditation, power of intention, and creating a powerful mindset to live a fulfilling life. She is also a Habitude Warrior Conference Speaker and emcee, and she is also a designated guest coach for Psych2Go, the largest online mental health magazine and YouTube Channel. Her mission in the world is to inspire people to live leading with L.O.V.E. (which stands for: laughter, oneness, vulnerability, and ease) and to ignite people's souls to live in a world of infinite creative possibilities and abundance.

Author's Website: *www.YuriChoiCoaching.com*
Book Series Website & Author's Bio: *www.The13StepsToRiches.com*

GRAB YOUR COPY OF AN OFFICIAL PUBLICATION WITH THE ORIGINAL UNEDITED TEXT FROM 1937 BY THE NAPOLEON HILL FOUNDATION!

THE NAPOLEON HILL FOUNDATION
WWW.NAPHILL.ORG

Global Speakers Mastermind & Habitude Warrior Masterminds

Join us and become a member of our tribe! Our Global Speakers Mastermind is a virtual group of amazing thinkers and leaders who meet twice a month. Sessions are designed to be 'to the point' and focused, while sharing fantastic techniques to grown your mindset as well as your pocket books. We also include famous guest speaker spots for our private Masterclasses. We also designate certain sessions for our members to mastermind with each other & counsel on the topics discussed in our previous Masterclasses. It's time for you to join a tribe who truly cares about *YOU* and your future and start surrounding yourself with the famous leaders and mentors of our time. It is time for you to up-level your life, businesses, and relationships.

For more information to check out our Masterminds:
Team@HabitudeWarrior.com
www.DecideTobeAwesome.com

BECOME AN INTERNATIONAL
#1 BEST-SELLING AUTHOR & SPEAKER

Habitude Warrior International has been highlighting award-winning Speakers and #1 Best-Selling Authors for over 25 years. They know what it takes to become #1 in your field and how to get the best exposure around the world. If you have ever considered giving yourself the GIFT of becoming a well-known Speaker and a fantastically well known #1 Best-Selling Author, then you should email their team right away to find out more information in how you can become involved. They have the best of the best when it comes to resources in achieving the best-selling status in your particular field. Start surrounding yourself with the N.Y. Times Best-Sellers of our time and start seeing your dreams become reality!

For more information to become a #1 Best-Selling Author & Speaker on our Habitude Warrior Conferences Please send us your request to: Team@HabitudeWarrior.com www.DecideTobeAwesome.com